PREVIOUS BOOKS BY DENNIS ADLER

Mercedes-Benz: Silver Star Century

Porsche 911 Road Cars

Chrysler

Fifties Flashback: The American Car

PORSCHE

PORSCHE

THE CLASSIC ERA

DENNIS ADLER

FOREWORD BY
FERDINAND ALEXANDER PORSCHE III

motorbooks

First published in 2016 by Motorbooks, an imprint of The Quarto Group, 100 Cummings Center, Suite 265-D, Beverly, MN 01915 USA. T(978) 282-9590 F (978) 283-2742 QuartoKnows.com

Motorbooks titles are also available at discounts for retail, wholesale, promotional, and bulk purchase. For details, contact the Special Sales Manager by email at specialsales@quarto.com or by mail at The Quarto Group, Attn: Special Sales Manager, 100 Cummings Center, Suite 265-D, Beverly, MN 01915 USA.

10 9 8 7 6

ISBN: 978-0-7603-5190-1

Library of Congress Cataloging-in-Publication Data

Adler, Dennis.
   The Classic Era / Dennis Adler.
      p. cm.
ISBN 0-375-50216-5
1. Porsche automobiles—History. 2. Porsche A.G.—History. I. Title.

TL215.P75A3524 2003
629.222'2—dc21
                        2003046506

Acquiring Editor: Zack Miller
Project Manager: Bryan Trandem
Art Director: James Kegley
Layout: BTDny
Printed in China

TO JEANNE, FOR HER BOUNDLESS ENCOURAGEMENT AND LOVE
THROUGHOUT THE YEARS AND IN MEMORY OF FERDINAND ANTON
ERNST FERRY PORSCHE AND FERDINAND
ALEXANDER "BUTZI" PORSCHE

FOREWORD

FERDINAND ALEXANDER PORSCHE III

Author's Note:

After this original Foreword was written by Butzi Porsche—the genius behind such legendary cars as the Porsche 904 and the original 911—he passed away at the age of 76, on April 5, 2012. I will always owe a great debt of gratitude both to Butzi and his father for their generous assistance in making both the original book and this revised edition possible.

"IN THE BEGINNING I LOOKED AROUND AND, NOT finding the automobile of my dreams, decided to build it myself." This was a statement of my father's about the creation of our company in a commercial in 1989, and it showed me how much entrepreneurial daring he had at a time when there seemed to be no future. To be dreaming of a sports car, tucked away in a remote Austrian Alpine valley two years after the end of World War II, was nothing less than boundless optimism or even—if one looks at it from today—temerity. His belief in the future, and his knowledge of the vitality and ability of the designers who attempted with him in Gmünd, Carinthia, to come to grips with postwar conditions—constructing, for example, winches and direct-flow turbines for agriculture—allowed his dream to become reality, to become the Porsche 356.

The dream once realized by my father set the stage for future successes. The company that was started up by my grandfather in 1931 as a limited-liability company, Dr. Ing. h.c. F. Porsche KG, through its experience designing and constructing automobiles, became a manufacturing company, and Porsche was now a manufacturer of its own cars.

My father was twenty-one when he became an assistant to my grandfather in the design office. He was there from the very beginning—a crown prince as an eager student among the technical specialists: Karl Rabe, the chief designer; Karl Fröhlich, responsible for the transmission; Josef Kales, for the engine; Josef Zahradnik, for the axles; and Erwin Komenda, for the body. I believe that the most important qualities that allowed my father to grow into his future responsibility were his constant willingness to learn, his ability to observe very closely and to listen, as well as his talent for recognizing how situations evolved within the company's administration.

Moreover, in a close family company, conditions were created that nurtured his talents through the clearness of its structure, the logic of its decision-making processes, and the efficiency of its

OPPOSITE: Ferdinand Alexander "Butzi" Porsche III in his studio at Porsche Design, his own firm, which he formed in Zell am See in 1972. Porsche Design has been responsible for everything from sunglasses to camera designs. Butzi also succeeded his father as chairman of Porsche AG's supervisory board in 1990.

way of doing business. There was, however, also the "human" component, which was present throughout the company from the very beginning and which also influenced my father. For one thing, there were emotional bonds between the employees themselves: there were also the employees' ties to the office, which knew how competent it was and which found itself in an upward trend. Finally, it was the human and professional leadership of my grandfather that united the team and, through his technical visions, kept providing impetus for the future.

The break with the past after World War II was complete, and it fell to my father to develop new strategies for the company. As Albert Prinzing told him on the occasion of his seventy-fifth birthday, my father's most consequential decision was "to develop a small sports car for a new type of customer in a world in which 'bigger and bigger' was thought to be the catchword. Ferry Porsche met that with a small, fast, and decidedly unadorned car with simple, well-proportioned lines. Many Americans lived by the motto 'to be different'; they desired to free themselves from their standardized world, which could be the explanation for Porsche's quick success in the largest of markets."

Of course, it was one thing to dream of such a sports car and another to make such a dream come true. However, this is what happened when my father moved the company back to Stuttgart, where he found the necessary conditions to produce cars in the facilities of Reutter and signed a contract with Heinz Nordhoff, the general director of Volkswagen, which provided for VW to supply parts for the sports car and allowed Porsches to be sold and serviced by VW agents and mechanics. In return, Porsche was to give design advice to VW.

This contract provided the material basis for the continuing existence of the company. No less important for the success of the company and for the special success of the Porsche automobile was the devotion the Porsche team had for their cars and the resulting spirit that infused the House of Porsche.

It almost sounds like a manifesto when one reads the forewords to the first issues of the house magazine, *Christophorus*. They give the priorities of principle that were written down by my father, Carl Otto Windecker, and Richard von Frankenberg. They deal with "Automobilism," "The Spirit of the House of Porsche," and "Porsche Automobile Sport."

What these articles show is a deep emotional relationship to the automobile—to the very concept of the automobile in general, and to Porsche in particular. These articles are so typical of the way of thinking of "car people" shortly after the war and had such an influence on the history of the Porsche company that they are worth quoting today without any further comment on their essential aspects.

Carl Otto Windecker, for instance, describes the phenomenon of "Automobilism" in this way: "The world of the automobile is a force field of nonmeasurable influence upon people who come within its aura. It is a phenomenon which fulfills and captures humans like a new religion. . . . No other vehicle manufactured by German carmakers has been supplanted or made redundant by the Porsche—for it is unique in the broadest sense. The Porsche has become the vehicle of believing fanatics in the new world appreciation of 'Automobilism.' . . . The sheer beauty of the Porsche releases it from the laws of everyday sober functionalism. Its power and the extraordinary speed it can travel at take it out of normal traffic and contribute to that feeling of liberation which can probably only be surpassed by the experience of flying."

Richard von Frankenberg, in his article "The Spirit of the House of Porsche," was captured by the far-reaching spirit of my grandfather: "There is a yardstick for this spirit today and in the future. This yardstick is based on a single question: 'Will the company continue to work in the spirit of the person who, with his technical pioneering work, established the fame of his name?' . . . Still another principle contributes to the special spirit of this house: that of pure achievement. Nobody has regarded achievement and accomplishment as much as the old professor; personal vanity meant nothing, work meant everything."

Finally, my father wrote about the relationship of his company to automobile sports: "The sporting line can be seen as a unifying theme throughout the creative period of my father. Whether it was the first Lohner cars with their electric motor, or (at Austro-Daimler) the Prince-Heinrich types, or the small Sascha sports car and the ADM with which Stuck drove his first mountain races, or the Daimler SSK, or the Auto Union Grand-Prix racing car—one can always see the same tendency."

If you ask, therefore, why we still participate so actively in sports events, the answer is that our house has a sporting tradition and has been in all phases of its development so closely connected with automobile sports that sports somehow belongs to designing and building cars and that, conversely, cars are built with the belief that they have to be successful in sporting competition. Or, to put it in the words of a journalist, "The Porsche people can't do anything else."

Change without sacrifice of principle is what distinguished Porsche in the past and will distinguish it in the future. My grandfather and my father created the basis for this tradition with their technical and entrepreneurial daring, their ideas and their dreams. The Porsche company will live on in that spirit of continuity.

ACKNOWLEDGMENTS

THERE ARE FEW AUTOMOTIVE ENTHUSIASTS MORE dedicated to their cars than Porsche owners and collectors, and it is with great appreciation that this book is dedicated to these resolute individualists. There are many collectors without whose dedication to preserving older 356 and 911 models, some of the most interesting cars to come from the Porsche factory would be absent from the motoring world and this book. I had the privilege of working hand in hand with three of the greatest Porsches collectors in America in writing and photographing this book, Chuck Stoddard, Kent Rawson, and Dr. Bill Jackson, without whose assistance there would be far fewer examples pictured. My special thanks also go to noted collector Bruce Meyer and Porsche restorer Dennis Frick for their invaluable help.

Many have followed the road from Zuffenhausen, and there are dozens of books on Porsche history which were used to research background on the models pictured, including Ferry

Porsche's autobiography, *Cars Are My Life; Excellence Was Expected,* by automotive historian Karl Ludvigsen, without whose work few of us could research the early cars; *Porsche 911 Forever Young,* the highly detailed chronicle of the 911 by Tobias Aichele; *Porsche Legends,* by Randy Leffingwell, *Porsche 356 Driving In Its Purest Form* by Dirk-Michael Conradt, *The 356 Porsche* by Dr. Brett Johnson, Porsche by Peter Vann, *Carrera 4* by Porsche AG, *Porsche Racing* by David & Andrea Sparrow, *Porsches For the Road* by Henry Rasmussen, *Porsche, The 4-Cylinders, 4-Cam Sports & Racing Cars* by Jerry Sloniger, and my own book, *Porsche 911 Road Cars.* I would also like to thank my colleagues Frank Barrett and Prescott Kelly for their assistance in preparing the chapter on Porsche collectibles and poster art. Both Frank and Prescott are consummate collectors of Porsche memorabilia and their contributions to the book are greatly appreciated.

The creation of any pictorial history also requires the assistance of the manufacturer, in this instance Porsche AG in Stuttgart-Zuffenhausen and Porsche Cars North America.

— DENNIS ADLER

February, 2016

CONTENTS

FOREWORD BY FERDINAND ALEXANDER PORSCHE III   ix

ACKNOWLEDGMENTS   xii

INTRODUCTION   xvii

CHAPTER 1

**THE FATHER: PROFESSOR
FERDINAND PORSCHE**   3

CHAPTER 2

**THE EARLY YEARS IN ZUFFENHAUSEN:
PORSCHE KG DESIGNS AND A WORLD
ONCE AGAIN AT WAR**   23

CHAPTER 3

**AFTER THE WINDS OF WAR:
THE EARLY DAYS IN GMÜND**   47

CHAPTER 4

**SELF-REPATRIATION:
FERRY PORSCHE AT THE HELM**   75

CHAPTER 5

**THE COACH-BUILT 356 PORSCHE:
RACING IMPROVES THE BREED**   97

CHAPTER 6

**BUTZI PORSCHE'S 901/911:
RE-CREATING THE PORSCHE IN ITS
OWN IMAGE**   125

CHAPTER 7

**THE SECOND DYNASTY:
THE 911 ERA BEGINS**   139

CHAPTER 8

RENNSPORT PORSCHES: THE RACE-READY 911   157

CHAPTER 9

**THE 911 ROAD CARS: THE AIR-COOLED COUPES
AND CABRIOS**   175

CHAPTER 10

**DRIVING ON ALL FOURS: EVOLUTION OF
PORSCHE ALL-WHEEL-DRIVE**   203

CHAPTER 11

A MOVE TO THE MIDDLE: 914 AND 914/6   221

CHAPTER 12

**PORSCHE RACING HISTORY: FROM
SCCA TO LE MANS**   233

CHAPTER 13

**PORSCHE IN PRINT: THE HISTORY OF
PORSCHE ADVERTISING AND POSTER ART**   257

INDEX   282

INTRODUCTION

SOUNDS CAN EVOKE VIVID IMAGES OF THE objects or of the people who create them. The haunting rhythm of a Fender Stratocaster played by Eric Clapton is unmistakable; so, too, the primitive rumble of a Harley-Davidson trying to catch its breath; the thwack of a Louisville Slugger thundering into the leather hide of a baseball; and the siren song of a Porsche boxer engine at full cry. Nearly seventy years ago, when the little bathtub sports cars from Germany were powered by retuned Volkswagen flat fours, the sound, then more a clatter than a blare, was still a Porsche beyond doubt.

As the most recognized sports car maker in the world, Porsche has a proud history dating back to 1931, when Professor Ferdinand Porsche established a design and engineering studio, Porsche GmbH, in Stuttgart-Zuffenhausen. Prior to that, Porsche had earned a reputation as one of Germany's leading automotive engineers, serving first as chief of design for Daimler and, after 1926, as chief designer for the newly allied Daimler-Benz concern.

Now, through the assistance of Porsche AG and the company's photographic archives, the story of a family dynasty unfolds to reveal the true heart of Porsche and its dedication to design and engineering, pioneered by Ferdinand Porsche and carried on by his son, Ferdinand Anton Ernst "Ferry" Porsche II; his daughter, Louise Porsche-Piëch; his son-in-law Ferdinand Piëch; his grandson Ferdinand Alexander "Butzi" Porsche III; and the Porsche family, which remains involved with the company to the present day.

The story of the early years in Gmünd, Austria, and the return to Zuffenhausen following World War II is a grand tale of commitment to an idea and an ideal that resulted in the first 356 models and the establishment of Porsche as one of Germany's leading automakers in a very short period of time.

Porsche: The Classic Era chronicles the complete history of Professor Porsche and the founding of the company as an independent automaker in 1948 by the Porsche family. The

OPPOSITE: Detail of a Pre-A Reutter-bodied 356 cabriolet. The fender styling of early 356 models such as this 1952 example was somewhat more elegant than that of the later 356A series car. (BATA MATAJA COLLECTION)

pre–World War II advances at Porsche included the very first prototypes of a sports car, the development of the Volkswagen by Professor Porsche in the late 1930s, and the creation of the first cars to bear the Porsche name, which were built in Gmünd, Austria.

With the assistance of the Porsche AG archives, the early history of the company has been beautifully depicted with rarely seen historical black-and-white photographs. Here, too, is the story of Max Hoffman, the Austrian entrepreneur who came to the United States and established a dealership in New York City, linking the German auto industry with affluent American sportsmen and establishing Porsche, among others, as one of the earliest European sports cars to successfully develop a niche in the U.S. marketplace.

The history of the 356 is outlined as the car is developed over more than a decade, including competition versions of the 356 and the evolution of the legendary Porsche 550 Spyder and 904 Carrera GTS. Here, too, is the story of the Porsche 911, one of the most compelling tales in automotive history because this venerable model has survived for nearly four decades—the longest production run of any postwar automobile design in history. *Porsche: The Classic Era* follows the development of the 911 prototypes in the early 1960s through the introduction of the car in 1964 and its evolution through the end of the air-cooled era in 1998.

Porsche's illustrious racing career in SCCA, World Manufacturer's Championship competition, at Le Mans, Sebring, and venues the world over are chronicled in a chapter dedicated to the company's renowned racing programs throughout the 1950s, 1960s, 1970s, and to the present day.

Porsche: The Classic Era is more than a comprehensive history of the marque; it is the story of the people who have created these remarkable sports and competition cars for some seven decades. Combined with photographs and technical information, this is a highly detailed history and reference book for collectors, restorers, and the more than one million Porsche owners and enthusiasts the world over. It is also a tale of ambition and dedication unlike any in the saga of the automobile.

PORSCHE

Ferry Porsche and Karl Rabe stood in the doorway of the small workshop listening to the sound of distant thunder. Across the room, Ferdinand Porsche sat with his elbows propped on the edge of a worktable, his chin resting on folded hands, and his bleary eyes closed tightly to block out the dismal image of Allied bombers and far-off battles.
His thoughts began to drift back to better times, before Hitler—before the ugly war—to the days when he was the most sought-after automotive engineer in all of Germany.
He had no idea what the future held in store. . . .

CHAPTER 1

THE FATHER

PROFESSOR FERDINAND PORSCHE

FERDINAND PORSCHE WAS BORN ON SEPTEMBER 3, 1875, just in time not only to witness the evolution of the automobile but also to participate in its development. When he was eleven years old, Ferdinand became fascinated with a new invention patented in 1886 by German machinist Karl Benz. In his Mannheim workshop Benz had created what historians regard as the first motorcar, but more important, he had inspired others to follow in his path, among them young Porsche.

Fourteen years later, as an engineer in the employ of the Lohner motorworks in Vienna, Ferdinand Porsche designed his first motorcar, the Lohner-Wagen, a small, four-person carriage powered by two electric motors, each developing 0.98 horsepower and turning the front wheels. While this would appear to make Porsche one of the earliest pioneers of front-wheel drive technology, his design was not influenced by any contemporary ideology promoting the advantages of front-driven wheels. In point of fact one could say that Porsche's design was conceived by using "horse sense." The motors replaced the horse, the horse pulled the carriage, and thus the electric motors were placed in the front. Interestingly, this was not the common practice at the turn of the century. Most early horseless carriages had their engines mounted in the rear, under the seat, with chain-driven rear wheels. In 1901, Wilhelm Maybach and Paul Daimler partly changed that tradition by positioning the engine under the front bonnet of the revolutionary new Mercedes, what was to be the first modern automobile. The drive, however, still went to the rear wheels via chains.

Despite the Mercedes' success, electric motorcars were more popular for a brief period in the 1900s than either steam-powered cars or those equipped with noisy, obstreperous internal combustion engines. In September 1900, intent on building even better electric motor wagons, Porsche had designed the Lohner-Porsche racing car, which was delivered to British sportsman E. W. Hart.

Porsche (far right) in a photo taken in 1897. He would soon get his first engineering job at the Lohner motorworks in Vienna.

This example used not two but four motors, one at each wheel. Almost ninety years later, Porsche's son Ferry would write of this design in his autobiography, *Cars Are My Life*: "[This] racing car designed by my father used the same mode of propulsion as was applied to the American 'moon car' driven on the moon by astronauts David R. Scott and James B. Irwin in July 1971."

That simple anecdote underscored Ferdinand Porsche's entire career. From the very beginning he looked beyond contemporary practice and searched for ways to improve what appeared to be in no need of improvement. This ideology was to serve him well in his first managerial position as technical director of Austro-Daimler.

The firm was established in Vienna in 1899 as the Austrian branch of Daimler-Motoren-Gesellschaft, which had become one

BOTH IMAGES ABOVE: By 1900, Porsche had developed a front-wheel-driven motor carriage powered by two electric motors. These Porsche-designed vehicles were manufactured by Lohner motorworks.

of Germany's most successful manufacturers of motor carriages and internal combustion engines. By the 1890s, D-M-G founder Gottlieb Daimler and his associate, Wilhelm Maybach, had developed a four-wheel motor carriage and the first motor-driven fire engines and general-purpose trucks (lorries), and had successfully completed experiments with dirigibles. This latter event was to play a significant role in Maybach's future.

The first designer at Daimler's Austrian branch, located in Wiener Neustadt, was Gottlieb's son Paul. Riding on the success of the 1901 Mercedes, Paul assumed his new position in 1902.

The most advanced electric vehicle of 1902 was the Lohner-Porsche four-wheel-drive racer built for British sportsman E. W. Hart (at the wheel). The Porsche racing car used the same mode of propulsion as was applied to the Lunar Rover driven on the moon by astronauts David R. Scott and James B. Irwin in July 1971.

He was instrumental in Austro-Daimler's early achievements, but by 1906 there was growing disharmony between Daimler-Motoren-Gesellschaft and its Austrian subsidiary. Paul had been called back to Germany in 1905, and the following year Austro-Daimler divorced itself from D-M-G and became an independent company.

In Germany the acrimony that had been growing between Paul Daimler and Wilhelm Maybach since his return to D-M-G finally became too much for the sixty-year-old engineer to endure. Maybach's closest friend and associate, Gottlieb Daimler, had died of heart failure in 1900, leaving him in control of the company's engineering department, the first product of which had been the 1901 Mercedes designed by Maybach and Paul Daimler. With his return to D-M-G, the friction between Paul and his late father's associate began to escalate, and following a lengthy disagreement over the design of a 1906 race car, Maybach decided to retire. In April 1907 he left the company he had helped bring into being with Gottlieb Daimler in 1890, and Paul assumed his position as chief engineer.

As for Wilhelm Maybach, afternoon tea and retirement were not what he had in mind when he departed from D-M-G. Having pioneered the development of the first motor-powered lighter-than-air craft in 1888, Maybach joined forces with Graf Ferdinand

Porsche posed for this portrait with his wife, Aloisia, in 1902.

Mercedes influenced Porsche's later front-wheel-driven electric car, shown here in 1902. Interestingly, the appearance of the Lohner-Porsche is similar to that of the revolutionary Daimler Phoenix, first seen in 1897, although it is lower to the ground in the 1901 Mercedes pattern. Porsche is behind the wheel.

BELOW: By 1911, when this family photo was taken on an outing, Porsche had become chief engineer of Austro-Daimler. This sporty yet elegant 1911 model was his design.

von Zeppelin in the development of a new aero engine for Zeppelin's giant airships. Maybach was given responsibility for overseeing the construction of all-new engines, and his son Karl (a gifted engineer in his own right) was appointed technical director. A separate company, Luftfahrzeug-Motorenbau GmbH (changed in 1912 to Maybach Motorenbau Gesellschaft), was established to produce the Zeppelin engines, and it would be from the M.M.G. factory in Friedrichshafen, Germany, that the first Maybach automobiles would emerge following World War I, to be marketed in direct competition—in revenge, one might say—with Mercedes.

These seemingly unrelated events all favored Ferdinand Porsche, who became chief engineer at Austro-Daimler following Paul Daimler's departure. Porsche would remain with the Austrian firm for seventeen years, during which time he created many of the company's most successful race cars. He also struck up a lasting friendship with a young race driver named Alfred Neubauer, who was himself destined to become one of the pivotal figures in German automotive history.

It was during his tenure in Austria that Porsche gained prominence as both an engineer and a designer. In 1909 he entered a trio of Austro-Daimler 28/36PS sports touring cars in the Prince Henry Time Trials, a successor to the Herkomer Trials and an important race for production automobiles of the time. One of the specially prepared Austro-Daimlers finished first in one stage of the event, and, thus encouraged, Ferdinand Porsche returned with a team of eight cars the following year, sweeping the first three places overall, with Porsche himself driving the winning car.

By 1916 he had risen to the position of managing director of Austro-Daimler. The Viennese Technical University presented him with an honorary doctorate for his advances in aircraft and automotive technology, after which he referred to himself as Professor Porsche, or *Herr Doktor*. In 1940, Porsche was also awarded an honorary professorship by the German Ministry for Science and Education, which gave him a great deal of pleasure.

Wars were to play a pivotal role in Porsche's life and career. The assassination in Sarajevo on June 28, 1914, of Archduke Francis Ferdinand, heir to the Austrian throne, ignited World War I. When the dual monarchy of Austria-Hungary declared war on Serbia on July 28, Germany sided with the Austro-Hungarian empire, and declarations of war began flying in every direction. Soon all of Europe was engulfed in a conflict that would last until November 11, 1918. Throughout the war Porsche concentrated his efforts on the design of aircraft engines, developing an in-line six-cylinder aero engine; an air-cooled opposed four (the fundamentals of which would reappear in Porsche's design for the Volkswagen), a rotary engine, and a variety of V-form and W-form aircraft engines. Long fascinated with aviation, he had developed the first Austro-Daimler aero engine back in 1911 and thus was already accomplished in their design when the company was called upon to manufacture aircraft engines for the war effort.

World War I brought about tremendous change within the German automotive industry when the potential of the motorcar in combat was realized for the first time. Mercedes-Benz historian and author Beverly Rae Kimes noted quite poignantly in *The Star and the Laurel* that the awakening came in September 1914, when General Joseph-Simon Gallieni ordered the use of French taxis to carry troops to the Marne front. The troop transport was born. Armored cars, particularly those produced by Rolls-Royce, played a significant role in battle, and the advent of the tank, perhaps the ultimate armored car, gave the British a marked advantage over the Germans, who found themselves sorely behind in the manufacture of military vehicles. Ironically, Paul Daimler had tried to encourage the development of armored cars years before the war, but his proposals had all been rejected.

"In 1918, when the war came to an end, we all faced a new situation as Austria became a republic," wrote Ferry Porsche in his memoirs. "The victorious powers demanded reparations, which led to considerable restrictions. The great Austro-Hungarian Empire had been replaced by a small country whose industry was now dependent to a considerable extent on exports."

These were difficult times for the German automotive industry, for Austro-Daimler, and for the Porsche family in particular. "My father's birthplace, Maffersdorf in Bohemia, was now in the state of Czechoslovakia, which had been newly created by the peace treaties of Versailles and St. Germain. This was actually a purely German area which had previously belonged to Austria-Hungary." The senior Porsche had decided to become a Czechoslovakian citizen after the war, thus allowing himself greater mobility throughout Europe. "As an Austrian, he would have been one of those who had lost the war. Thus, for example, it would not have been possible for him to go to Paris, where the most important international automobile exhibition, the Paris Salon, took place in the Grand Palais. For the general manager of an automobile factory, but particularly for an engineer as closely involved as my father was with the development of the motorcar, the opportunity to attend such an important exhibition was absolutely essential. Moreover, my father felt that Maffersdorf was his native territory, the place where he felt at home, and that he should not change his allegiance to this part of the former Austro-Hungarian Empire as he might change his shirt."

Following the Treaty of Versailles in 1919, the value of the German mark began to plummet. In 1914, before the war, the mark had traded against the U.S. dollar at 4.20 to one. Now it took sixty-two marks to equal one U.S. dollar! By 1920 the failing German economy had brought the nation's automotive industry to its knees. Fuel shortages and the general instability of the economy saw more cars parked along the side of the road than on it. People were out of work, and automakers were banned by the conditions of the Versailles Treaty from any military production, including the manufacture of aircraft engines. The economic impact on Austro-Daimler, Benz & Cie., and Daimler was devastating.

In the early postwar years Austro-Daimler struggled to regain market share and Porsche led the company into the 1920s with the introduction of a 4.4-liter, six-cylinder motorcar capable of delivering 60 horsepower. Fitted with sports coachwork, the cars sold well abroad and, noted Ferry Porsche, "brought in precious foreign currency. This foreign currency was the cause of the first serious tensions between the shareholders and my father which were to lead later to a parting of the ways."

While most regarded the elder Porsche as a difficult man, he was at the same time a gentle-hearted, almost doting father who was dedicated to his family and the education of his two children, Ferdinand "Ferry" Porsche, and his older sister, Louise. Both would grow up in the automotive industry, and Ferry would one day assume control of the family business. In 1920, however, he was only eleven but already an automotive enthusiast. Ferdinand Porsche catered to Ferry's infatuation with automobiles, and for

Christmas 1920 he presented his son with a scaled-down, two-person roadster powered by an air-cooled, four-stroke engine. To his father's dismay, when the little auto was moved outside and the engine started, Ferry slipped behind the wheel and drove off! "He certainly hadn't reckoned that. I had, of course, already secretly learned to drive, since there were always opportunities for 'maneuvering' a car on the factory premises or in the garage at home." From that moment on it was a certainty that Ferry would follow in his father's footsteps.

Under Ferdinand Porsche's guidance, Austro-Daimler continued to prosper in the 1920s; however, there was growing dissension between the board and Porsche over *what* the company should build. Austro-Daimler continued to produce only large, prestigious cars, while Porsche longed to pursue his idea of a small, affordable car. He had always

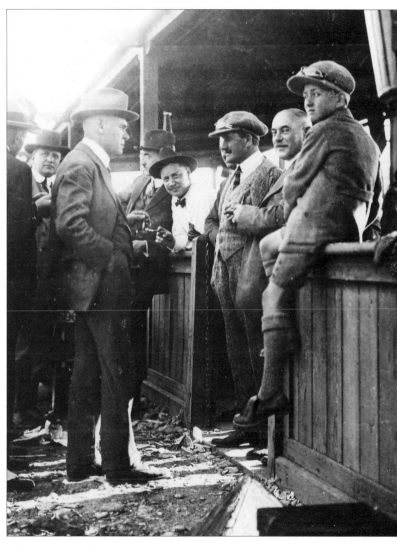

Ferry Porsche (far right) in 1921. He was already a constant companion of his father (with matching racing hat and goggles).

NEAR RIGHT, ABOVE AND BELOW: Ferdinand Porsche and co-driver with Austro-Daimler race cars in 1921.

FAR RIGHT, ABOVE: Alfred Neubauer joined Austro-Daimler as a race driver. He is seen behind the wheel of the 1.5-liter Sascha race car in the 1922 Targa Florio Italian road race. Ferdinand Porsche is standing directly behind the numeral 6 on the hood.

FAR RIGHT, BELOW: Racing was one of Porsche's first concerns after arriving at D-M-G. This 1924 supercharged race car developed 160 horsepower. It was driven between 1925 and 1927 by legendary racers Christian Werner, Rudolf Caracciola, and Otto Merz.

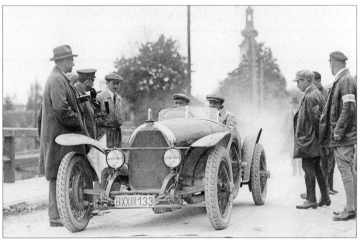

envisioned a compact motorcar as a realistic means of providing reasonably priced personal transportation for the masses. One such example developed by Porsche was the Sascha, what Alfred Neubauer described as a forerunner of the Volkswagen. Neubauer raced one of the little 1.5-liter sports cars in the 1922 Targa Florio in Sicily, at the time the most grueling road race in the world. He finished sixth in the racing car class, which was won by a larger 4.5-liter Mercedes driven by Count Giulio Masetti. Neubauer's teammates won the category for production cars up to 1,100 centimeters in a smaller 1.1-liter Sascha touring car that Porsche had also developed. The touring model very likely would have been successful as a lower-priced Austro-Daimler, but the com-

pany directors would not consent to a production version. Porsche's persistent nature led to the manufacture of the Sascha as both a racing and a sports car but never the touring model he truly wanted to build. By 1922 it was clear to him that the creative and technical freedom he had enjoyed over the years was being denied him. "My father was not the type to allow himself to be constrained within narrow limits," wrote Ferry. "Finally [this] pushed him into leaving Austro-Daimler."

Once more Ferdinand Porsche's fate was to be allied with that of Paul Daimler's. At the same time that Porsche decided to leave Austro-Daimler, Paul, having fallen out of favor with the supervisory board of the company founded by his late father, felt he no longer belonged and tendered his resignation with short notice. Suddenly, here was Daimler-Motoren-Gesellschaft with an

opening for a chief engineer and Ferdinand Porsche out of work for the first time in seventeen years. As in 1906, Porsche stepped in to assume a position vacated by Paul Daimler.

Porsche arrived from Austria in April 1923 to become D-M-G's chief engineer. The first great sporting cars designed for Daimler by Porsche included a supercharged 2-liter straight eight (the first eight-cylinder car built by D-M-G), finished in 1923 and raced at Monza in October 1924, and two six-cylinder supercharged touring cars, the 15/70/100 and the 24/100/140, introduced in December 1924.

The political and economic repercussions of World War I were weighing in heavily by the early 1920s, and the German automotive industry was struggling for survival. Even the two largest automakers in the country, Daimler-Motoren-Gesellschaft and

ABOVE LEFT: The Targa Florio was regarded as one of the most grueling road races in Europe. Car No. 10, a Mercedes Model K derived racer, was driven by Christian Werner in the 1924 event.

ABOVE RIGHT: By 1924 the agreements between Daimler and Benz were already in effect, and this example of a Daimler-Benz 2-liter, eight-cylinder race car designed by Porsche was also raced in the 1924 Targa Florio.

RIGHT: Under Porsche, advancements in engineering and design were swift, and by 1927 the Model S had been fully developed as both a touring car and a race car. At the July 1927 Nürburgring Grand Prix, a pair of the sleek, new supercharged Mercedes were driven by Caracciola and Werner.

Benz & Cie., could feel the tightening of belts. Having already agreed in principle to a mutually beneficial sharing of resources in the early postwar years, by 1924 Daimler and Benz found themselves in still greater need of each other's assistance. On May 1 they entered into an Agreement of Mutual Interest, a noncompetitive and cooperative arrangement that established the groundwork for their merger two years later, in June 1926. The formation of Daimler-Benz AG consolidated the individual engineering and production capacities of D-M-G and Benz into the largest automobile company in Germany, and at the same time it thrust Ferdinand Porsche into the spotlight as chief engineer for what was now the world's oldest and most respected automotive marque, Mercedes-Benz.

The first product of Daimler-Benz AG was the Model K, introduced in 1926. The Model K was more of an evolutionary design than a completely new luxury automobile. Based on the 1924 Type 630 Mercedes 24/100/140 PS, the Model K was principally the work of Porsche, who improved upon Paul Daimler's pioneering design of an overhead camshaft, six-cylinder engine and Roots-type supercharger, giving the massive K models unparalleled straight-line performance. Specified by Daimler-Benz to attain a top speed of 90 miles per hour, it was the fastest standard production model of its type in the world.

The supercharger was the foundation for an entirely new and more powerful generation of Mercedes that would emerge in the late 1920s and flourish throughout the following decade. The Roots supercharger, however, was not invented for the automobile. In fact, it is older. When brothers Francis and Philander Roots patented the design in 1860, the two Connersville, Indiana, inventors had no idea that their device would have any use other than to improve the performance of the water turbine at their spin-

Rosenberger and Caracciola competed with the Model S Mercedes in the June 19, 1927, Nürburgring race.

ning mill. Nevertheless, their patent laid the groundwork for the Roots-type superchargers in use to this day throughout the automotive industry.

Having gained some experience with supercharging aircraft engines during World War I, Paul Daimler was the first to attempt combining a supercharger with an automobile engine. Shortly after the war he mounted a Roots-type blower to the Knight sleeve-valve engine of a Mercedes 16/50 hp model, which proved to be an unsuitable host. Continued experiments with the larger 7.3-liter six used in the 28/95 series proved successful, and in April 1922, Daimler factory driver Max Sailer drove the first supercharged Mercedes race car to victory in the Targa Florio, the same race in which Porsche and Neubauer entered the Austro-Daimler Sascha.

The Mercedes superchargers were driven by the engine's crankshaft, and in a model like the 630K, for example, they were geared to rotate at a speed greater than that of the engine. Installed ahead of the carburetor, the blower forced precompressed air into the carburetor, which was then enriched with the fuel. The net result was immediately increased horsepower; however, the supercharger could be engaged for only short bursts of speed without fear of damaging the motor or blowing it up completely, as overzealous race drivers occasionally did. When judiciously applied, in that brief span when the engine cried its siren song, a supercharged Mercedes was breathtaking both in sight and sound. As Mercedes-Benz poignantly noted in *The Fascination of the Compressor*, a 1998 book on the history of the company's supercharged cars, "The sound and appearance of the Mercedes-Benz engines were testimony to the raw power beneath the hood. This was innovative technology encased in the most elegant car bodies of the time. The high-gloss chrome exhaust pipes that peeked from the side of the hood became synonymous with superchargers, the symbol of power and glory. These mighty machines were like creatures from ancient legends. The only way to escape their beguiling melody, their aura, their fascination, was to hide yourself away and stop up your ears." Such was the image Ferdinand Porsche had fashioned for Daimler-Benz.

As to the road manners of the new Model K, any change over the earlier car, however small, would have been considered an improvement. The stiff underpinnings—semi-elliptic leaf springs at all four corners and a cumbersome channel-section chassis—of the older model had imparted all the ride characteristics of a truck. The K introduced Porsche's improved suspension design on a shorter wheelbase, 134 inches compared with the 630's 147.5 inches.

The "K" designation in this specific instance stood for *Kurz* (German for short) rather than for *Kompressor* (supercharged) as on later Mercedes-Benz models utilizing the "K" classification, such as the 540K.

Besides putting less overall weight on a more responsive suspension, Porsche also increased the output of Daimler's supercharged six, which had previously made 100 horsepower with an additional 40 horsepower delivered by depressing the throttle pedal fully to the floor to engage the blower. The Porsche-enhanced engine delivered a maximum of 160 horsepower, the increase derived from a higher compression ratio (5.0:1, up from 4.7:1) and better ignition through Porsche's use of two spark plugs per cylinder. With a bore and stroke of 94 × 150 millimeters ($3^{11}/_{16}$ × $5^{29}/_{32}$ inches), the K's engine displaced 6.24 liters (381 cubic inches). As a transitional model during the Daimler and Benz consolidation, the 630K paved the way for Porsche's all-new S and SS series launched in the late 1920s.

The S series was particularly successful in racing, and with drivers such as Rudolf Caracciola, Christian Werner, Otto Merz, Manfred von Brauchitsch, Adolf Rosenberger, and Hans Stuck, it achieved many important international successes for Daimler-Benz. The Model S and subsequent SS and SSK were built on a new drop-center frame with a 133-inch standard wheelbase. To improve the handling over the Model K, Porsche's new design moved the radiator and engine about a foot rearward on the chassis, resulting in better front and rear weight distribution and a lower center of gravity. This lower chassis also encouraged more rakish, open coachwork.

With chassis improvements came greater performance, 120 horsepower under normal aspiration, and 180 with the super-

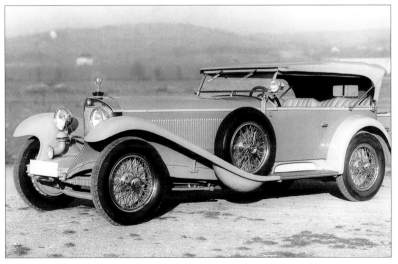

During the summer of 1927,
Porsche (seated in the stern) took
a break from Daimler-Benz to go boating
with his secretary, Ghislaine Kaes, his daughter
Louise (second from right), and son Ferry.

On June 28, 1928,
Louise Porsche married
Anton Piëch, who was
to become Ferdinand
Porsche's closest associate
in the late 1930s and a
principal in the creation
of the Volkswagen. The
Piëch family remained
associated with both
Porsche and Volkswagen
through their children,
and to this day the two
firms are still closely allied.

charger engaged. The updated engine in the Model S, the single strongest tie to Daimler, had its bore increased from 94 to 98 millimeters. With a 150-millimeter stroke, this brought displacement up to 6,789 centimeters, a massive 414 cubic inches. The SSK, powered by a 170/225-horsepower (increased to 180/250-horsepower in 1929) Roots supercharged in-line six, was capable of reaching the magic century mark, a speed that for the time every builder of luxury and sporting cars claimed to achieve. Porsche had assured that a Mercedes could.

Racing versions of the S and SS with higher-compression engines running on Elcosine—an alcohol-fuel mixture used for competition—attained speeds well in excess of 100 miles per hour. In one of these competition versions, the great Rudolf Caracciola surpassed 120 miles per hour in the 1927 Belgian Speed Trial and won the opening event of the Nürburgring. The culmination of the S Series was the SSKL, which arrived in 1931 as a lighter, more powerful version purposely built for motor sports yet equally at home on the open road.

While Porsche has always been given credit for the entire Model S series, many of the later changes that appeared on the SSK and SSKL were the work of Dr. Hans Nibel, who had been chief engineer at Benz prior to the merger and was Ferdinand Porsche's successor at Daimler-Benz in January 1929.

Porsche had originally been hired by D-M-G prior to the merger, and he left Daimler-Benz AG in December 1928 when the term of his contract expired. He returned to Austria, where he accepted a position as technical director at Steyr, but after a year he resigned, moved back to Stuttgart, and established his own design and engineering firm, Dr. Ing. H.c. F. Porsche GmbH.

Throughout the 1930s, Ferdinand Porsche's counsel as a designer and engineer as sought by many German automakers,

By the late 1930s, Porsche's counsel was being sought by Germany's leading automakers, and his fortunes were about to change with the development of the car he had longed to build since the 1920s: a small, affordable automobile that would come to be known as the "People's Car," the Volkswagen.

including Daimler-Benz. The greatest achievement of Ferdinand Porsche's career, however, would come about at the behest of history's most unlikely automotive enthusiast, Germany's chancellor Adolf Hitler.

OPPOSITE AND RIGHT: The Model K was the most powerful production car in the world in 1926. Daimler-Benz specified that it could attain a top speed of 90 miles per hour.

RIGHT: The supercharged 1926 Model K Mercedes presented an imposing image of the new Daimler-Benz concern. The revised Daimler model was the work of Ferdinand Porsche. This example was bodied in France by Hibbard & Darrin.

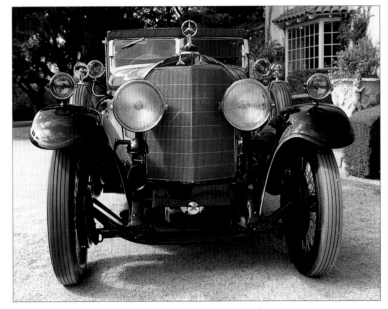

With the Model K, Porsche had taken the first step toward redefining Daimler-Benz, creating a new high-performance line that was suitable for both competition and touring. Although the Model K was a large automobile, Porsche's revised suspension and more powerful six-cylinder engine endowed the car with unrivaled performance.

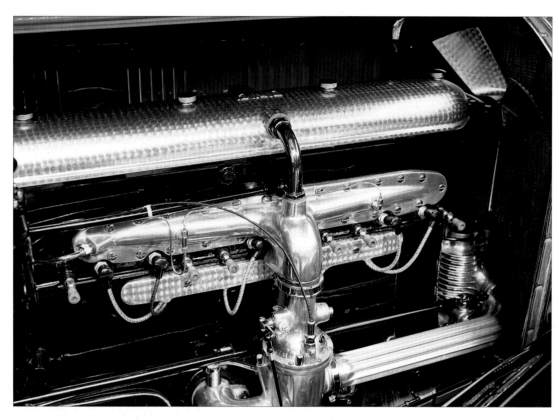

Porsche redesigned Paul Daimler's supercharged six, which now delivered a maximum of 160 horsepower; the increase was derived from a higher compression ratio of 5.0:1 and better ignition through Porsche's use of two spark plugs per cylinder. The Model K engine displaced 6.24 liters, or 381 cubic inches. The supercharger can be seen directly below the beautifully engine-turned radiator fan.

OPPOSITE: The evolution of design from the Model K to the 1927 Model S is evident in the new, lower profile and the position of the grille and engine farther back on the frame. Porsche's new design resulted in a faster and better balanced automobile suitable for competition even in touring form as pictured. This particular example was built for American song and dance man Al Jolson.

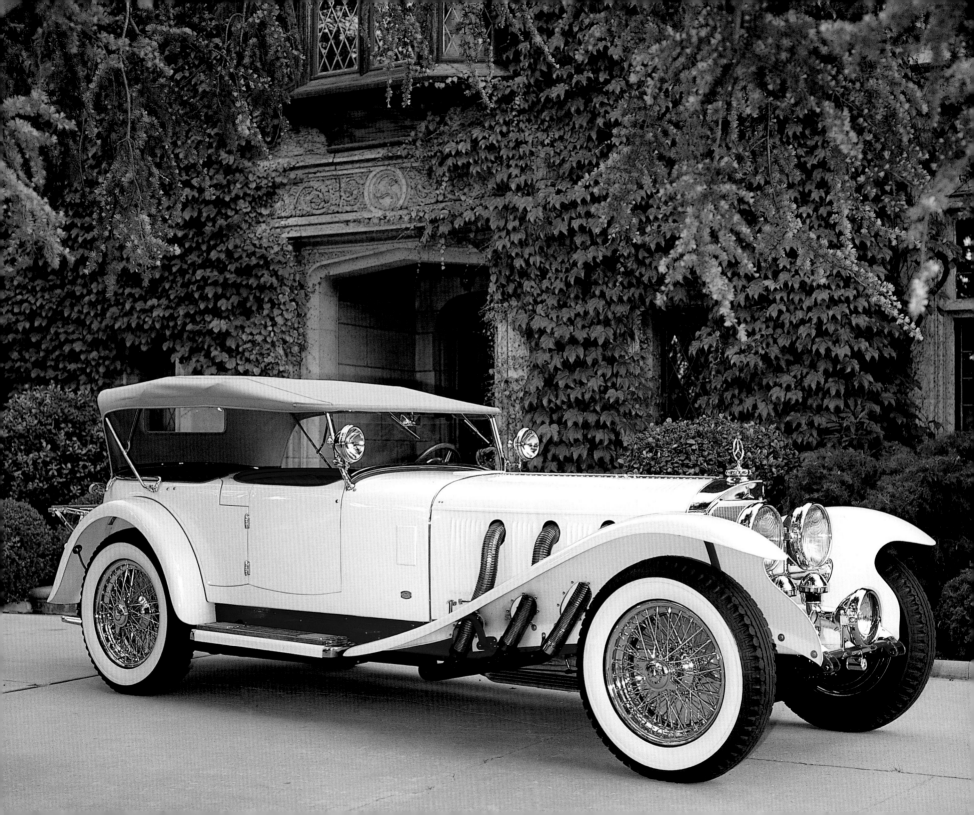

CHAPTER 2

THE EARLY YEARS IN ZUFFENHAUSEN

PORSCHE KG DESIGNS AND A WORLD ONCE AGAIN AT WAR

T HAD TAKEN FERDINAND PORSCHE NEARLY A QUAR-ter century to come to the realization that he could not work for others, at least not in a traditional sense. When he was called upon to develop an engine, a chassis, or some innovative means of over-coming a problem, his business relationships were almost exem-plary, but in the long run he ultimately found himself in conflict with those of authority. A true visionary when it came to automo-tive engineering, Ferdinand Porsche was equally shortsighted and unable or unwilling to accept decisions that were in conflict with his own. This obstinate nature led to his resignation from Austro-Daimler in 1923, from Daimler-Benz in 1928, and from Steyr in less than a year, following that company's acquisition by Austro-Daimler late in 1929. Thus in 1930 he was faced with a difficult decision: going into business for himself or seeking another engi-neering position. He had already worked for the most prestigious automakers in Germany and Austria, so his options were few. "My father naturally thought very carefully about the path he should now pursue," wrote Ferry. "He received offers from Skoda, the well-known Czech company, and from General Motors, but in the end he decided to go it alone and set up his own design company."

Porsche's departure from Daimler-Benz brought an end to his association with Alfred Neubauer, who had become head of the racing department, a position he could not afford to vacate in order to follow Porsche as he had from Austro-Daimler. Neubauer would remain with Mercedes for the rest of his career, becoming one of the most respected and influential racing managers in auto-motive history. He owed much of that success to his early associa-tion with Ferdinand Porsche.

Others whom Porsche had worked with in the past decided to follow him, including Karl Rabe, his oldest colleague, whom he had taken on at Austro-Daimler in 1913. Along with Rabe came Josef Mickle; from Steyr came gearbox specialist Karl Fröhlich and engine designer Josef Kales; from Mercedes-Benz also came race driver Adolf Rosenberger and the brilliant automotive stylist

OPPOSITE: Pictured with his father in 1934, Ferry Porsche was learning every aspect of automotive design and engineering at his side. Over the next decade Ferry would become the compelling force behind Porsche GmbH and lead the company from postwar ruin to international acclaim.

and deputy director of car body design Erwin Franz Komenda, who would be responsible for every Porsche model built from the 1930s to the 1960s.

Ferry, now twenty-one years old, became his father's assistant, and on April 25, 1931, their new design firm opened its doors at 24 Kronenstrasse, on the outskirts of Stuttgart. Ferdinand Porsche, his son-in-law, Dr. Anton Piëch, and Adolf Rosenberger were equal partners in the daring new venture. In all, Porsche had brought twelve of his former colleagues with him from Austria to Stuttgart, ensuring a highly skilled team of designers, engineers, and assemblers. Ferry, still receiving private tutoring in mechanics, physics, and engineering after leaving the Institute of Technology in Vienna, devoted most of his time to the company by learning every facet of its operation.

The Porsche design studio soon had commissions from several of Germany's leading automakers, but the very first came in 1930 from Wanderer, solely on the merits of Porsche making public his intentions to set up an independent design studio. Wanderer was interested in a medium-size car with a six-cylinder engine of between 1.7 and 2 liters capacity and an output of 35 to 40 horsepower. Work began in late December, and the design proposal was delivered on April 1, 1931. By then Wanderer had merged with Horch, DKW, and Audi to form the great German Auto Union, which was to become one of Porsche's most important clients. Ironically, Paul Daimler was now chief designer for the Auto Union, so once more the paths of Daimler and Porsche crossed. The Porsche studio was initially assigned work on models for Wanderer while Daimler pursued development of a new eight-cylinder Horch, intended to compete with Mercedes-Benz.

In 1932, Ferdinand Porsche received an unprecedented invitation from the Soviet Union to visit the country and tour its automotive manufacturing facilities. He was given the red carpet treatment and granted access to every Russian assembly plant, including those for aircraft and military vehicles. It was uncommon for a westerner to have such access, but the Soviets had an ulterior motive. At the end of his tour the Russian government offered Porsche the position of national director of development and design for the Soviet motor industry. Although flattered by the proposal, Porsche declined, feeling that at the age of fifty-seven it was more responsibility than he wanted to undertake. One can only imagine the course Eastern European automotive history might have taken had Ferdinand Porsche accepted.

Back home, the fire still burned within Porsche to design a truly affordable car, and the opportunity finally presented itself in 1932 with a commission from the German NSU motorcycle factory. They wanted to try building a small car, and Porsche was free to use whatever ideas he wanted just as long as the vehicle remained within budget. The result was a design known as the Model 32, a true predecessor to the Volkswagen. The NSU utilized an air-cooled, flat-four (horizontally opposed) engine mounted in the rear, with a body designed by Komenda that could best be described in appearance as a stretched VW. The car also introduced a new torsion bar suspension system developed by Porsche. Ferry noted, "Historians of the motor industry have seen it as an important stage in the history of automobile technology." Unfortunately for the Porsche Model 32, NSU motorcycle sales soared in 1933, and with production at capacity, the Model 32 was never manufactured. The foundation had been laid, however, for Porsche's small car, and virtually all the technology developed for the NSU would later be utilized on the VW prototype.

Germany had finally rebounded from the aftermath of World War I, but by the early 1930s the European economy was beginning to feel the aftershock of Wall Street's collapse. The loss of sales abroad was taking a toll on every industry, but once again it was the automotive sector that was feeling the greatest pinch.

German auto sales had fallen from 62,563 in 1931 to 44,448 by 1932, a decline of more than 25 percent in one year. Similar declines were being experienced by American automakers, but in Germany this incident marked a significant turning point in the history of the automotive industry. For the first time since the dawn of the motorcar, the automobile and the national infrastructure necessary to support it were about to be politicized. The new chancellor of the German reich, Adolf Hitler, believed that the automobile was a means of reaching the German people. His plan was to breathe new life into the country's declining automotive marketplace by having a car built that was within the financial grasp of the average man. Hitler first eliminated taxes on all new cars registered on or after April 1, 1933, and then he instituted a vigorous renovation of the German highway system and revealed plans for a new national motorway, the autobahn. The news had the desired effect: By the end of 1933 automobile sales had rebounded to 92,226.

There was, however, a sinister and immoral undertone to Hitler's plans for a new Germany. This was the wanton persecution of Jews, which had already begun by the early 1930s. Ferdinand Porsche's partner, Adolf Rosenberger, wanted to quit the firm and leave the country. Rosenberger was Jewish and quite understandably saw no future for himself in Germany under the new political system. He was part owner of Porsche GmbH, and his shares had

to be bought out. Porsche and Piëch immediately went looking for an investor, but none were found. Piëch finally persuaded a wealthy would-be Austrian race driver named Hans von Veyder-Malberg to purchase Rosenberger's interest in the company, but it was too late. Rosenberger had already been arrested and imprisoned by the Nazis. Feeling a responsibility to his friend and partner, Ferdinand Porsche used his influence to appeal for his release. Hitler complied. Once out of prison, Rosenberger immigrated to America, where he spent the rest of his life. Though he was now

The Porsche house in Stuttgart in 1929, a year after Ferdinand Porsche (far left) had resigned from Mercedes-Benz. He was now in the employ of Steyr, but that would last less than a year. At the senior Porsche's side are his son, Ferry, Anna Porsche, and two Steyr employees with a new model.

One of the highlights of Ferdinand Porsche's career as an automotive designer was the 1934 Auto Union race car. It is pictured here at the Nürburgring in July with driver Hans Stuck.

The body design of the Auto Union race car is clearly shown in this view during a pit stop. Porsche had created something entirely new with this car—a challenger not only to Mercedes-Benz but to the world of motor racing.

out of harm's way, his departure was a blow to Porsche, and his racing experience and business acumen would be sorely missed. Now the ugly underbelly of Hitler and the Third Reich were appallingly revealed to Ferdinand Porsche, but he was indebted.

Porsche's next and perhaps most historically significant project was the design and construction of a new race car for the German Auto Union. The organization, headquartered in Chemnitz in Saxony, regarded racing as the most effective means of attracting

public attention to its united brands, symbolized by the four intertwining rings of the Auto Union insignia—the emblem still used today by Audi. This was a bold undertaking, and Porsche brought to bear all his design and engineering resources to create a novel and remarkable race car. It was also a very expensive one, and the Auto Union petitioned Berlin for a state subsidy.

At the onset Hitler had only intended to back one manufacturer in motor racing, Mercedes-Benz; however, the alliance of

The forward-cabin seating position of driver Hans Stuck is clearly shown in this view. With the engine mounted behind the driver, the car's weight distribution and handling characteristics were unique.

The Auto Union race car at the Nürburgring in June 1936, with driver Ernst von Delius.

Germany's most dashing race driver was Bernd Rosemeyer, shown here with the Auto Union race car at Roosevelt Raceway on Long Island. The car was shipped over in 1937 to compete in the Vanderbilt Cup race.

A rare photo of the Auto Union race car at rest in 1934. Porsche's design for the Auto Union set new standards for design, engineering, and performance with a sixteen-cylinder engine mounted behind the cockpit.

Porsche and the Auto Union was too tempting, and he ordered the Ministry of Transport to underwrite the project. Thus, Mercedes-Benz received 500,000 reichsmarks and Auto Union 300,000, thereby turning the two companies into rivals. To further increase the competition between them, each was given another 300,000 reichsmarks in 1934, and from 1935 to 1939 the sum of 400,000 annually. This was all part of Hitler's plan to prove German superiority through motor sports, and it was extraordinarily successful: Mercedes-Benz and the Auto Union dominated Grand Prix and sports car racing throughout Europe until 1939.

Porsche's design for the Auto Union was a Grand Prix car powered by a sixteen-cylinder engine mounted behind the driver. The fuselage-shaped body was what one might call an early cab-forward design, placing the driver closer to the front wheels. The cars made their first appearance in 1934 and were a sensation. Drivers Hans Stuck, the Prince of Leiningen, and August Momberger set three world records on the Avus course, reaching a top speed of 180 miles per hour and averaging 134.93 miles per hour.

In its first year, 1934, the sixteen-cylinder Auto Union race cars had some impressive successes, including victories in the German Grand Prix at the Nürburgring, the Swiss Grand Prix at the Bremgarten circuit in Bern, and the Czech Grand Prix at the Masarykring in Brno, all with the factory team driver Hans Stuck. In the 1930s, Ferry had also become quite skilled behind the wheel of a race car, testing the notoriously difficult to handle Auto Unions at competition speeds—this to the absolute disparagement of his father, who preferred him behind a drafting table. "My father was not keen on my racing," Ferry explained in 1984. "He used to say he had many drivers . . . but only one son."

Porsche's success with the Auto Union brought another important project to his company's doorstep, not from a manufac-turer but from the Führer himself. Porsche was now to design a "people's car," a "Volkswagen."

At the opening of the 1934 Berlin Motor Show, Adolf Hitler had given a speech in which he called upon the German automotive industry to develop a new small car, one that was affordable and economical to run and repair. This was the very description of the car Porsche had designed and prototyped for NSU. This was the car he had wanted to build since the Sascha. It was unfortunate that his long-awaited benefactor turned out to be Hitler.

As Ferry Porsche recalled, the entire project was virtually handed to his father following a meeting with Hitler in the spring of 1934. "At this meeting my father presented his plans for the people's car to Hitler, who agreed with his technical design but requested that the sale price of the vehicle should not exceed 1,000 reichsmarks. A basic decision had thus been taken, and our design office immediately began work, although there was still no agreement in writing. The new project went into the company's files as the Type 60."

In order for Porsche to get a written agreement, the project had to officially pass through the German Automobile Manufacturers Association (Reichsverband der Automobilindustrie, or RDA), and the association was not at all pleased that Hitler had given the Volkswagen project to Porsche. In their view it was a fait accompli, but several of the association members also had small-car projects of their own in their production schedule and regarded the Type 60 as "posing a real threat to them." Nonetheless, the RDA reached an agreement with Porsche GmbH, and a contract commissioning the Volkswagen was signed on June 22, 1934. It provided the company with a monthly fee of 20,000 reichsmarks for a period of only ten months, by which time the project was to be completed. The time frame was too short. Ferdinand Porsche realized he was being set up to fail. When he left the building, he was approached by two association members, and Ferry Porsche recalls that one said, "'Herr Porsche, if you spend the money and then say that it can't be done, that will be exactly what we expect from you!' To this my father replied, 'Then you have given the contract to the wrong man, because it can be done!'" The industrialist then declared, "'But, Herr Porsche, the people's car is a bus. What does each worker need his own car for?' My father walked away."

Although they had been given the 20,000-reichsmark monthly subsidy, it was not enough to fund the entire developmental project, and Ferdinand and Ferry Porsche, along with a dozen of the company's designers and engineers, ended up building the first prototype in the Porsche family garage. "Both money and time were in short supply, and even today I am still amazed that we actually managed to complete the project," wrote Ferry in 1989, more than fifty years after the first Volkswagen prototype was completed.

Initially, two versions of the car were preprototyped: a saloon (a two-door coupe) and an open top (a convertible coupe), designated V1 and V2. In December 1934 the Porsches were given approval to build a trio of test cars, designated the V3 prototype series and later referred to by the Roman numerals I, II, and III. The cars had four-wheel independent suspension with spring torsion bars in the front axle tubes and, at the rear, a floating axle with a longitudinal control arm on either side and transverse spring torsion bars in the axle tube. There was a central tubular frame, and

Ferdinand Porsche (left) and engineer Karl Rabe reviewing the final design for the Volkswagen in 1938.

the engine was mounted behind and the four-speed gearbox in front of the rear axle. (These same features would later become the underpinning of the Porsche 356.)

The project appeared to be going well, but the prototypes were not roadworthy by April 1935, the end of the ten-month agreement. The RDA immediately accused Porsche GmbH of breach of contract and declared that the VW would be built as a common effort among its members. In July Daimler-Benz undertook the responsibility of designing an experimental body while other automakers attended to engineering calculations. Porsche

Not the Volkswagen. Two years before the VW was put into prewar production at Wolfsburg, the German Automobile Manufacturers Association had leveraged control of the project from Porsche GmbH and Daimler-Benz had been commissioned to build thirty VW prototypes. At the same time, Daimler-Benz was also developing its own version of a "people's car," which just happened to debut ahead of the VW and shared virtually all of Ferdinand Porsche's engineering designs and Erwin Komenda's body styling. Introduced in 1936, the Mercedes Type 170H was the last rear-engine model produced by Daimler-Benz.

GmbH was still involved, but the RDA had opened a Pandora's box. The end result was that Daimler-Benz built thirty preproduction prototypes that were completed by the spring of 1937, a year *after* the debut of the Mercedes-Benz Type 170H, which in no small way resembled the VW!

It is ironic that one of Ferdinand Porsche's ongoing disputes with Daimler-Benz management in the late 1920s was over his de-sire to design and build a more affordable car. Under Porsche's direction Daimler-Benz had begun experimenting in 1927 with rear-mounted engines, swing axles, and unibody construction, but nothing had come of it by the time of his resignation in December 1928. Now, two years prior to the Volkswagen's debut, here was Mercedes with the 170H, a rear-engine saloon with nearly identical specifications to the VW and a body all too coincidentally evoca-tive of Komenda's final design, which was completed on January 18, 1936, and affixed to VW prototype III. The unmistakable simi-larity between the last rear-engine model to be produced by Daimler-Benz and that of the Volkswagen left little doubt that Fer-dinand Porsche was facing strong opposition from not only the RDA but his former employers as well.

Although Daimler-Benz had stolen some of the Volks-wagen's thunder, the 170H was still a Mercedes, and price would ultimately separate the two cars—that and Hitler's support for the VW, a design in which the Führer had taken a personal interest from the beginning. Even more revealing was that the contract to produce the cars was not given to an established manufacturer, as Daimler-Benz had anticipated in 1937 after building the thirty pre-production prototypes at the RDA's request. Instead, a new fac-tory for the people's car was to be erected at Fallersleben in Wolfsburg under the direction of Ferdinand Porsche. Financed by the German Labor Front and owned by the state, the facility was officially known as the KdF assembly plant. It was here that the first prewar cars following Porsche's design were produced in 1939; however, when World War II began, production at the KdF quickly switched over to Volkswagen-based military vehicles de-signed by Porsche GmbH.

Two years earlier, in an effort to exhibit the superiority of German technology, the sixteen-cylinder Auto Union race car was

The Porsche test crew stops for a little roadside celebration after a successful trial run of the Type 60 V1 cabriolet and V2 saloon in 1936.

BELOW LEFT AND RIGHT: The 1936 VW Type 60 V3 prototype at the Porsche villa in Zell am See. Komenda had not yet rendered the final version of the body design. This example lacks a rear window.

ABOVE LEFT: By October 1936 the familiar shape of the VW was realized.

ABOVE RIGHT: Another pair of prototypes, the W30 (left) and the V3 III, are pictured outside the Porsche villa in 1937. Note that the doors are still hinged at the rear and open to the front.

sent to the United States to compete in the famous Vanderbilt Cup Race. Driven by popular German race driver Bernd Rosemeyer, the Auto Union was once again victorious, drawing the desired attention to the German automotive industry that Hitler had wanted. Ferdinand and Ferry Porsche had traveled to the United States to attend the race and to visit American automakers, in particular Henry Ford.

While in Detroit, Ferry took note of the way doors were hinged on most American cars. The thirty VWs assembled by Daimler-Benz had their doors hinged to the center post and opened toward the front of the car. Americans often referred to this as a "suicide-style door." In the United States, observed Ferry, the majority of production cars had their doors hinged at the front and opened to the rear; thus if a door became unlatched in traffic, it would not be blown open. When the VW finally went into production, Porsche made use of this American-inspired design.

The visit with Henry Ford was one of Ferry's most memorable experiences because Ford directed some of his more note-

worthy questions to him rather than his father. Ford was interested in the opinions of a young man, and Ferry responded with enthusiasm about the VW project as a car for the people, something to which Ford could relate, having done much the same with the Model T in the early 1900s. However, when Ferdinand Porsche extended an invitation to Ford to visit Germany, he made a gesture of refusal, saying, "Unfortunately, that won't be possible because there's going to be a war!"

"His tone was very persuasive, and his words did not fail to have an effect on us," wrote Ferry. "In 1937, who was thinking of war? I was twenty-eight years old at the time, and it made a deep impression on me, giving me plenty of food for thought. Our trip had given me a feeling of freedom and shown me the opportunities offered by a free economy, emphasizing how different it all was at home. Many years later, when we built our own factory and were able to operate in accordance with the principles of the free economy, I often cast my mind back to that visit in 1937. However, there was a long, hard road to struggle along before we reached our current level of achievement." Indeed, there was going to be a war, and the Porsches were going to find themselves right in the middle of it. The machinations of Adolf Hitler and the Third Reich were becoming clearer day by day.

On March 12, 1938, Germany annexed Austria, and on May 26 a great celebration was held in Wolfsburg at which Hitler laid the foundation stone for the new Volkswagen factory. "To the great surprise of all of us," said Ferry Porsche, "Hitler renamed the VW the KdF car after the Strength Through Joy (*Kraft durch Freude*) section of the German Labor Front, which had taken the place of the labor unions [and financed the VW factory]. I was horrified by this renaming since numerous press reports had ensured that the VW trademark was already internationally known. Volkswagen, or People's Car, was a readily understandable name, while the same could hardly be said of KdF." It was done, however; Hitler had spoken, and nothing could change it.

Porsche had brought three VW prototypes to the groundbreaking ceremony, and afterward Ferry was asked to drive Hitler to the train station in a VW cabriolet. The German chancellor sat in the backseat with Ferdinand Porsche, and all along the route crowds lining the road cheered them and tossed garlands of flowers into the new people's car. "Hitler did not seem to be bothered by this; he just beamed and waved to the cheering crowd," said Ferry. His personal endorsement of the VW made people take notice. It aroused in them a hope that they would soon have a KdF car of their own. It was a hope that would not soon be realized.

On the drive to the train station Ferry thought again about his trip to America the previous year and the impression it had made on him. Perhaps Hitler, he mused, should be sent on a trip around the world. Maybe then he, too, would see things through different eyes. A few years earlier it might have made a difference,
but by the summer of 1938 too much had already changed in Germany. Henry Ford had been right: There was going to be a war.

With projects from both the Auto Union and Daimler-Benz, among others, the Porsche *Werk* (factory) had expanded from only nineteen employees to over one hundred. In 1936, Porsche GmbH acquired property in Stuttgart-Zuffenhausen, and in June 1938 the entire operation moved into a new design and manufacturing facility. Now owned entirely by members of the Porsche family, the company became a limited partnership, or *Kommanditgesellschaft* (in German one keeps adding letters until you get the word you want), at which time the firm was renamed Porsche KG. Today this building is the site of Porsche Werk I.

The "People's Car" was simple. The efficiency of interior design shown on this W30 prototype dictated a single-combination gauge and two cubbyholes for storage. The final version was more elaborate and had two instrument fascias and glove box doors.

In the interim, Karosserie Reutter in Zuffenhausen had assembled another series of thirty KdF cars for Porsche to be used as sales demonstration models while the Wolfsburg factory was being completed. All these models had their doors hinged at the front and opened toward the rear of the car, as Ferry had observed. He had also become involved, along with his father and Erwin Komenda, in the design of a VW-based sports racing car, the Type 64 60K10.

The so-called Berlin-Rome axis, an alliance formed by Hitler and Mussolini, set in motion an ambitious plan for a road race between the two capital cities. Even before this announcement,

Porsche and Komenda had been at work on the design for a streamlined race car based on the Volkswagen platform. It was a logical progression: the same chassis fitted with a more powerful version of the VW flat four and surrounded by an aerodynamic body that would achieve both greater speed and fuel economy. "The VW," said Ferry, "provided an almost perfect basis for further development in this direction."

The idea had been briefly explored with the Type 114, a design exercise for a rear-engine V-10 sports car, and the Type 64, a VW-based streamliner. This was to be fitted with an engine bored out to 1.5 liters and an aluminum body with a lower coefficient of drag. Ferry wrote, "We had, of course, submitted our plans for making a sports version of the VW to the leaders of the German Labor Front, but they rejected them out of hand. They were unable to go along with plans of that kind. Later we hit upon the idea of making our own car based on VW components, which could have been supplied to us by the Wolfsburg factory, but this proposal was not favorably received, either. As an entirely state-run enterprise, VW did not want to make available components from the KdF car for private initiatives." Fortunately, Hitler and Benito Mussolini's plan for the Berlin-Rome race, to be held under the auspices of the National Sporting Authority (ONS), provided the opportunity to develop a few VW competition models with the state's approval and financing.

Volkswagens cruise through Berlin in 1939. Note that the cars now have front-hinged doors. Ferry incorporated the design in 1937 after returning from his trip to America, where he observed that most U.S. cars were built in this fashion.

ABOVE LEFT AND RIGHT: A preproduction Volkswagen cabriolet with a body by Reutter for use as a demonstrator. The car was used by Ferry Porsche to drive Hitler to the Wolfsburg train station following groundbreaking ceremonies for the KdF assembly plant on May 26, 1938. **BELOW LEFT:** Karosserie Reutter in Zuffenhausen built the bodies for the first thirty Volkswagens produced by Porsche as demonstrators in 1938. **BELOW RIGHT:** In May 1940, Ferdinand Porsche was photographed in one of the early prewar Volkswagens. Note the sliding Webasto fabric-covered roof. The top fabric could be folded back along rails to open the interior. Similar tops were popular on Mercedes in the early 1950s, and VW models were shown in KdF-Wagen sales brochures published before the war.

In 1941 production at *Werk I* in Zuffenhausen consisted of a combination of Volkswagen-based military designs.

The Type 64 60K10 would combine features developed for the VW (Type 60), Type 114, and Type 64, the K denoting the use of an aluminum body coach-built by Reutter. Komenda designed streamlined coachwork for the car; it was nearly identical to that of the proposed Type 114, which bore little resemblance to a Volkswagen but looked remarkably similar to his first postwar design for the 356. With limited time and resources the Porsche *Werk* was able to build only three examples of the Type 64 60K10 prior to the scheduled race.

The route was to follow part of the new Berlin-Munich motorway (autobahn) and then lead from Munich through the Bren-

ner Pass into Austria. A series of closed-off Italian motorways would then provide the route into Rome. The total distance was 808 miles. In road tests the Porsche race cars achieved a top speed of 87 miles per hour and averaged 81.25 miles per hour in timed runs between Berlin and the VW factory at Fallersleben in Wolfsburg. Ferry lamented that "the Berlin-Rome race was to take place in September 1939, but like so many other things intended to serve peaceful ends, it, too, fell victim to the war."

On September 1, Hitler's forces invaded Poland; two days later, on Ferdinand Porsche's sixty-fourth birthday, England and France declared war on Germany, and every hope of peace in

Europe vanished. So did production of the VW and Porsche's plans for the Type 60K10. They were never raced. Two remained at the Porsche *Werk*, while the third prototype was written off after being involved in a collision. Raced or not, the Type 60K10 had sown the seeds for a Porsche sports car. While the company was committed to the design of VW-based military vehicles throughout the war, the idea of a sports car never faded from Ferry Porsche's thoughts.

Completely apolitical, the Porsche father and son found themselves in an almost untenable position with Hitler's reich during the war. The German chancellor liked Ferdinand Porsche, referring to him at the opening of the 1935 German Motor Show as an "outstanding designer." Hitler also had a great deal of respect for Porsche, and some say the Führer looked up to him with almost father-figure admiration. He requested Porsche's counsel and expertise

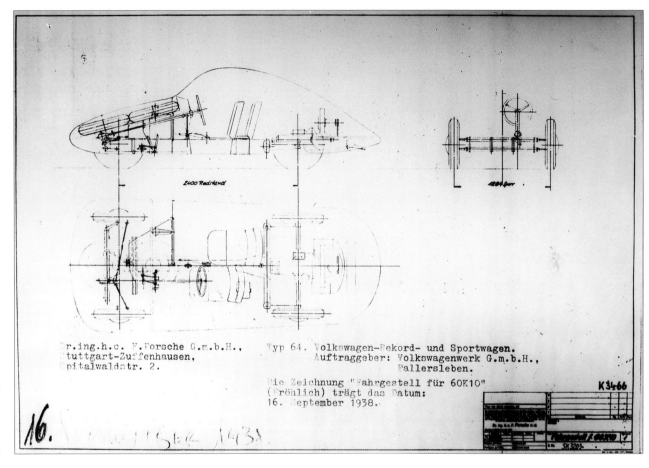

Dr.ing.h.c. F.Porsche G.m.b.H., Stuttgart-Zuffenhausen, Spitalwaldstr. 2.

Typ 64. Volkswagen-Rekord- und Sportwagen. Auftraggeber: Volkswagenwerk G.m.b.H., Fallersleben.

Die Zeichnung "Fahrgestell für 60K10" (Fröhlich) trägt das Datum: 16. September 1938.

as a designer more than anyone else's, although this was likely influenced by the variety of military vehicles that could be produced using the Volkswagen's platform. From 1939 to 1945, Porsche KG was asked to design everything from amphibious VW Schwimmwagens to tanks and tank destroyers. In 1939, Ferdinand Porsche was made manager of the Volkswagen factory; his son-in-law, Anton Piëch, become Porsche's deputy; and Ferry took over management of the Zuffenhausen design office.

Another indication of Hitler's favoritism was the appointment of Ferdinand Porsche as reich auto designer and a decision to grant the contract for the design of a cross-country vehicle to Porsche KG. The Porsche proposal had, of course, been based on the KdF car that Hitler personally favored. Because of Ferry's involvement with the project he was exempted from military service, allowing him to continue design and engineering work. The Porsche-designed VW Kübelwagen, or "bucket car,"

In September 1938, Ferry Porsche and Erwin Komenda were working on the design for a Volkswagen-based sports car. The Type 64 60K10 had been approved by the state for development as a competition car to race in the 1939 Berlin-to-Rome event.

ABOVE LEFT AND RIGHT: From drafting board to sheet metal, the evolution of the first Porsche-designed sports car, the Type 64 60K10, took about a year. The result was three examples of the higher-performance Volkswagen platform surrounded by Komenda's streamliner body. The contours that would become the Porsche 356 can be seen in these 1939 photos.

Developmental work on the VW-based sports car continued into 1941, when prototype 1 of the 60K10 streamliners was wrecked in this collision. The remaining two cars were moved to Gmünd, Austria, in 1943 to protect them from bombing raids over Stuttgart-Zuffenhausen.

as the soldiers called it, became the German equivalent of the American Jeep.

Ferry found it ironic that the VW had earned this reputation. He wrote that "the Volkswagen was conceived as a means of mass transport; it was designed with the aim of offering the man on the street a little bit of independence by making it possible for him to afford his own car. With the outbreak of World War II, this aim unfortunately passed completely out of sight. Nevertheless, it was to become a reality after the war when democracy was restored."

It was obvious that Ferdinand Porsche had Hitler's ear, and you have to wonder how an engineer's mind functioned in an environment where all reason, if not sanity, had been abandoned. Ferry believed that Hitler had gone mad. He was known to ignore the advice of his generals and, in matters of military vehicle design, the counsel of Ferdinand Porsche as well, demanding new tanks of such massive size that they were impractical. In response to one such request, the elder Porsche made an astonishing proposal to Hitler in the presence of the internationally renowned tank expert General Heinz Guderian: Rather than larger tanks, smaller soldiers should be used, with a maximum height of 5 feet 3 inches, so that smaller, more maneuverable tanks could be built! Ferry attended the meeting and was equally astonished by Hitler's response. "There's something in that," said the Führer with conviction, "and what's more, small men are more courageous than big ones. Look at Napoleon and Prince Eugene!" Hitler himself was short of stature, and no one was really certain whether Porsche had been serious, but Hitler appeared to have taken it that way. As Ferry wrote years later, "The matter never went any further." Porsche KG did design the 68-ton Jägdpanzer tank destroyer and, as Hitler had wanted, a land battleship, the biggest tank of World War II, the 180-ton Type 205 Maus. Despite argu-

A handful of KdF-Wagens were built for military use during the war. This cabriolet was built in 1943.

The Volkswagen was a versatile platform suitable for a variety of different bodies and uses. This was the prototype for a small truck.

ments from the Army regarding the impracticality of such an immense tank, Hitler ordered two built and the contract awarded to Porsche. It is believed that both, built in 1944, were captured by the Allies and taken away.

Neither Ferdinand nor Ferry Porsche was a military man. Both were designers and engineers, sportsmen and dreamers who were suddenly faced with an unwelcome task. The vehicles of war designed by Porsche KG were no less a necessity of the times than

ABOVE LEFT AND RIGHT: The KdF Type 287 was a full military version of the Volkswagen. The rear-engine design and the weight of the car made it suitable for traversing difficult terrain. Note the Porsche-built tractor in the background.

BELOW LEFT: The Volkswagen-based Kübelwagen, or "bucket car," as the soldiers called it, became the German equivalent of the American Jeep, capable of transporting personnel over varied terrain regardless of the weather.

BELOW RIGHT: The Volkswagen at war was often more than the sum of its parts; on occasion, however, there were more parts. This is a Type 155 Kübelwagen modified to a half-track.

those built by Rolls-Royce, Ford, General Motors, Packard, and Chrysler for the Allied forces. War is blind in that respect. The eyes of American and British bombardiers, however, were not, and the Porsche facilities, the VW plant in Wolfsburg, and those of Daimler-Benz were regarded as primary targets. During an Allied bombing raid in 1943, a nearby explosion blew the roof off Ferdinand Porsche's house, which was situated on a hill overlooking the city. "When we returned from the air raid shelter," recalled Ferry, "there was a fiery glow in the valley: Stuttgart was burning." A single bomb had struck the Porsche plant in Zuffenhausen, doing only minor damage to the building but destroying the archives that contained all of the company's original design illustrations. Fortunately, there were duplicates at the Porsche villa and in the house of Ghislaine Kaes, Ferdinand Porsche's personal secretary.

Porsche also designed an amphibious version of the Volkswagen aptly named the Schwimmwagen.

This necessitated Porsche's move at the end of 1943 from Zuffenhausen to the small Austrian village of Gmünd in Kärnten, about twenty-five miles north of the Italian border in the Malta Valley. Ferry was responsible for the move and decided to set up manufacturing facilities at an old sawmill in Gmünd as well as small workshops in the hangars at a flight school not far from the Porsche family's Austrian estate in Zell am See. He also made the decision that Porsche KG headquarters should remain in Stuttgart-Zuffenhausen even though design and manufacturing would be conducted elsewhere. "The evacuation lasted until well into 1944," wrote Ferry. "My organization of the removal was based on an old Jewish saying: 'Divide your possessions into three, then you will always have something to start again with.' So it was in the converted sawmill that the Porsche family and associates would sit out the remainder of the war, far removed from the battle and free to work on new designs.

For Hitler's reich the end of the conflict was in sight. For the German automotive industry the end had already come by 1944. The KdF assembly plant in Wolfsburg had been heavily damaged, and the Mercedes-Benz facilities in Mannheim, Sindelfingen, Gaggenau near Baden-Baden, and Untertürkheim were nearly leveled to their foundations.

Ferry Porsche and Karl Rabe stood in the doorway of the small workshop listening to the sound of distant thunder. Across the room, Ferdinand Porsche sat with his elbows propped on the edge of a worktable, his chin resting on folded hands, and his bleary eyes closed tightly to block out the dismal image of Allied bombers and far-off battles. His thoughts began to drift back to better times, before Hitler—before the ugly war—to the days when he was the most sought-after automotive engineer in all of Germany. He had no idea what the future held in store.

On May 8, 1945, the war in Europe ended. Zell am See and Gmünd were occupied by American and British forces, and to Ferry's amazement one of the first U.S. soldiers to arrive at the Porsche house in Zell am See was driving a Volkswagen! Two officers arrived later in an American Jeep. Both of them knew Ferdinand Porsche. One was an English lieutenant colonel named G. C. Reeves, a former race driver who had followed Porsche's success with the Auto Union race car; the other was an American major named Torre Franzen, a former Chrysler engineer who had met Porsche on his first visit to the United States in 1936. Ferry was relieved by their arrival, but for the Porsche family the trials of war had just begun.

Ferdinand Porsche was not a military man; he was a designer caught up in a world at war. He is shown here in 1940, at age sixty-five, with one of the early Reutter-bodied Volkswagen prototypes.

After the bombing of Stuttgart-Zuffenhausen in 1943, the Porsche *Werk* was moved to Gmünd, Austria, and set up in an old sawmill.
The buildings housed design and prototyping. Workshops were also set up at the flight school near Zell am See.

OVERLEAF: The Porsche Type 64 60K10 streamliner was built for the Berlin-Rome race, which was scheduled for September 1939. With Germany's invasion of Poland on September 1, England and France declared war on Germany two days later, and the race was canceled.

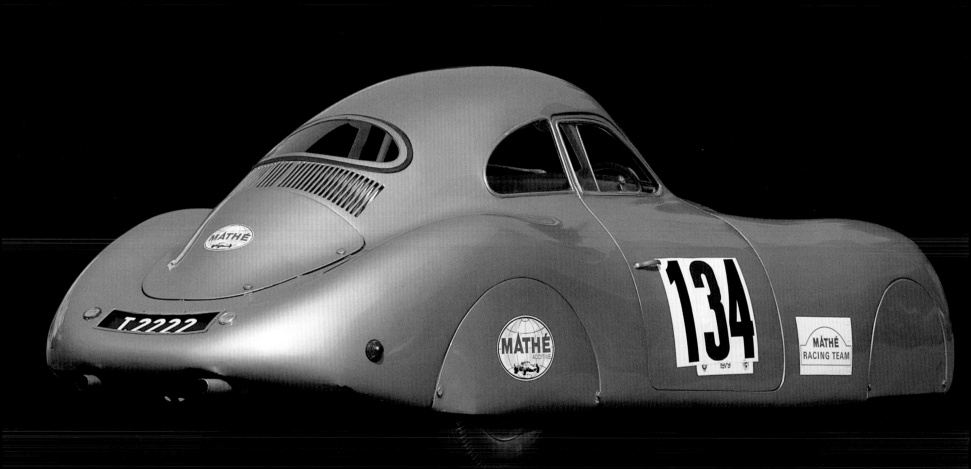

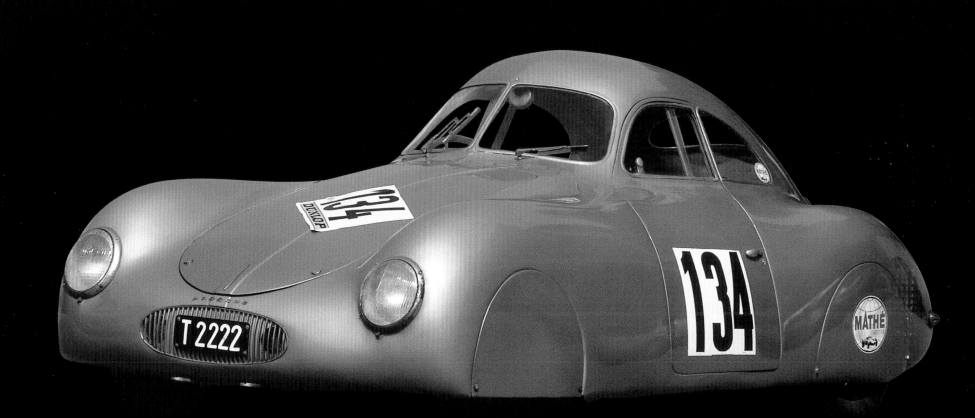

CHAPTER 3

AFTER THE WINDS OF WAR

THE EARLY DAYS IN GMÜND

G ERMANY LOST MORE THAN A WAR IN 1945. Hitler's Third Reich, with its perverse political ideology, unspeakable atrocities, and brazen aggression toward its European neighbors, had turned the world against Germany for the second time in the twentieth century. However, unlike after World War I, when the country had merely been humbled by its defeat, its industries restricted, and its borders redrawn by provisions in the Versailles and St. Germain treaties, this time German cities had been pummeled from the skies by Allied saturation bombing. Its factories, roads, and rail networks were reduced to rubble, and its industry, government, and military were dismantled by the occupation forces. This was a nation in total despair, a country divided in two and occupied by the Americans, French, British, and Russians. Germany would have to rebuild from its own ashes, some still warm to the touch.

What remained of the KdF factory in Wolfsburg was now under British jurisdiction. Factory workers were permitted to re-turn in the summer of 1945, and a handful of surviving prewar VWs were repaired for use by the occupying forces. New VW construction would resume later in the year under British authority, making VW one of the first German automakers to begin postwar manufacturing. By the end of 1946 more than ten thousand VWs had been produced!

Porsche KG headquarters in Stuttgart-Zuffenhausen was first occupied by the French and then turned over to the Americans, who used it as a transit camp for Russian prisoners of war awaiting repatriation. The U.S. military then started using the Porsche assembly shops as repair facilities for their trucks and Jeeps. Thus, by 1946, Porsche was a company divided not only by the Americans and British but also by two countries, Germany and Austria. Porsche KG would not regain use of the Zuffenhausen *Werk* until the 1950s.

Germany was facing a similar problem of division and ownership after the war. The country was to be divided into the West

OPPOSITE:
Erwin Komenda's 1948 design for the 356-2 coupe body relied heavily on his prewar styling of the Type 64 60K10 Berlin-Rome streamliners. The aerodynamic profile of the car has evolved over the past fifty-five years into the current Porsche coupe, a still familiar silhouette.

Part of the restored Porsche *Werk* in Gmünd as it appears today. It is now a historic sight.

German Federal Republic, still occupied by the Americans, British, and French; and the German Democratic Republic (East Germany), which would remain under the control of the Russians. This separation and the indissoluble Soviet hold on East Germany was to keep the country divided for the next forty-five years.

Fortunately for Daimler-Benz, they were on the right side of the division after the war ended, although nearly all their manufacturing plants had been badly damaged or destroyed. Mercedes-Benz introduced its first postwar models in 1946 and had most of its factories rebuilt by 1948.

BMW, which had built engines for the Luftwaffe jet fighters used late in the war, fared even worse. Its major automotive manufacturing facilities were located in Eisenach, now considered part of Eastern Germany. They were appropriated by the Russians and

managed by the Soviet automotive consortium Auto Velo, which began producing prewar-designed BMW models by the end of 1945. It would take until 1951 before BMW was able to rebuild itself in West Germany, regain sole rights to its name from the Soviets, and introduce its first postwar automobiles.

Overall, Porsche had fared much better than most of its contemporaries. Although the Americans occupied the Porsche factory in Zuffenhausen and the British controlled the VW factory in Wolfsburg, Porsche was permitted to resume design work in Gmünd, Austria, by the end of 1946. Ferry's division of company assets into three locations had proven to be a wise decision. The visit from the British and American officers had also been a pleasant surprise for the Porsche family. Such would not have been the case had the Russians or French arrived first. In fact, the United States stationed guards to protect the Porsche family house should either Russian or French officers and troops arrive to interrogate them. Neither Lieutenant Colonel Reeves nor Major Franzen regarded any of the information and technical drawings they were given by the Porsches as the business of either the French or the Russians. "If these people do turn up," Ferry was told, "you are not obliged to give them any information at all."

All the Porsche military documents were taken to British-occupied Gmünd. There Reeves and Franzen locked the materials away for safekeeping. However, the question remained: From whom were the Americans and British keeping Porsche's designs for tanks and military vehicles? Certainly not the Germans.

The British command permitted Karl Rabe to take charge of the small Porsche factory in Gmünd, which, due to its remote locale, had remained undamaged throughout the war, as had the two remaining Type 60K10 streamliners and a handful of VW prototypes that had been kept from harm's way in Zell am See and at the sawmill in Gmünd. Unfortunately, not long after the occupation, some American soldiers discovered one of the Berlin-Rome cars in a hangar at the Zell am See flight school. It was summer, and the soldiers decided to make the aluminum-bodied aerodynamic streamliner coupe into a convertible with a pair of metal cutters! Racing up and down the runway, the car lasted only a few days because the soldiers failed to check for oil in the engine, and it ran dry and seized up. Now only one of the three Type 64 60K10 streamliners remained. That car is now in a private collection.

The Porsche family was permitted to remain at their Zell am See estate, which was now under American jurisdiction. Ousted from the main house, which was used for living quarters and as an operations center by the American military command, the Porsche family was forced to live on the property as best they could. Food, gasoline, and diesel fuel were all in short supply. "Millions of our fellow countrymen were far worse off," wrote Ferry, but a reversal of fortune awaited not only the Porsches but also the men who had worked at Gmünd during the war.

The first incident occurred in the summer of 1945 when a German informer, who, as Ferry wrote, had "insinuated his way into favor with the British," became chief of police in Wolfsburg. Seeking to strengthen his political position, he accused Ferdinand Porsche of murder after two bodies were found in the house that Porsche had used when visiting the KdF factory. The trumped-up charges were unsubstantiated since no one from the Porsche family had been any-

where near Wolfsburg for several months. However, the police chief persisted and convinced the chief of the American military police in Zell am See that the Porsches were murderers. Ferry considered the whole affair preposterous until a unit of American MPs arrived and arrested every male member of the Porsche family except Ferdinand Porsche, who was in Gmünd visiting Karl Rabe. Erwin Komenda and most of the factory workers living on the estate grounds, thirty-two people in all, were also taken into custody and carted off to a prison in Salzburg.

Unbeknownst to any of the family members in Zell am See, Ferdinand Porsche was also taken into custody and was under

During the early postwar years, the Porsche family estate in Zell am See was occupied by the American command, but the family was permitted to remain on the property, which is totally restored today. It was here, in the home he had known all his life, that Ferry Porsche passed away on March 27, 1998, at age eighty-eight.

house arrest at Gmünd until early August. He was then driven in his own car to Schloss Kransberg, a castle near Bad Nauheim that had been turned into an internment camp by the occupation forces. There, Porsche was kept along with senior members of the German ministry, including Albert Speer, Hitler's minister for armaments and war production. Everyone held at Schloss Kransberg was under suspicion of war crimes, and it was here that the Allies would ascertain who would be sent to trial at the Nuremberg Court. Those sent to trial, including German Field Marshal Hermann Göring and ten other Nazi Party leaders, were sentenced to death in 1946.

Knowing that Porsche had not been involved in any political activity during the war, Speer strenuously defended him before the military tribunal. As a result, Porsche was cleared of any suspicion of complicity in war crimes and given an official document stating that no charges were to be brought against him. When he returned to Austria, shortly after his seventieth birthday, he discovered that his son and all his associates were in prison, accused of a crime they not only had not committed but of which they had no knowledge. Ferry and the others had been interned for thirteen weeks, and not once had any of them been questioned about the incident in Wolfsburg.

Recalled Ferry, "My father eventually succeeded in convincing the British of our innocence, and he secured our release from the American military government in Vienna." It was November 1, 1945, and when Ferry arrived back in Zell am See, he believed that the worst was over. "We were to be proved hopelessly wrong," he said.

Sentiments toward Germany were hard-hearted, much worse than they had been after the Great War. The Morgenthau Plan, named after Henry Morgenthau, Jr., Franklin D. Roosevelt's Secretary of the Treasury (1934–45) and the son of a wealthy U.S. financier and statesman who was born in Germany, was a harsh peace settlement that called for the total dismantling of German industry, the closure of mines, and the conversion of a highly industrialized nation into an agrarian state. Allied bombing attacks beginning in 1943 had almost assured the first decree; nevertheless, by the end of summer 1945, the Allied occupation forces were allowing the German automotive industry to begin the slow process of cleaning up and rebuilding. This was about the time a young French lieutenant named Henri LeComte arrived at the Porsche estate in Austria.

"Lieutenant LeComte had first gone to our Zuffenhausen factory and discovered that we were living in Austria. LeComte claimed to be working on behalf of Marcel Paul, the French minister for industry," wrote Ferry. "Paul was a member of the French Communist Party. He wanted to obtain the Volkswagen factory as part of Germany's reparations payments to France. Of course the agreement of the Americans and, more important, the British, in whose zone the factory was, had to be obtained." What the French needed even more was Ferdinand Porsche's help, or so it first appeared when LeComte came knocking on Porsche's door. At his bequest, in mid-November Anton Piëch and the Porsches, along with their cousin Herbert Kaes, drove to Baden-Baden, which was now in the French-occupied zone of West Germany. There they met at the Hotel Müller with government representatives who told them that France was planning to build a state-owned automobile factory which would include half of the manufacturing equipment from the VW plant in Wolfsburg as reparations payments. The Porsches were needed to supervise the removal and relocation of the Volkswagen tooling and to oversee construction of the new manufacturing facility in France. The French representatives, led by LeComte's superiors, Major Trevoux and Major Maiffre, had gone so far as to draft a contract in advance for Ferdinand Porsche to sign. Trevoux requested that he do so before leaving. Although the plan appeared to have some merit and had obviously piqued Porsche's curiosity, he told Trevoux that he needed to think it over before agreeing to the proposal.

Back in Zell am See, Ferry expressed serious doubts regarding Marcel Paul's plan and the sincerity of the French to build a German car, but his father had become enthusiastic about the project in the weeks that followed. He told Ferry, "It looks as if the French are pretty serious about this business." Early in December the Porsches, Piëch, and Kaes once again made the drive to Baden-Baden to resume discussions with Trevoux. They had no idea that the political situation had changed between November and December and that they were now walking into a trap.

The French accommodated the Porsches in the Villa Bella Vista, and a meeting was arranged again at the Hotel Müller. When they arrived, however, Trevoux was not there. In his place was a Colonel Lamis, who barely showed any interest in the discussions and asked seemingly irrelevant questions of Ferdinand Porsche. The meeting concluded rather abruptly, and the Porsches were sent back to their rooms. "My father gradually became more and more impatient," recalled Ferry, "and decided to go back to Zell am See the next day. That same evening Maiffre and LeComte were dining with us when two Frenchmen in civilian clothes suddenly appeared and told us that we were under arrest. LeComte acted surprised and said, 'The whole thing is a misunderstanding, believe me! Please remain calm and don't get excited. We'll have the matter cleared up by Monday!'" Monday would be too late. The order had come from the French minister of justice, Pierre-Henri Teitgen, and on Sunday, December 16, 1945 Ferdinand and

Ferry Porsche and Dr. Anton Piëch were taken to the prison in Baden-Baden. Kaes, who had decided to skip the dinner on Friday and go to the cinema instead, managed to escape arrest. Staying at the house of a relative, he remained nearby to observe the events as they unfolded.

The Porsches were imprisoned now for the second time in as many months. Knowing of the document clearing his father of any war crimes, Ferry was at a loss to understand their unprovoked arrest. His answer came the next day when a series of charges were leveled at his father and brother-in-law, this time for misconduct with respect to prisoners of war and workers at the Peugeot plants that had come under the control of VW during Germany's occupation of France. The rationale was that Ferdinand Porsche and Anton Piëch had been in charge of the KdF *Werk* during the war, thus they were responsible for the acts of the Gestapo who had brutalized French workers. The accusations were as thin as the paper on which they were written. The Porsches and Piëch had merely become pawns in a battle between two factions, and their arrest was part of a politically motivated conspiracy by French automakers and those in the French cabinet to sabotage Marcel Paul's plan of building VWs in France. Ferry's early apprehensions about the sincerity of the French had been correct. "They had hoped to achieve their aim by taking us out of circulation," he said. And it had worked. The accusations, false or otherwise, were far more serious than they first appeared.

The charges against his father, as Ferry later recounted, were based on half-truths and the mistaken beliefs about events that occurred at the Peugeot factory in Montbéliard. "My father was accused of being a war criminal on the grounds that, after a few incidents of sabotage at Peugeot factories, some French people had been arrested by the Gestapo at my father's instigation. There was alleged to be evidence that a few Peugeot managers had been thrown into prison during the German occupation. This was all contained in charges brought against my father, which we would have dismissed as ridiculous if the situation had not been so serious. In reality, my father had intervened on behalf of the Peugeot managers and had complained bitterly to the Gestapo that cooperation would be impossible if the Peugeot management was locked up in jail. The managers were subsequently released. However, when shortly afterward there were further acts of sabotage at Peugeot, several managers were thrown back into prison. My father intervened again, but this time the strength of available evidence meant his efforts were in vain. One of the managers died during his imprisonment."

Similar accusations were made against Anton Piëch and Ferry. It was soon proven that Ferry had never been associated with the management of the KdF *Werk* or Volkswagen, and he

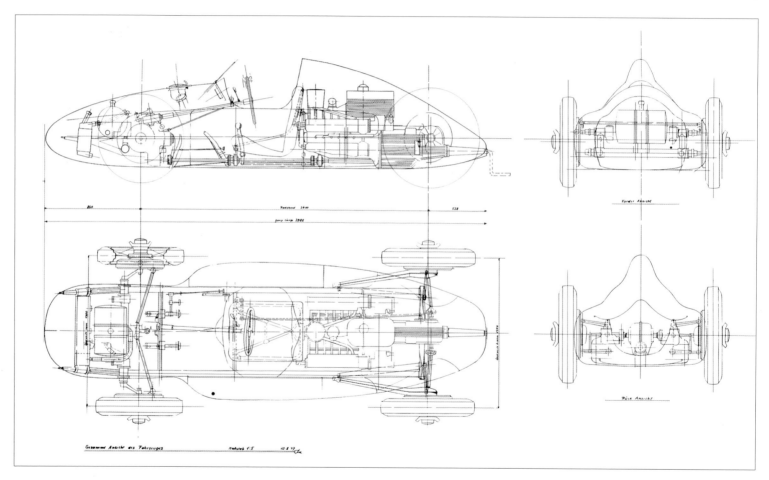

RIGHT AND OPPOSITE:
Ferry Porsche and the staff in Gmünd completed the design for the Cisitalia Type 360 by October 1947. The innovative design utilized all-wheel drive, which Porsche KG had pioneered during World War II. The engine was mounted amidships, a practice that was copied numerous times in Porsche's history.

was released from Baden-Baden prison in March 1946. However, he was still detained by the French and not permitted to return to Austria until July. Ferdinand Porsche and Anton Piëch were also released from prison but were likewise detained as "guests" of the French.

Despite protests from within the French cabinet, Marcel Paul continued to lobby for the production of Volkswagens in France, and thus the struggle raged on into 1946. In May both Porsche and Piëch were driven to Paris where they were accommodated in the servants' quarters of the Renault villa. They were later met by a team of Renault engineers and asked to review drawings for the new 4CV model and to assist Renault in setting up the production line. Porsche and Piëch cooperated fully and even worked in the Renault assembly shop on preparations for the production of the

4CV, but after more than a year and repeated pleas for their release, in February 1947 they were jailed again. Events had suddenly gone from bad to worse.

Marcel Paul had lost his seat in the French cabinet, thus ending the debate over producing the VW in France, and Minister of Justice Teitgen, who signed the original arrest warrant, had become even more powerful within the cabinet. Perhaps as a result, Porsche and Piëch were transferred to the prison in Dijon, one of the worst in France. The cells were unheated even in the middle of winter, and at age seventy-two the elder Porsche's health soon began to fail. A physician declared him too ill to remain incarcerated, and Porsche was transferred to the prison hospital where he slowly regained some strength but remained in despair over his situation.

Several months later Porsche was interrogated once again by French authorities, only this time there were two Peugeot managers present, both of whom spoke on Porsche's behalf and confirmed that he had had nothing to do with the mistreatment of French workers. A former Gestapo officer had also been questioned, and he, too, confirmed that Porsche had absolutely no involvement with French prisoners being sent to Germany as forced labor at the KdF. Ferdinand Porsche's long winter appeared to be coming to an end. With these new revelations the French finally agreed to free both Professor Porsche and Dr. Piëch, but first a bail of one million francs was to be posted. It was an impossible sum of money for the Porsche family to obtain.

Throughout the ordeal in France, Karl Rabe and Louise Porsche-Piëch had kept things going at Gmünd by supervising the repair of prewar VWs and VW bucket cars. Toward the end of 1946 there were more than two hundred employees working at the Gmünd facility, which Ferry and Louise had wisely reorganized as

Renowned Italian race driver Tazio Nuvolari is pictured at the wheel of the Cisitalia Type 360 in 1948.

him, and in 1946 he bankrolled the development of an entire class of single-seat race cars known as Cisitalia, the contraction for Consorzio Industriale Sportivo Italia. He hired a talented Fiat engineer named Dante Giacosa, who designed a simple, Fiat-based race car that could be produced profitably in reasonable numbers. Dusio also employed former Fiat experimental engineer Dr. Giovanni Savonuzzi to put the car into production and also the great Piero Taruffi to road test the first sample. By August 1946, Cisitalia had produced seven of the new Type D46 Monopostos, and in their debut race a trio of Cisitalias finished first through third.

Among Dusio's cadre of racing luminaries was the legendary Tazio Nuvolari. As fate would have it, Nuvolari had driven for the Auto Union before the war and was familiar with Professor Porsche and the magnificent cars he had designed. When he decided to resume his Grand Prix racing career, both Nuvolari and Dusio found their way to Porsche's doorstep through mutual friends: Carlo Abarth, who was married to Anton Piëch's former secretary, and Rudolf Hruska, who had worked with Porsche in 1939. It was only after making contact with Louise Piëch and Ferry Porsche, however, that Dusio discovered the plight of their father and offered to provide the necessary funds to secure his release. He had one million francs delivered to the French authorities through his friends, celebrated race drivers Louis Chiron and Raymond Sommer. On August 1, 1947, Ferdinand Porsche and Anton Piëch were released after almost two years in and out of French prisons. The money used to buy their freedom was the payment for designing the Grand Prix car for Dusio, but he was generous

an Austrian company under the name Porsche Konstruktionen GesmbH. It was still tough going, but in September 1946 fate at last turned in Porsche's favor when Italian industrialist and amateur race driver Piero Dusio entered their lives.

Dusio had made his fortune selling war matériel to the Italian government. Even being on the losing side had been profitable for and contracted additionally for Porsche to design a small farm tractor, a sports car, and a water turbine. Of the three, only the tractor was produced.

"The commission from Piero Dusio was of great significance to us," said Ferry. "It meant that we once again had a future in the automobile industry. The Grand Prix car, which we also called Cisitalia after Dusio's racing designs, was to have a supercharged 1.5-liter engine in accordance with the Grand Prix formula valid at the time. We had to follow the formula laid down, but otherwise we had a free hand. We planned a mid-engine car with a twelve-cylinder boxer engine and four-wheel drive. It was to be a very advanced design, and of course we were able to draw on our wealth of experience with the Auto Union P racing car."

Although history remembers Ferdinand Porsche as the designer of the Cisitalia Grand Prix car, the design had been nearly completed by Ferry and his staff prior to his father's return to Gmünd. "He came to Gmünd and inspected what we had been doing during his absence, particularly the Cisitalia," wrote Ferry. "He scrutinized the technical drawings for the racing car without saying a word. I was of course impatient to hear his verdict. Finally I asked, 'So what do you think of our work then?' He replied, 'I'd have gone about it in the same way as you!' and laid his hand on my shoulder. I hardly need to say that I was very proud of this judgment from my father, who was always so critical in matters of engineering."

While Porsche was working on the Grand Prix car, Dusio commissioned renowned Italian stylist Battista "Pinin" Farina to design a Fiat-based sports car, the Cisitalia 202. When it appeared at the 1947 Villa d'Este

Concours d'Elegance, the automotive world was astounded both by the simplicity of its design and its fresh approach to sports car styling. The Cisitalia 202 would become one of the most important automotive designs of the twentieth century.

Unfortunately for Dusio, he would not share in the glory. His unbridled enthusiasm had blinded him to an impending financial disaster. The costs of developing and producing the Type D46 Monoposto race cars, the Cisitalia 202, and the Porsche twelve-cylinder Grand Prix car had exhausted his finances. Despite the success of the Cisitalia sports car design and the Monoposto race cars, by 1949 Consorzio Industriale Sportivo Italia was bankrupt. Dusio was forced to sell the remains of Cisitalia, and then he

The first Porsche sports cars were virtually hand-built in the shops at Gmünd. Here the body for a coupe is being fabricated. In the background is the wooden styling buck over which aluminum panels were formed for the body.

BOTH IMAGES ABOVE: The very first Porsche 356 was the 356-1 roadster. The prototype utilized a tubular space frame and a VW-based engine mounted amidships.

hastily departed for Buenos Aires, along with the Porsche-designed Grand Prix race car! He never returned, and Cisitalia's new owners failed in their efforts to revive the marque.

Dusio's legacy was securing the freedom of Ferdinand Porsche and the future success of Porsche KG. In addition, the design of the Cisitalia 202 ignited the *granturismo* movement within Italy: a body conceived as a single profile rather than as a construct of separate panels—the traditional prewar blueprint of hood, fenders, body, and trunk being individual components. The sleek envelope styling exemplified by the Cisitalia gained momentum throughout Europe in the 1950s, particularly in the realm of high-performance sports car design, where coachwork had to satisfy both the eye of the customer and the ideals of the engineer. Looking at the spectacular Cisitalia design in 1947, hardly anyone noticed that the graceful Granturismo Berlinettas were built on top of simple Fiat 1100S mechanicals. Hardly anyone.

Watching Dusio build the Cisitalia 202 using essentially off-the-shelf Fiat components rekindled Ferry's desire to build a Porsche sports car doing essentially the same thing with VW parts. "It is certain," said Rudolf Hruska later, "that when Porsche built their own sports car, they were very influenced by what Cisitalia did with the Fiat parts." In 1947, almost a decade after the design had been completed, the plans for the Type 64 60K10 were about to be removed from their steel cases and dusted off. Porsche was going to build a car of its own.

At Gmünd, Ferry Porsche, Karl Rabe, and Erwin Komenda began the design of a sports car built around Volkswagen components. The project was officially named the Type 356. In his design Ferry Porsche used Volkswagen steering and braking systems, suspensions, transmissions, and engines with slight modifications. Komenda and Ferry designed the first body, which was mounted

Porsche's production manager, Otto Huslein, was photographed with the first Porsche 356 in 1948 just outside the town of Gmünd, Austria.

Ferry Porsche (left) and his father with the Gmünd roadster in 1948. The elder Porsche's twenty-month imprisonment had taken a toll on his health. He was seventy-three years old when his son and the staff at Gmünd completed the first car that had the PORSCHE name across its hood.

space frame and an engine mounted in the rear rather than in the middle. Although the Gmünd roadster was never put into production, one could regard the 356-1 as the original concept for the legendary 550 Spyder of 1953 and, currently, the highly successful Porsche Boxster, which also uses a mid-engine layout.

The Type 356-2 utilized a newly designed frame consisting of a welded steel platform strengthened through the cockpit area by boxed square-section side sills and a small center tunnel (the latter used to contain the shifter, fuel lines, brake line, and emergency brake cable). A front box was joined to the side sills by angled panels that distributed the stresses. The box completely enclosed the foot well and suspension spring housings, and extended forward to the nose of the car. At the rear a sheet steel structure rose up and back from the side sills and arched above the space that would be occupied by the engine and axles. As in a race car, various support structures were also utilized to direct either cool or hot air. For example, the sills and cowl were to serve as built-in ducts through which warm air from the engine could be used to heat and defrost the passenger compartment. Following the design his father had established with the Volkswagen, Ferry positioned the flat four-cylinder boxer engine behind the rear axle. The body for the car was all aluminum except for the doors, which were steel. Completed in July 1948, the 356-2 would be the final preproduction prototype.

Porsche planned on producing both coupe and cabriolet versions of the 356, and Komenda's design for the 356-2 coupe was even more accomplished than his rendering of the Gmünd cabriolet. The coupe featured a classic fastback roof design similar to the

on a tubular space frame. The aerodynamic lines of the open two-seater were based almost entirely on the Berlin-Rome car. The first 356 roadster body was hand-formed by Friedrich Weber, a brilliant metal craftsman who had joined Porsche in April 1948. Weber began his career in 1922 at Austro-Daimler, where Ferdinand Porsche had told him he should train as a coach builder because they were always in demand. And here he was, twenty-six years later, building the body for the very first Porsche sports car.

Completed on June 8, 1948, the mid-engine 356-1 Gmünd roadster would become a test bed for the new sports model. For series production, however, Porsche and Rabe had already decided on a more practical platform than the roadster's hand-formed

It wasn't exactly mass production at the Gmünd facility in 1948. Virtually hand-assembled chassis were built in the small workshops one or two at a time.

BELOW, LEFT AND RIGHT: The Porsche 356-2 was built on a welded steel platform strengthened through the cockpit area by boxed square-section side sills and a small center tunnel. A front box was joined to the side sills by angled panels that distributed the stresses. The box completely enclosed the foot well and suspension housings, and extended forward to the nose of the car. The fuel tank was mounted forward of the cowl (the fuel filler cap can be seen on top of the tank). At the rear a sheet steel structure rose up and back from the side sills and arched above the space in which the engine was mounted. Ferry Porsche looks on as chassis number 12 is being completed outside the Gmünd workshop in 1948.

An early 1948 Gmünd coupe body is shown in the paint shop. The bodies of the cars were aluminum, except for the doors, which were steel. Continual changes were made from car to car as the design and manufacturing process was refined during the first year of production.

Early in 1948 the first 356-2 chassis was driven into the town of Gmünd to test the engine and suspension. It caused quite a stir in the small Austrian village.

The beginning of the Porsche legend, the original 356-1 and 356-2 models, outside the Gmünd *Werk* in 1948.

Three of the most important men in the history of the sports car: Ferdinand Porsche (right), design engineer Karl Rabe (center), and renowned stylist Erwin Franz Komenda, at Gmünd in 1949.

From humble beginnings Porsche launched a sports car dynasty. Pictured in 1949 with two production models, the coupe and the roadster, are (from left to right) Henrich Kunz, Hans Orsini, Ferry Porsche, Bernhard Blank, Louise Porsche-Piëch, and Ernst Schoch.

BELOW LEFT: Ferdinand Porsche's health was failing by 1949 when this intimate photo was taken of the company's founder with two of his grandchildren, Ferdinand Piëch (left) and Ferry's son, Ferdinand Alexander "Butzi" Porsche. Butzi would grow up to become one of the most influential designers in the company's history.

BELOW RIGHT: Something that few sports car enthusiasts remember about Porsche is their production of farm tractors in the postwar era. Ferdinand Porsche and Ferry Porsche are shown here along with colleagues at the debut in Frankfurt of the Type AP 17 tractor.

Berlin-Rome streamliners and Pinin Farina's evolutionary Cisitalia 202. The result was a unique design that Porsche would continue to use with only minor alterations for more than a decade.

Despite the lack of a wind tunnel to prove his design theories, Erwin Komenda's years of experience as a stylist at Daimler-Benz and as a race car designer at Porsche KG had allowed him to create an incredibly aerodynamic profile. Ferry often told the story of the poor man's wind tunnel test, that of taping tufts of wool to the 356-2 and driving it at speed past Komenda and the design staff to see if the tufts lay flat against the body. They did, proving that the flow of air over the car was undisturbed by its shape.

By the summer of 1948 the first 356 Porsches were completed in Gmünd, although there had been numerous difficulties, particularly with obtaining parts from VW and acquiring the sheet aluminum from which body panels were hand-formed over wooden styling bucks. Almost everything Porsche required was delivered to Gmünd by way of Switzerland through the cooperation of two Swiss businessmen, Rupert Von Senger, who owned a Zurich advertising agency, and his associate, Bernhard Blank, who had a successful automobile dealership. As Swiss nationals they were free to travel and trade internationally, thus providing Porsche

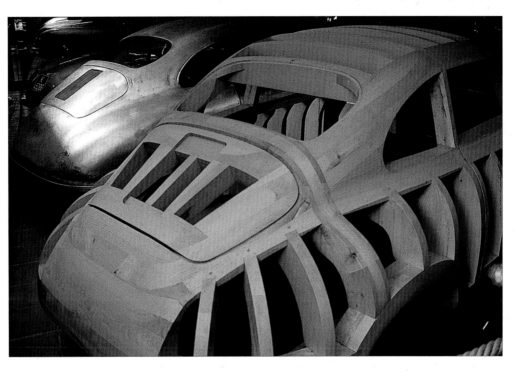

The original wooden styling buck for the 356-2 body is now displayed at the Porsche museum in Gmünd. (PORSCHE WERKFOTO)

with a pipeline for supplies that would otherwise have been denied them in the early postwar years.

Despite the numerous obstacles encountered throughout the year, the first 356 Porsches were of excellent quality; each was

The original drafting room was restored at Gmünd and is part of the museum tour. (PORSCHE WERKFOTO)

OPPOSITE: The sixth Gmünd coupe built in 1948; this is the lowest serial number car extant except for the 356-1 roadster in the Porsche museum.

virtually handmade under the watchful eyes of Ferry Porsche, Karl Rabe, and Erwin Komenda. The assembly process at Gmünd was very slow since the 356 was in a continual state of change in 1948 with various alterations to the suspension, the body, and particularly the VW-based engines, which were modified by Porsche engineers to deliver performance better suited to a sports car. Not only were they more powerful and capable of propelling the 356 to speeds in excess of 80 miles per hour, but they were also more fuel efficient than the VW Beetle's, averaging 30 to 34 miles per gallon.

The majority of the time was spent building the coupe and cabriolet bodies. These were fabricated by the same men who had made prototype and race car bodies for Porsche KG since the 1930s. "We had one real artist," recalled Ferry, "Friedrich Weber, who could make every part of the body in half the time the others could. But he often failed to come in on Monday because he'd been so drunk over the weekend. Nevertheless, he more than

OPPOSITE AND RIGHT:
The advantages of Komenda's streamlined body design were substantiated in the 1970s when a wind tunnel test of an early 356 coupe revealed that it was more aerodynamic than any new car being built at that time. As noted by the license plate, this is the seventeenth example produced.

Minor details often varied from car to car. For example, comparing the rear of the ninth Gmünd coupe to the seventeenth shows a different lighting arrangement.

The limited materials available after the war required that Porsche use whatever supplies were available to complete the 356 models. Almost everything, from the rubber trim around the windshield to the door seals and interior switches, was purchased from other automakers. All early 356 models featured trafficators, or signal arms, built into the front fenders.

ABOVE LEFT: A single bench seat was all that Porsche offered in the first cars; the area behind the seat was carpeted, however, and all the interior trim, doors, seat, floor, and kick panels exhibited exceptional workmanship. The Gmünd coupes had unsynchronized transmissions, mechanical brakes, quick but crude steering, and lever action shocks. Everything was basically World War II Volkswagen.

ABOVE RIGHT: Early Porsches used gauges made in Vienna, Austria, by F. Hetterich in Wien. The speedometer was centered on the dashboard behind the steering wheel. The only other instrument was a small oil temperature gauge. There was no fuel gauge. A 13.2-gallon fuel tank was good for about 400 miles. When the car ran out of gas, the driver flipped a lever to release a reserve fuel supply that was good for approximately 30 additional miles.

RIGHT: Porsche designed the Volkswagen engine utilized in the 356. The horizontally opposed, four-cylinder boxer engine—so named for the pistons' reciprocating movement, toward and away from each other like two boxers sparring—displaced 1,131 cubic centimeters (75 mm × 64 mm bore × stroke) developing 46 horsepower at 4,000 revolutions per minute. Even with this modest output the 356 coupe could attain a top speed of 88 miles per hour, thanks in part to its wind-cheating profile.

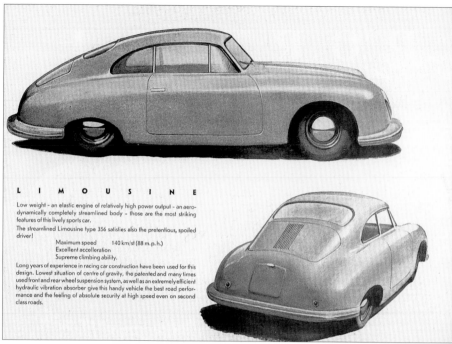

ABOVE AND OPPOSITE: The English version of the first Porsche sales brochure published in Vienna in 1948. This marked the official birth of the Porsche sports car and the beginning of a new era in the history of the automobile. (PHOTOS FROM THE PRESCOTT KELLY COLLECTION)

caught up with the others during the rest of the week." Ferry once remarked that he had been amazed Porsche was able to succeed in producing forty-six cars the first year. The majority of these were sold in Switzerland through Blank's dealership, the rest in Austria.

Several important events began to reshape West Germany by the end of 1948. On June 20 the new German deutsche mark replaced the devalued prewar reichsmark. The new currency helped

wash away the stigma of the Third Reich, and to stimulate the lagging economy, every German citizen was given forty deutsche marks. The Marshall Plan proposed by U.S. Secretary of State George C. Marshall in 1947 was also pumping millions of dollars into Europe to help countries rebuild their war-torn industries, including Italy and Germany. The controlled economy implemented after the war was also abolished and a free market economy introduced in 1948 to encourage German trade and industry. For

Porsche this led to a significant turn of events. A contract was signed in September with Volkswagen AG to provide the parts necessary from Wolfsburg for the manufacture of the 356. In addition, VW agreed to sell and service Porsche sports cars through its dealer network. More important, since Porsche KG had originally designed the Volkswagen, the company would now receive a five-deutsche-mark royalty on every VW produced. This was a historic milestone. "The VW was now our intellectual property," wrote Ferry, whose dream of building his own car had finally come true.

The first Porsche catalog, a simple four-page folder, appeared in the late summer of 1948. Published in Vienna, in German, English, and French, it contained drawings of both the coupe and cabriolet. The following March, Porsche cars were exhibited for the first time at the 1949 Geneva Automobile Show. For the Porsche family the war was finally over.

CHAPTER 4

SELF-REPATRIATION

FERRY PORSCHE AT THE HELM

AFTER A SUCCESSFUL BEGINNING IN 1948 WITH the Gmünd coupe, Ferry decided the time had come to reestablish Porsche KG in Germany. The Americans, however, were still occupying the Zuffenhausen factory that had been Porsche's headquarters since the 1930s. "I contacted Dr. Arnulf Klett, the new lord mayor of Stuttgart, and asked for his help in our attempts to reclaim our old factory in Stuttgart-Zuffenhausen from the Americans," wrote Ferry, "but in 1949 it just wasn't possible." Undeterred, he established an office in the garage of the house his father had built on the outskirts of Stuttgart in 1923 when he was chief engineer for Daimler-Motoren-Gesellschaft. Albert Prinzing, a former economics professor at the University of Berlin and an old school friend of Ferry's, agreed to become administrator of the Stuttgart operation while Ferry tended to matters at the factory in Gmünd, which was working at capacity to keep up with demand for the 356. By 1949 it had become impera-

tive that production be expanded in order for the company to survive, and it was no longer possible to hand-build every car.

If there was a silver lining to the gray cloud hanging over Zuffenhausen, it was that the Americans were paying Porsche rent on the factory, which was now being used by the U.S. Army to house the motor pool. With the Americans' recompense, combined with modest sales of the Gmünd models and the licensing fee that Porsche was receiving for every Volkswagen built, the company was finally erasing years of red ink.

Determined to begin series production, Ferry now sought another solution—a quid pro quo arrangement with Reutter, the Zuffenhausen-based coach builder with whom Porsche had collaborated before the war. Porsche rented five thousand square feet in the Reutter facility for use as a production area and in November 1949 placed an order with Reutter for the manufacture of 500 Type 356 bodies based on Erwin Komenda's redesign of the Gmünd

OPPOSITE: The Porsche factory had come a long way by 1960, when coupes and cabriolets were streaming off the small moving assembly line in Stuttgart-Zuffenhausen.

coupe. For the new production models he refined the design of both the coupe and cabriolet with somewhat smoother, more rounded lines, creating the unmistakable Porsche silhouette. The new cars were to have steel bodies rather than aluminum like the Gmünd Porsches. The workers at Reutter were more adept at manufacturing steel body panels, and for their production purposes it was a more cost-efficient method. At the same time, Porsche commissioned 250 Type 356 cabriolets to be built in Ullersricht by Karosserie Gläser. Owned by the Erich Heuer Body Factory, it was last the remnant of the original Gläser of Dresden, one of Germany's oldest coach builders. Founded in 1864, the Gläser *Werk* was expropriated from the Gläser-Heuer family after the Soviet occupation of East Germany. The company reestablished itself in Ullersricht in 1950, and Porsche became their largest client.

The first 356 coupe was completed by Reutter early in 1950, and Ferry anxiously took his father to examine it. "When we arrived, my father inspected the body closely, walking around it without saying a word and finally sitting down on a stool right in front of it," recalled Ferry. "There was general astonishment. The Reutter people perhaps thought that my father was tired, then he said suddenly, 'The body will have to go back to the workshop. It's not right. It's not symmetrical!' The body was measured, and indeed it was discovered that it had shifted 20 millimeters (0.78 inch) to the right away from the central axis." Even at age seventy-four, Ferdinand Porsche's eye for detail had not failed him.

By 1950 production was finally under way at Reutter, and Professor Prinzing called a dealer meeting at VW headquarters in Wolfsburg where a new 356 coupe and cabriolet were shown to prospective dealers. He came away with thirty-seven firm orders.

Remarkably, the deposits paid by the VW dealers were the exact amount needed by Porsche to cover the first production run at Reutter. The company was at last on the road to success, and as Ferry wrote of that first order for thirty-seven cars, "Who would have thought after this modest but nonetheless promising start that we would eventually produce 78,000 Type 356s?"

Frustrated by the Americans' extended occupation of Zuffenhausen, by the end of 1950 the Porsche and Piëch families had pooled their finances and established a new headquarters building near the old factory. Although the small 1,100-square-foot prefabricated wood structure accommodated only a design and sales office, it was a vast improvement over the garage at Ferdinand Porsche's house. At the same time, Porsche and Piëch also reorganized the company as "Dr. Ing. H.c. F. Porsche KG," the KG signifying a limited partnership, which it had been before the war. It wasn't Zuffenhausen, but the company was back on German soil, and just in time for Ferdinand Porsche to celebrate his seventy-fifth birthday, in September 1950. The following month he decided to travel to Paris for the annual Motor Show, which was again being held at the Grand Palais. It was to be one of the most prophetic journeys of his life. It was here in the City of Light that he would meet an Austrian-born auto dealer named Maximilian Hoffman.

It seems there is hardly a postwar European sports car story that can be told which does not in some way involve Max Hoffman. Born in Vienna, Austria, he was an avid sportsman who began an amateur racing career in the 1920s riding DKW and AJS motorcycles. He eventually graduated to sports cars and continued to race professionally until 1934 when, at age thirty, he decided to retire and step from the cockpit to the sales floor, becoming a dealer and importer in Austria for Auburn, Cord, Duesenberg, Lancia, Pontiac, and Vauxhall. He later added such renowned marques as Rolls-Royce, Bentley, Alfa Romeo, Talbot, Delahaye, Volvo (the first importer in Europe), and Hotchkiss to the lines marketed through Hoffmann & Huppert. (In America, Hoffman dropped the second "n" from his surname and occasionally used his entire first name, Maximilian. As he once noted, "It was more fitting in New York for a purveyor of exotic motorcars.")

The rise to power of the Third Reich and the stranglehold Hitler had on Germany and Austria deeply concerned Hoffman, who could find no common ground with the Nazi Party or their policies. Fearing the worst, in the late 1930s he moved his business to Paris; this lasted until France declared war on Germany, prompting him to pack his bags and book passage on the first ocean liner headed for New York. After December 7, 1941, even that proved to be a problem. With America entering the war, the U.S. automobile industry seemed to vanish almost overnight, and there was certainly little need for an importer of German automobiles. To make ends meet Hoffman launched a new venture, manufacturing costume jewelry made out of metal-plated plastic. Like almost everything Max Hoffman touched, this, too, turned to gold—or rather, gold plate. In his first week of business he booked $5,000 in orders!

By the time the war was over, New York City had become Max's home, and while the jewelry business had been a financial windfall in the 1940s, he longed to get back to his automotive roots. He had come to this country with the intention of importing cars from Europe, and in 1947 he decided to do just that. With the profits from his jewelry business he was able to open the Hoffman Motor Car Company with a spectacular showroom located in

the heart of Manhattan, at the corner of Park Avenue and Fifty-ninth Street.

America in the postwar era was an incredible place to be. Soldiers were returning home, industry was booming, and Americans were car starved. To quell those pangs of automotive hunger, beginning in 1947 Max Hoffman dished up some of the finest imported cars built in Europe. Initially he sold French Delahayes, Italian Lancias, and a handful of British makes, including the stunning new Jaguar XK120, one of his personal favorites. By the early 1950s he had become the sole United States importer and dis-

On the occasion of his seventy-fifth birthday, a celebration was held in Ferdinand Porsche's honor at the castle Solitude. Porsche (at right), along with friends, factory workers, and Porsche owners from Germany and Austria, was regaled with a parade of Gmünd coupes and cabriolets. (PORSCHE WERKFOTO)

It was the first benchmark in Porsche history: the completion of the five-hundredth 356 coupe at Reutter on March 21, 1951. The car was proudly displayed in the Reutter parking lot along with two cabriolets and several other 356 coupes. Note that these early cars all bore split windshields

Chinetti had come to the United States as chief mechanic for Rene Dreyfus and Rene Le Begue, who were racing Maseratis in the 1940 Indianapolis 500. When World War II broke out, Chinetti decided to remain in the country, taking up residence in New York and becoming a U.S. citizen in 1946. An entrepreneur at heart, that December he took his wife and young son to Europe to visit friends, among them Enzo Ferrari. As the result of a Christmas Eve meeting in Modena, Italy, Ferrari was convinced that his sports cars could be successfully marketed in the United States. It was the beginning of Ferrari's postwar renaissance and Luigi Chinetti's career as the first Ferrari importer in the United States.

At the same time, Hoffman was building a power base comprised of the leading German makes, and after his chance meeting with Ferdinand Porsche in 1950, he believed that the sporty VW-powered 356 coupes and cabriolets would be a hit in the American market. As in most things regarding automobiles, Max Hoffman was absolutely right. He took delivery of three 356 Porsches in 1950, two of which he sold to famed American sportsman Briggs Cunningham. Hoffman took the third to the Concours d'Elegance at Watkins Glen in New York, where the Porsche won the trophy for "The Most Interesting Car." With its rear-mounted, horizontally opposed, air-cooled four-cylinder engine and aerodynamic body styling, the 356 was nothing if not interesting!

With Hoffman's exclusive clientele, the 356 coupes and cabriolets he had imported in 1950 and 1951 found their way into the hands of wealthy would-be American racers, and by the end of the 1951 racing season a small but enthusiastic body of Porsche

tributor for both Mercedes-Benz and BMW, and was soon to become the principal dealer for the Volkswagen, which made its U.S. debut on July 17, 1950, at Hoffman Motors.

Max had already heard good things about the 1948 Gmünd Porsche sports car from his friends in Austria, and he had known Anton Piëch since the 1930s. The purpose of his trip to the 1950 Motor Show in Paris was to find new and interesting European cars to import to America. Since the end of the war both he and Luigi Chinetti, Sr., had been creating a market for imported sports cars in New York, catering to a clientele of wealthy American sportsmen anxious to test their skills with the finest European marques that money could buy. Chinetti was an accomplished race driver and mechanic, and a former colleague of Enzo Ferrari. They had worked together at Alfa Romeo, where Ferrari got his start. In 1940, owners had been created who were successfully entering 356 Pre-A models in production sports car classes across the country. In 1952, Hoffman returned to Watkins Glen driving a new 356 Pre-A cabriolet; he proudly walked off with the award for the "Best Looking Car," a marked improvement over "Most Interesting" only two years earlier.

The cabriolet was Porsche's new top-of-the-line model, and 1952 was the first year that Hoffman offered it for sale in the United States. This was a luxury model, and in German it was referred to as the *Dame*, literally lady or queen, and came equipped with a fully upholstered and carpeted interior, more comfortable seating, a convertible top with a full, padded headliner, and amenities such as an interior dashboard light and an optional Telefunken (tube-type) radio with push-button tuning. To maintain the clean lines of the Porsche, the Telefunken radio featured a unique antenna that was built into the driver's outside mirror! Presumably the mirror got good reception.

The Pre-A designation was actually added later in Porsche history to distinguish the earlier 356 models from the 356A series introduced in October 1955. These so-called Pre-A models are actually more interesting to examine because of their unique styling, which differed noticeably from later models. One of the more distinguishing characteristics was the rear fender treatment; it had a wider, more graceful wheel arch, covering

more of the tire than on the 356A models. Other production changes that occurred, particularly in 1952, included redesigning the bumpers, which were originally integrated into the body and by mid-year were separate pieces mounted through the body. Other changes included replacing the original split windshield with curved one-piece glass and dropping the temperamental four-speed crash box for a new synchromesh transmission. Mid-year models were also among the first to come equipped with the more powerful 1500 Super motor. The cabriolet was an elegant car worthy of the soubriquet *Dame*, or *Die Damen*, and in 1952, Reutter produced 294 cabriolet bodies and 1,056 coupes, while Gläser added another 123 cabriolets to the year's total.

Three Gmünd coupes were specially prepared for the 24 Hours of Le Mans in 1951; however, by the June race all had been involved in wrecks. On race day Porsche had only one repaired car left to run on the Circuit de La Sarthe. One was enough: The lone fender-skirted Gmünd coupe won its class and finished twentieth overall with drivers Auguste Veuillet and Edmond Mouche.

LEFT: In April 1952, Ferry set sail for America on the *Queen Elizabeth*. There he met with Max Hoffman to cement the relationship that would make the United States Porsche's largest market.

BELOW LEFT: The second and third Porsche dynasties: Ferry with his sons, Ferdinand Alexander "Butzi," Gerd, Wolfgang, and Peter, in 1953. Butzi would become one of Porsche's greatest designers in the 1960s.

BELOW: The men who created the 356, Ferry Porsche (left) and Karl Rabe, in 1953.

This is a rare photo of the triumvirate responsible for the 356 Porsche: Karl Rabe (left), Erwin Komenda (center), and Ferry Porsche, taken at the Porsche factory in 1956. Their collective efforts were responsible for every Porsche design from 1948 through early 1964.

By 1954 the 356 had further evolved. Ferry is shown with a line of new models featuring the one-piece curved windshield and the bumper design introduced mid-year in 1952. Porsche was on its way to another production milestone that year, the completion of the five-thousandth car in March, just thirty-six months after building its five-hundredth car.

RIGHT: Production at Zuffenhausen was moving along at an incredible rate. On April 16, 1956, Ferry Porsche (far left) presided over the presentation of the ten-thousandth 356.

Ferry Porsche (center) with a 356 competition coupe in front of the Zuffenhausen *Werk* in 1958. With Porsche are renowned race drivers Huschke von Hanstein (left) and Jean Behra.

It was a long way from the converted sawmill in Gmünd to the Porsche factory in Zuffenhausen, but Ferry Porsche (foreground) had been determined to succeed, and by 1960, when this picture was taken, production was racing along. Hardly what one imagines when talking about an "assembly line" nowadays, each car still had that personal, almost hand-built quality about it.

Half a world away, in New York City, Max Hoffman was selling 356s as quickly as Porsche could deliver them. In 1952 he also received the first of sixteen specially built "America roadsters" that were designed to his specifications and intended for sale exclusively through Hoffman Motors. The cars were delivered to privateer racers such as Briggs Cunningham, who purchased the first one, Richie Ginther, Phil Walters, John Bentley, Jack McAfee, and John and Josie von Neumann.

The America roadster is perhaps the least known of all early Porsches. The lightweight, aluminum-bodied racers were to become the predecessor of the famed 356 Speedster. True to proven Porsche philosophy, established with the Gmünd roadster, the Americas had the lowest possible weight, compact dimensions, agile handling, and good aerodynamics, providing the ideal sports car with which to challenge the likes of Jaguar, Healey, Allard, and MG.

The America was noticeably different from other 356 models. The new body was actually closer to the conventional postwar notion of what a sports car should look like. Hoffman had more than a passing influence on the car's design, and the modest but undeniable resemblance between the America and the XK120 Jaguar is no coincidence. The America had a far more graceful, sweeping fender line than the typical 356 and cut-down doors, and its rear fender treatment was similar in shape to the Jaguar's, although the fenders were unmistakably Porsches from the front and rear views.

Basically a custom 356, its chassis and inner construction were that of the cabriolet, and it was bodied in aluminum rather than steel. Equipped with Porsche's new 75-horsepower 1500S engine,

For a family portrait, Ferry posed with his sister, Louise Piëch, and their mother, Aloisia, in January 1958.

IMAGES ON FOLLOWING SPREAD: American importer Max Hoffman had a hand in the design of the America roadster, which has contours distinctively different from the Gmünd coupe and roadster. The car has a more sweeping rear fender line and cut-down doors suggestive of the Jaguar XK120. Indicative of all early 356 models built before mid-1952, the America has a two-piece windshield.

The cockpit of the Porsche America roadster was all business: speedometer, tachometer, and clock. A wide cubbyhole was cut into the right side of the dashboard for storage, and there were small compartments in the hollows of the door panels.

The split windshield used on all early Porsches was easily removed from the America's cowl and replaced with a small aeroscreen for racing. Midway through 1952 production, Porsche switched to a one-piece curved windshield on the 356 coupe and cabriolet. All sixteen Americas used the earlier windshield design.

the America weighed only 1,580 pounds. Since it was intended strictly for racing, there were no frills in the cockpit. For storage there was an open cubbyhole in the simple dash and hollows in the doors, and instead of roll-up windows, snap-in plastic side curtains were used. This was the same formula Ferry Porsche would use for 356 Speedsters, which were also inspired by Hoffman.

Built for both road and track, the America could easily be stripped down for competition. The windshield was removable and easily replaced by a small curved plastic aeroscreen, the canvas top was simply sprung into place by two pins, and even the bumpers could be unbolted in a matter of minutes. By additionally removing the baggage compartment, jack, tool kit, and wheel covers, a total weight reduction of more than one hundred pounds could be achieved. On the track, a stripped America could overtake a Jaguar XK120 up to around 70 miles per hour and easily out-corner and out-brake anything in the genuine sports car line that was anywhere near its $4,600 price. In the inaugural SCCA race weekend at Thompson, Connecticut, in the fall of 1952, Hoffman had three Porsche America roadsters on the track for the 1500cc race.

When you look at a car like this today, you are drawn to admire its simplicity and unaffected styling, but you have only to sit behind the wheel and drive a few miles to be reminded of how utterly primitive it was. Take a few declining radius turns at high speed, and you begin to wonder how sports car club racers in the 1950s managed to do as well as they did on those tall, skinny tires and quirky VW-derived suspensions. Back in the 1950s, though, the America roadster was on the cutting edge. Author and race driver John Bentley owned the first America roadster built—chassis 10465, engine 40020—which he purchased from Briggs Cunningham in 1953. His commentary on the car's capabilities, published in *Auto Age* magazine, were quite to the point. Bentley wrote, "[The America] is an incredibly versatile and adaptable sports car. In the matter of handling, the roadster is neither more nor less sensitive than the other models. The reduced weight enhances its excellent roadability, provided you observe the same basic precautions as with any other Porsche. That is, always get your breaking and shifting over and done with before you enter a corner, and go through under moderate power, wishing (rather than steering) the car around to compensate for the marked feeling of oversteer. Follow this simple rule," Bentley advised, "and you can out-corner anything but an OSCA; ignore it and you may find yourself in serious trouble. Roughly handled, the Porsche will swap ends faster than your quickest reaction can anticipate this ma-

neuver." In his road test, Bentley's America accelerated from rest to 60 miles per hour in 9.3 seconds, covered the standing quarter mile in 17.9 seconds, and reached a maximum speed of 110 miles per hour.

Production of the America was so limited—in total only sixteen cars were bodied for Porsche by Gläser—that they were never formally cataloged by the factory and were totally unpublicized in Europe. The market for the America roadster was the United States, and specifically Hoffman, who would ultimately purchase all but one. Today, the few remaining examples are

The America roadster was the last Porsche to be bodied by Gläser. The company lost money on every one of the Americas produced as well as 250 Porsche cabriolets. The Erich Heuer Body Factory, which had resurrected the prewar Karosserie *Werk* in Weiden in 1950, went out of business in December 1952.

The Pre-A Reutter-bodied 356 cabriolets had a wider, more graceful fender arch and covered more of the tire at the rear than the later 356A models. The beehive lenses were used on both the front and rear fenders of the early models. Later ones featured two beehive lenses at the rear and did away with the rectangular Hella taillights, which were too easily broken.

ABOVE AND RIGHT:
Rear seating? Yes, it was there, but could you actually sit on it?

considered among the rarest of all 356 Porsches, even though historically Porsche barely acknowledged their existence.

Unfortunately for Gläser, the America roadsters were the last Porsches to bear their historic builder's emblem. The Porsches were, in fact, to be the company's final undoing. Eager to get work after the war, the Heuer body factory had inaccurately estimated production and shipping costs, and in order to fulfill their contract with Porsche, they lost money on every body they built, including the 250 cabriolets. In December 1952, Gläser quietly went out of business, leaving all Porsche coachwork to Reutter, which was now averaging better than two cars a day.

Ferry Porsche's efforts were now focused on making improvements in the car's design and developing a more powerful engine for the 356 series. The engines in the first production cars had been modified VW motors displacing up to 1,300 cubic centimeters and fitted with new aluminum cylinder heads. Porsche had next increased the flat four's swept volume to 1,500 cubic centimeters, as used in the America. This was achieved by lengthening the stroke and using a new die-forged crankshaft; however, the VW engine had now been taken as far as its design would permit. Porsche would have to begin building their own engines if they wanted to go beyond this capacity. Chief engineer Dr. Ernst Fuhrmann had already begun to tackle this problem in 1950 under the product designation "Carrera," the Spanish word for race, which by the end of the decade was to become synonymous with the Porsche name.

As the 1950s began to unfold, everything was finally going

One of the options for the new 1952 cabriolet was a Telefunken push-button radio with built-in speaker. Although it took some time for the tube-type radio to warm up, it had good reception. The antenna was hidden inside the driver's side-view mirror.

Ferry Porsche's way, but the past was about to catch up with him one last time. In November 1951 he took his father to tour the VW plant, and the elder Porsche finally saw his life's work accomplished: the People's Car, which he had endeavored to create throughout his entire career, had become a reality. "This journey certainly inspired my father," wrote Ferry, "particularly in view of the great injustice that had been done to him during his imprisonment." Tragically, it was to be Ferdinand Porsche's final trip. Although his mind remained remarkably keen, he had never fully recovered from being imprisoned in France, and on November 19, the night after their return from the VW plant in Wolfsburg, he suffered a massive stroke.

After being bedridden for more than two months, Ferdinand Porsche passed away on January 30, 1951, at the age of seventy-five. He was laid to rest on February 5 in the chapel at the family estate in Zell am See.

In 1951 it was unlikely that many people outside of Germany realized how influential Ferdinand Porsche had been. Throughout his entire adult life, better than half a century, he had given himself to this mechanical contrivance called the motorcar. One way or another, Ferdinand Porsche had been involved in the design of nearly every great automobile and race car produced in Germany since the turn of the century. His legacy was not only the great Daimlers, Mercedes, and Auto Unions that he had breathed upon but also the most successful automobile since Henry Ford's Model A: the Volkswagen Beetle.

Even though his name would be forever linked to these legendary German marques, to automotive enthusiasts in America, PORSCHE wasn't the name of a man, it was seven chrome letters across the prow of a remarkable new sports car. Throughout the United States, the Porsche was gaining fame in sports car club racing competition, and sales were strong both here and in Europe. Ferry noted that much of this success had come from racing, even though the 356 was not a race car—not in the pure sense, at least. It was at best a road car that could be raced. But that was the Porsche's greatest strength. Realizing this, Ferry decided the time had come to take the next step. In the summer of 1951, Porsche entered a 356 Gmünd coupe in the Vingt-Quatre Heures du Mans (24 Hours of Le Mans), the most important sports car race in Europe.

For the race at Le Mans, the factory chose to run older, lighter-weight, alloy-bodied Gmünd models rather than the new steel-bodied Reutter coupes. The alloy cars were the last to be assembled at the Austrian *Werk*, which had ceased production by March 1951. Three cars were prepared for the June race, each fitted with full fender skirts to further reduce aerodynamic drag, larger capacity fuel tanks, finely tuned engines, and sturdier suspensions.

But before the race one of the cars was involved in a wreck on the autobahn, another was badly damaged during practice, and the third was written off after driver Rudolph Sauerwein crashed at White House during night practice in the rain. On race day Porsche had only one repaired car left to run on the Circuit de La Sarthe.

Thus far it had been a bittersweet year for Ferry due to the sadness of losing his father in January and the joy of celebrating the completion of the five-hundredth 356 in March. This was the company's first milestone as an automaker, an event that Ferry wished he could have shared with his father. Then three months later came Le Mans, with Porsche's high hopes dashed by the succession of shunts, but in the end there was cause for yet another celebration when the lone fender-skirted Gmünd coupe won its class and finished twentieth overall with drivers Auguste Veuillet and Edmond Mouche.

The important class victory in France was a major triumph. Not only had Porsche been the first German team since the war to take part in the 24 Hours, but it was the first German team to compete in any race in France since 1945. And they had won! The editors of the respected British publication *Autosport* wrote that Porsche had "surprised everyone by its speed and reliability at Le Mans." What a difference a day makes. After Le Mans the Porsche name would be known the world over, and the demand for their cars would begin to multiply.

With the Porsche name being spoken in more places and in more languages, by 1952 the first steps were taken toward creating a Porsche emblem or coat of arms. "Max Hoffman had been urging us to do this for some time," recalled Ferry. "He cited the example of the English and said what beautiful emblems they had and that we should produce something similar. He considered this

Ferry Porsche and Max Hoffman met in New York to establish a marketing partnership that would lead to the United States becoming Porsche's largest market.

Porsche in U.S.

FERDINAND PORSCHE, son of the late Professor Porsche, is now in America to explore the market for the Porsche company. Prices in the U.S.A. for these cars range from about £1,285 to £1,465.

important for the American market. He made the suggestion to me one day while we were lunching together in New York, and I quickly sketched out a piece of heraldry on a napkin. I said to Hoffman as I was drawing, 'If all you want is a coat of arms, you can get one from us!'" Ferry then sketched the crest of the House of Württemberg and in the middle put the coat of arms of the city of Stuttgart: a rampant horse, above which he placed the Porsche name. (Enzo Ferrari had also used the rampant horse for his personal emblem since 1923, when the Countess Paolina Baracca presented the Stuttgart coat of arms to Ferrari after his victory in the Circuit of Savio race.) Upon his return to Stuttgart, Ferry gave the napkin to Erwin Komenda and asked him to draw a clean copy. "We then took the design to the state government and the City of Stuttgart and requested that they authorize the design for use as our emblem. The authorities raised no objections, and so from 1953 onward Porsche cars bore their own emblem, to the great pleasure of all concerned," said Ferry. Today, both Porsche and Ferrari still use the rampant horse as part of their company emblem.

In 1950 there had been serious talk about the Americans relinquishing the Zuffenhausen factory that September, and it would probably have happened had the Korean War not started in June. As a result, the United States found it necessary to retain all of its vehicle facilities in Europe, and the Porsche factory was among them. The company, however, was expanding at a rate far exceeding anyone's expectations. Over the next four years production soared at Reutter, and in March 1954, just thirty-six months after the five-hundredth car had been completed, Ferry Porsche watched as the five thousandth 356 model rolled off the Reutter assembly line. In America, Hoffman alone had sold nearly six hundred Porsches in 1954. No longer able to wait for the Americans to relinquish control of the Zuffenhausen facilities, Ferry decided to construct a new factory in Stuttgart and another in Friedrichshafen, on Lake Constance. The Friedrichshafen *Werk*, which opened its doors in January 1956, was to be home to Porsche-Diesel-Motorenbau GmbH. It was established to build Porsche diesel engines and diesel-powered tractors, which had become another thriving enterprise for the Porsche family. Werk II, Porsche's new automobile assembly plant, was to be completed in December 1955, the twenty-fifth anniversary of the founding of Porsche GmbH. Then on December 1, Ferry received news that the Americans had derequisitioned the factory in Zuffenhausen. He noted with some irony, "It happened at the same time as the [new] factory designed by architect Rolf Gutbrod became ready for occupation. At that time we had a workforce of 616 people." Since 1945, Porsche had been without its own factory, and now in a day it had two. Always the optimist, Ferry concluded, "We now had sufficient space for future expansion."

With the departure of the American military, the last vestiges of World War II were gone. After waiting a decade, Porsche had finally returned to Zuffenhausen.

CHAPTER 5

THE COACH-BUILT 356 PORSCHE

RACING IMPROVES THE BREED

F ONE WERE TO LOOK BACK AT THE EARLY 1950S AND the vast number of Porsches competing in sports car club events across America, the 356 would appear to be a very raceable car. Still, with the exception of the America roadster, and then only in a modest way, Porsche was not building genuine race cars but, rather, street cars that could be raced. In the right hands they were undeniably competent for rallying and amateur competition, but the 356 was in no sense a real racing car, a term that to Porsche implied a very different type of machine. Though successful in America, in Europe the 356 was barely competitive against the refined high-performance sports-racing cars being manufactured by Porsche's competitors for use in hill climbs and short-course races. Thus, as the design of the 356 progressed during the 1950s, Porsche ventured off into the development of higher performance engines and a series of race cars that would become the most celebrated competition models of the era: the 550 Spyders.

While Porsche can be considered the father of the 550, the Spyder's delivery was, so to speak, through the hands of a mid-wife—the Volkswagen and Porsche distributor in Frankfurt, Walter Glöckler. An avid motorsports enthusiast and racer, Glöckler and his chief designer, Hermann Ramelow, built a race car around the 1.1-liter Porsche engine, VW running gear, a simple ladder-type tubular frame, and a roadster body similar in shape to the 356, fabricated by Karosserie C. H. Weidenhausen in Frankfurt. Glöckler followed the same design principles used by Ferry Porsche in his 1948 prototype—placing the engine ahead of the rear wheels in a mid-ship position. Glöckler's handsome single-seat sports car managed a string of victories in 1950 and again in 1951, with Walter and his brother, Helm Glöckler, Ramelow, Hermann Kathrein, and Heinz Brendel sharing stints behind the wheel.

The success of this single car led to an informal mutual assistance pact between Glöckler and the Porsche factory in 1951 wherein Porsche would supply 1.5-liter engines to Glöckler and the cars produced beginning in 1951 would wear the Porsche

OPPOSITE: Detail of the 356C interior, which was the most stylish of the entire 356 series, with its leather-upholstered dash, door, kick panels, and seats standard on the cabriolet. Also note the deluxe steering wheel with full horn rim.

Although the 356 had been raced successfully, it was not a race car. For serious competition Porsche developed the Type 550, a sports model engineered for racing. Here a 550 Spyder from 1954 is shown at Karosserie Wendler with Ferry Porsche (left), race driver Kurt Ahrens, Porsche racing director Wilhelm Hild, Porsche engineer Ernst Fuhrmann, and race driver Huschke von Hanstein. (PORSCHE WERKFOTO)

nameplate. The early Glöckler-Porsches were victorious in virtually every type of event in which they were entered, and in 1951 they established a new international 1500cc class record at 187.73 kilometers per hour (116.60 miles per hour) for 500 kilometers, 185.63 km/h (115.30 mph) for 1,000 kilometers, and 184.11 km/h (114.35 mph) for six hours.

By 1953 the success of the Glöckler cars in competition was drawing attention to Zuffenhausen since they were now publicly referred to as Porsches. At the same time, factory engineers were involved in two new projects: a racing engine, the Type 547, and a new car, the Type 550, a Porsche-designed race car patterned after the mid-engine Glöcklers.

The first trial for the 550 prototype was the Eifel Races at the Nürburgring on May 31, 1953. The team driver was Helm Glöckler, who managed to pilot the car to victory in spite of heavy rains throughout the race and a malfunctioning carburetor, which kept engine speed limited to 5,400 revolutions per minute instead of 6000. The Nürburgring victory was all the sweeter for Porsche since the car had been entered merely to shake out the bugs in preparation for the next and most important race in Europe, the 1953 Vingt-Quatre Heures du Mans. At Le Mans, Helm Glöckler and Hans Herrmann were teamed in the 550-01 car, and race driver–journalists Richard von Frankenberg and Paul Frère shared the 550-02 prototype, which handily won the 1500cc class, crossing the finish line just moments ahead of the Glöckler-Herrmann car.

The two 550 prototypes shared brief but remarkable careers, with a string of victories that followed their Nürburgring and Le Mans triumphs. By year's end Porsche had another feather in its cap, the coveted German Sports-Racing Championship.

The production version of the 550 Spyder was introduced at the Paris Salon in October 1953. The 01 and 02 prototypes had opened the door, but what came next was a car completely different from the first Glöckler-based 550s. The new body was a work of purposeful art penned by Erwin Komenda. The sweep of the fender line was far more graceful and the contours more visually appealing, accented by raised rear fenders, which was Komenda's tip of the hat to the tailfin designs appearing on American automobiles. The 550/1500RS would also be the first Porsche to combine the benefits of a mid-placed engine and a trailing rear suspension geometry.

Bodies for the Spyders, produced by Karosserie Wendler in Reutlingen, were made of aluminum and weighed a mere two hundred pounds. A tubular ladder frame, based on the 1954 Le

Porsche designated the production models as the 550/1500RS, which stood for the type, 550; the approximate engine displacement, 1,500 cubic centimeters; and the designation, Rennsport, or sports racing. The Spyder epithet was Max Hoffman's idea; he believed that a name rather than a series of numbers would be more marketable. Among sports car cognoscenti, the Spyder (or Spider) classification was already familiar, having been used to describe very light, sketchy two-seater competition sports cars since the 1930s. Hoffman, once again, was correct.

At the heart of the 550/1500RS was the latest version of the Type 547 four-cam engine developing 110 horsepower. With its lightweight body and frame, the dry weight of the 550 Spyder ranged between 1,320 and 1,350 pounds, depending on the equipment fitted. As for price, the cars boasted a delivery nearly twice that of a standard 356, exceeding $6,800 in the United States. To put that in some perspective, a brand-new Cadillac Eldorado sold for $5,738 in 1954.

FAR LEFT: An avid motor sports enthusiast and racer, Walter Glöckler (second from right), and his chief designer, Hermann Ramelow (far right), built a race car around the 1.1-liter Porsche engine and VW running gear in 1951. Pictured with Glöckler and Ramelow are race driver journalist Richard von Frankenberg (far left), Ferry Porsche, and race drivers Huschke von Hanstein and Petermax Müller.
(PORSCHE WERKFOTO)

Mans design, carried the lightweight coachwork and Porsche's latest version of the 547 four-cam engine. Although introduced at the Paris Salon as a finished car, the final version of the 550 Spyder required another year of revisions before going into limited production. According to historian Karl Ludvigsen, it is estimated that anywhere from twelve to twenty-two cars were built, in addition to eight 550 prototypes, before series production began in 1954. By that time the cars were known throughout Europe and abroad as formidable competitors, having won their class in virtually every event in which they were entered, including the 1953 and 1954 Carrera PanAmericana, the Mexican equivalent of Italy's grueling Mille Miglia and the namesake of the 547 engine and every high-performance Porsche model to the present day.

The Glöckler Porsche used a simple ladder-type tubular frame and a roadster body similar in shape to the 356. Glöckler followed the same design principles used by Ferry Porsche in his 1948 prototype—placing the engine ahead of the rear wheels in a mid-ship position. The car with license BN 85-3049 is shown during testing in 1952.
(PORSCHE WERKFOTO)

The 550 Spyders came with either a racing screen for the driver, with a passenger-side tonneau cover, or a full-width low racing screen. The car could also be ordered with a conventional aluminum-framed safety glass windscreen and a simple canvas top, a combination seldom seen these days.

The production class 550 was joined by the 550A/1500RS race car in 1956, which was succeeded in mid-1957 by the 718 RSK Spyder and in 1960–61 by the 718 RS60 and 718 W-RS models, the last of the four-cylinder Spyder variants. They were all highly successful in competition and by 1961, Porsche sports cars had won more than five hundred races around the world.

Of all the people who owned 550s, the most recognized was film star James Dean, who purchased his car from John von Neumann in September 1955. A few weeks later, on his way to a race in Salinas, Dean was killed on a remote California highway just outside the small town of Cholame, his 550 struck nearly head-on by a Ford. The small car careened off the road and came to rest against a fence, a distorted tangle of aluminum and steel, its famous driver fatally injured. Dean's passenger, Rolf Wütherich, a Porsche factory mechanic who was in California instructing and troubleshooting for von Neumann, was miraculously thrown clear and survived the accident. Were it not for that ill-fated event, the 550 Spyder might not be as well remembered as it is today. Then again, even if James Dean had never owned a Porsche or died in one, the 550 Spyder would still have been the most celebrated Porsche race car of the 1950s. Dean's tragic death unfortunately underscored an unsettling truth about the production Spyder: It was just too much for most drivers to handle and really demanded the skills of a professional at the wheel. Many loyal Porsche enthusiasts weren't altogether taken with the limitations of a road-going race car, either, and turned to Porsche for a more practical sports model equipped with the 550's four-cam engine.

In August 1953, Porsche decided to test the four-cam in the 356 to evaluate its compatibility with the rear-engine platform. Seven months later the prototype 356 four-cam proved to be a match that made its own case. Overlooking the fact that the Type 547 four-cam had been intended exclusively for racing, Ferry Porsche bowed to the wishes

The Porsche RS 60 was first raced in 1960. A further development of the original 550, this is one of three cars entered at the Nürburgring 1000km in May. The Bonnier-Gendebien RS 60 finished second. (PORSCHE WERKFOTO)

of his customers and in the fall of 1955 introduced the four-cam Carrera model as part of the new 356A series, which made its debut at the Frankfurt Auto Show.

The higher-performance push-rod engine offered in the 356A was a new, more powerful version with a swept volume of 1.6 liters (1582 cubic centimeters) available in either 1600 or 1600 Super versions (Types 616/1 and 616/2, respectively). Their greater displacement allowed Porsche to increase compression ratios, taking full advantage of the newer high-octane fuels available in the mid-1950s. The 356A also fit nicely into the Fédération Internationale de l'Automobile (F.I.A.) class established for 1600cc touring and grand touring cars, putting Porsche in an even better position for sports car competition. With the new push-rod 1600s, Porsche could stress smoothness and flexibility rather than sheer neck-snapping power. This was possible because Porsche engineers had also improved the body, chassis, and running gear on the 356A. Among the changes was a new tire-wheel relationship; tires with a smaller rim diameter and a larger section (5.60 × 15 rather than 5.00 × 16) were fitted with lower recommended tire pressure. In concert with the new tires, strengthened steering tie-rods and ball joints were utilized. The position of the steering linkage was also changed to impart a roll understeer effect—a slight

steering outward of the outside front wheel when the car leaned into a turn—and the caster angle was doubled. This reduced some of the tendency for the car to swap ends when driven hard into a turn. Thus, the majority of changes introduced with the 356A had to be experienced rather than seen.

On April 3, 1962, Porsche produced its fifty-thousandth Type 356 at the new Werk II facility. Every factory employee was on hand for the milestone event. (PORSCHE WERKFOTO)

OPPOSITE: In April 1954, Porsche introduced the horn grilles positioned inboard of the parking lights, allowing the new Bosch horns to be better heard. The arched hood handle was also adopted in 1954 from the first Speedsters. Pictured is a rare Pre-A Carrera 4-cam coupe. They were produced beginning in July 1955, just prior to the debut of the new 356A Carrera in September.

RIGHT ABOVE AND BELOW: The new Carrera engine lived beneath the same rear-deck lid as the standard 1500 and 1500S engines, all sharing a single grille. Only the gold *Carrera* script on the fenders and tail panel announced the new, more powerful Type 547 engine developing a rousing 110 horsepower.

From behind the wheel the 356A was a decidedly different car from its predecessors, not only in performance and handling but in appearance as well. The floor pan had been lowered 1.4 inches by doing away with the false floorboards previously used. The hand brake lever had been relocated from under the dashboard on the driver's right, where it had proven to be a frequent obstacle, to the left side, where it was out of the way. The dashboard was a completely new design, with three large gauges positioned directly within the circumference of the steering wheel —speedometer to the left, tachometer in the center, and combination fuel and oil temperature gauge to the right. An interesting footnote to the new design was the use of foam rubber padding under the dashboard cap upholstery, one of the first modern attempts to add a safety feature to interior design.

The 1600S was a true 100-miles-per-hour-plus car, and it endowed the 356A with qualities that were simply uncanny for the 1950s. Most drivers were surprised to find the tail-heavy feeling of the Pre-A models all but gone. The 356A was a more tractable car than its predecessor, one capable of endowing average drivers with above-average abilities, a fact bemoaned by those who had finally mastered the unpredictable handling of earlier Porsche models. Uli Wieselmann, editor in chief of Germany's prestigious *Auto, Motor und Sport,* wrote, "Now, even dear granny can take a turn faster with a Porsche than with an average car." Still, one had to drive a 356 with respect because its 45/55 percent front-to-rear weight distribution and swing axle rear suspension could still encourage the rear end of the car to assume the position of the front if driven too aggressively through a turn. In a 1955 *Mechanix Illustrated* review, Tom McCahill, America's most bombastic automotive scribe, said of the 356A, "These are fantastically roadable cars, up to a point. . . ."

OPPOSITE ABOVE AND BELOW: The Pre-A interior was different from that of the new 356A models. The instrument panel still featured two hooded round gauges and a large radio mounted in the center of the dash. On models without the radio, such as the example shown, a Porsche faceplate filled the opening. A new steering wheel with a large horn ring was introduced in 1954 along with the dual Bosch horns. Interiors were beautifully upholstered, and seating was quite substantial for a sports car.

RIGHT: Erwin Komenda's design for the 356 was remarkably aerodynamic for a car that was created without the use of a wind tunnel. In 1957, nine years after the initial design, a 356A Carrera 1500 GS was tested in the wind tunnel at Daimler-Benz. It was exactly as Komenda said it would be. (PORSCHE WERKFOTO)

Then he cautioned prospective owners, ". . . And the fact that they are so easy to handle has caused some people to go beyond the back-off point. It is quite easy and requires no skill to flip one of these bugs while hitting a bump in a rough stretch of road the wrong way."

For those desiring even greater performance, there was the four-cam Type 547/1 engine introduced in the 1955 Carrera 1500 Grand Sport. The Porsche Carrera engine was almost identical to that used in the 1500RS Spyders, with the exception of a lower compression ratio and adjustments to allow the engine to be mounted in the rear rather than in the middle. Based on the earlier air-cooled, four-cylinder motor developed for the 356, the Carrera engine had, in addition to dual overhead cams, a Hirth built-up crankshaft, twin choke Solex carburetors, dual ignition, and dry sump lubrication. Noted Wieselmann in *Auto, Motor und Sport*, "With this model, Porsche are offering the four-cam engine from the Spyder, which has countless racing victories to its credit, in a comfortable and luxurious touring car. The power of this long established and foolproof engine has been reduced from 115 to 100 horsepower, while the compression ratio has been cut back from 9.5:1 to 8.7:1. This engine will power the coupe to a top speed of about 200 km/h [125 miles per hour]. Its handling, combined with its truly outstanding engine, will give all those with the feeling for it a pure driving experience that cannot be matched by any other car that I know of!"

Although the four-cam was a far more difficult engine to build and maintain, Porsche offered it as an option on all 356A models in 1955—coupe, cabriolet, and Speedster—each signified by the gold Carrera script on the front fenders and rear-deck lid. The four-cammers also displayed dual exhaust pipes and a rousing increase in performance compared to the push-rod 356s.

In 1956–57 the Carrera models were further distinguished from the push-rod models with the addition of twin grilles on the engine cover.

Beneath the otherwise inconspicuous 356A body work, the Carreras were equipped with modified suspensions utilizing stronger stabilizers, improved track rods, a hydraulic steering damper, wider track and larger 15-inch wheels. Although the new 356A Carrera was a heavier car by about one hundred pounds, it had more responsive handling than standard Zuffenhausen fare and could exceed 125 miles per hour.

The Speedster was the most exciting of the new 356A models, a more civilized version of Hoffman's 1952 America roadster. Like the America, the Speedster was a tinny blithe spirit of a car with two poorly hinged doors, a leaky canvas top, flimsy side curtains, an unpredictable (better get ready for the turn before you get there) Volkswagen-based suspension, and an engine that sounded as though it was about to burst at every shift. For its time it was *Pur Sang*. A modern-day Porsche Carrera will easily tease the 200-miles-per-hour mark and propel itself from rest to 60 miles per hour in a matter of seconds. The 356 Speedster with its flat-four engine could have achieved such speeds only if dropped from a very great height! It was, nonetheless, one of the greatest sports cars of the era and one of the few foreign cars to become an American icon of the 1950s.

The Speedster, first introduced in the Pre-A series, was essentially a bare-bones sports model requested by Max Hoffman. Ferry recalled, "At the time Hoffman was always anxious to have the cheapest Porsche on display in his showrooms. His price was less than $3,000, to which he added all the 'extras,' which even included the V-belt, the tire pressure gauge, and the heating, although no cars were sold without heating. This way of doing

OPPOSITE: Racing improves the breed. The Type 550 was Porsche's first thoroughbred competition car. Designed by Komenda, the sleek roadsters (shown in this unusual overhead view) were ideally suited to sports car racing because of their lightweight bodies and mid-mounted engines. The cockpit and seating were ample but unfretted.

The team of Jack McAfee and Pete Lovely competed with a 550 Spyder at Sebring in 1956. (PORSCHE WERKFOTO)

business was actually not so unusual in the U.S.A. The aim, of course, was to use the low price displayed on the car to tempt the customers into the showroom, where the salesman could then demonstrate his skills. I well remember an experience I had on my first visit to the U.S.A. in 1937. At the time the small eight-cylinder Ford cost exactly $600. However, this price did not include the bumpers, the spare wheel, or the tool kit. These 'extras' pushed the price up to $680. So you can see that Hoffman's tactics were based on some distinguished precedents." The Speedster was an attrac-

Race driver-journalists Richard von Frankenberg and Paul Frère drove this factory-prepared 550 coupe at Le Mans in 1953. (PORSCHE WERKFOTO)

Beautifully restored, this 1953 Type 550, now in the Porsche Museum, was originally raced by Hans Herrmann in the 1954 Carrera PanAmericana. (PORSCHE WERKFOTO)

the 356 Speedster started at $2,995 in 1954 with the standard 55-horsepower, 1.5-liter 1500 engine. The 1500 Speedster was the lowest priced Porsche ever sold in the United States. Another $500 upgraded the car to the powerful 1500S, 70-horsepower, roller-bearing engine, which shaved almost two seconds off zero-to-60 and quarter-mile times, and pushed the car's top speed to over 100 miles per hour.

On March 25, 1956, Porsche GmbH celebrated the twenty-fifth anniversary of the company's founding in Stuttgart-Zuffenhausen by Ferdinand Porsche, Dr. Anton Piëch, and Adolf Rosenberger. The event was marked by the production of the ten-thousandth Porsche, which Ferry's youngest son, Wolfgang, drove off the Reutter assembly line. And Porsche had a new sales slogan in 1956: "Years ahead in engineering, miles ahead on the road."

The sales office estimated that 70 percent of all Porsches produced were being exported by 1956, with the majority being sold in the United States. Ironically, after one year of producing the much demanded 356A Carrera, Porsche discovered to their dismay that the customers who had wanted such a car were not only dissatisfied with it but divided on the issue of whether the Carreras were any more suitable for the road than the 550s had been.

The success of the 550 led to a demand for the 4-cam engine in other production Porsche models, including the 356A Speedster. Intended to be a low-priced sports model for the American market, the Carrera Speedster was something of a contradiction because it was considerably more expensive with the four-cam engine.

tive sporty car that brought people into the showroom, where they were often persuaded to buy a coupe or cabriolet that could be ordered with an economical 44-horsepower or 60-horsepower engine or the more powerful 75- and 100-horsepower engines, the latter being the 1500 GS Carrera. As mandated by Hoffman,

OPPOSITE: Aside from the rarefied Carrera Speedsters, the 1958 1600S Speedster was the fastest production car you could purchase from Porsche. This was a true 100-miles-per-hour sports car, and it endowed the 356A Porsche with qualities that were uncanny for the 1950s. The Speedster styling was distinctive, with its lower windshield, flat boot, and gold Speedster emblem along the front fenders.

ABOVE LEFT: Dashboard designs changed several times in the Pre-A series, and in the 356A there were two basic designs, the sportier of the two being the Speedster. There were early and late Speedster designs; this example is the latter, with its three large gauges in an arc centered behind the steering wheel.

ABOVE RIGHT: A gold Speedster emblem was placed along the front fenders. The Reutter body plate was mounted at the bottom of the fender just behind the wheel arch. This Speedster is equipped with the optional Rudge knock-off wheels frequently used on competition cars.

LEFT: Positioned just below the 110-horsepower Carrera engine, the 1600 Super engine delivered 75 horsepower at 5,000 revolutions per minute. Cataloged as the Type 616/2 engine, the early 1600 S used Solex 40 PBIC carburetors; the later 616/2 used 32 NDIX Zeniths, an 8.5:1 compression ratio, and a 74 × 82.5 mm bore × stroke for a swept volume of 1,582 cubic centimeters (1.6 liters). The cars could easily surpass 100 miles per hour.

ABOVE: In 1958, Porsche switched to Zenith 32 NDIX carburetors, which allowed the use of the same basic carburetors on both 1600 Normal and 1600 Super engines. The black fan shroud indicates a 1600 Normal engine.

RIGHT: Yes, that is the trunk. With the spare tire and fuel tank occupying most of the available space, luggage area was at a premium. Most serious travelers opted for a rear-deck lid luggage rack or stuffed as much as possible behind the seats.

OVERLEAF LEFT:
At Porsche there has always been a fine line between race car and road car. In 1959, Zuffenhausen rolled out the most luxurious of all 356 Carrera models, the 1600 GS. Only forty-seven were built; twelve were cabriolets, and of those only two were hardtop cabriolets. Arguably a contradiction in terms, the unique pair of Carrera cabriolets was fitted with a removable hardtop painted in a contrasting color.

OVERLEAF RIGHT:
The hardtop provided a wider curved glass backlight for better visibility, and in cold climates it provided a warmer roof over one's head than that of a canvas top.

LEFT: The Convertible D was so named for its coach builder, Karosserie Drauz, in Heilbronn. Each of the D models bore the coach builder's emblem on the front fender. **ABOVE LEFT:** With the top raised the Convertible D still retained much of the Speedster look, but it had a more accommodating interior and an elegant profile. The 356A Convertible D was produced for one year and then replaced by the further improved 356B Roadster in 1959. The Convertible D sold for $3,695. **ABOVE RIGHT:** Deciding to make a clean break with earlier model designations, the Speedster D became the Convertible D when it was introduced. The new model combined the best attributes of both the Speedster and the cabriolet, with a high windshield, and thus a high roof line and more headroom with the top raised; more luxurious and comfortable seating; and glass roll-up windows in Speedster-style doors. **BELOW RIGHT:** The Convertible D interior was a full-dress version of the Speedster and had more comfortable seating, better carpeting and trim, and roll-up windows—all of the creature comforts that had been lacking in the original Speedster models.

OPPOSITE: From the beginning Ferry Porsche was skeptical of the Speedster as an entry-level model, saying that "stripping a car only degrades it without achieving the intended result." Though Hoffman initially proved him wrong, the Speedster was neither a comfortable nor a convenient car, and in August 1958, Porsche discontinued the design and replaced it with a more civilized model first known as the Speedster D.

The 1963 Carrera 2 engines, model 587/1 and 587/2, used 40 PII-4 and W 46 IDM/2 carburetors, respectively. Output from the 9.2:1 compression 587/1 was 130 horsepower at 6,200 revolutions per minute and from the 9.8:1 compression 587/2 it was 160 horsepower at 6,900 rpm. It was quite a leap to make in fifteen years from the 40-horsepower VW-based flat fours that had powered the earliest 356 models.

Arguably, the first Carreras had been a compromise, neither light enough for racing nor luxurious enough to be considered a touring car, so with Solomon-like wisdom, Ferry solved the problem in 1957 by creating two versions. First was the Deluxe, equipped with a full leather interior and every luxury feature Porsche could fit into the car, and the other was the GT, a full competition model available only in Speedster and coupe body styles, and equipped with bucket seats, plastic windows, lighter bumpers, a Nardi wood-rimmed aluminum steering wheel, and 60-millimeter Spyder front brakes. No creature comforts were afforded the GT at all—not even a heater! The Carrera was now an eligible GT racer, and in competition the 356A Carreras surpassed many purpose-built race cars of the era.

Right below the Carrera was the 1600S Speedster, somewhat of a mixed metaphor on wheels. It was the embodiment of the Porsche principle, yet it was also the least luxurious and most scarcely appointed model in the 356A line. The average Porsche customer wanted performance without sacrificing comfort or luxury, and for that Zuffenhausen offered the cabriolet and coupe. The Speedster was built for purists, indomitable individuals who threw caution to the wind (quite literally in a Speedster) and didn't give a damn about anything that wasn't purposeful. Aside from the high-performance four-cam Carrera Speedster, the 1600S was the fastest production car one could purchase from Porsche.

The 1958 models were introduced at the biennial International Auto Show held in Frankfurt. The 1958 series, carrying the internal designation T-2, were revised mechanically but looked essentially the same as the previous year's models. Starting with the T-2 series, however, the roller connecting rod bearings and the Hirth built-up crankshaft were eliminated in the 1600S engine. Along with the standardization of plain-bearing crankshafts, the T-2 series also incorporated a new oil cooler design and the first use of Zenith 32 NDIX carburetors in place of the Solex 32 and 40 PBIC carburetors used in the earlier 1500 and 1500S engines. The Zeniths allowed Porsche to use the same basic carburetors on both the 1600 Normal and 1600 Super. Internally, the size of the venturi was the only significant difference, 24 millimeters for the Normal and 28 millimeters on the Super. The two engines were visually distinguished by the color of the fan shroud, black for Normal and silver for Super.

The 356C/1600 SC cabriolet had a fully-lined top and more than ample headroom, but top down was the way to really enjoy the car.

OVERLEAF, LEFT: The 356 SC cabriolet was the top of the luxury line in 1963. Introduced in July, it was the first of the new C series models. The cars had reached their final evolution, and waiting in the wings for introduction as a 1964 model was the all-new Porsche 911. The 356C models remained in production through March 1966, when the final 356C/1600 SC was completed, bringing to an end eighteen years of 356 series production.

OVERLEAF, RIGHT: The 356C interior was the most stylish of the entire 356 series, with its leather-upholstered dash, door, kick panels, and seats standard on the cabriolet. Also note the deluxe steering wheel with full horn rim and seats with headrests, all available options.

However refined they were, the 1958 model year was to be the last for Zuffenhausen's austere 1600S Speedsters. In August 1958 the lightweight two-seaters were superseded by the all-new and luxuriously appointed 1959 356B model, originally named the Speedster D (D for Drauz, which was the coach builder). By the time of its introduction Porsche had renamed the new model the Convertible D, in order to make a clean break with the older, less sophisticated Speedster series. The D combined the best attributes of the 356A Speedster with a more stylish, comfortable, and practical interior that included a higher windshield, to reduce the draft

The luxurious 356C came equipped with a deluxe wood-rimmed steering wheel with full horn rim. Also note the padded dash panel.

and allow more headroom with the top raised, and roll-up glass windows rather than drop-in plastic side curtains. The convertible D 1600 sold for $3,695, making it pricey but not overpriced. *Road & Track* wrote in 1959, "[It is] the best buy in a highly desirable line and [one that] will probably give more driving pleasure per dollar than almost any car you can buy." For 1960 the model was improved once again and renamed the 356B roadster.

Back in 1958 and 1959, Drauz at Heilbronn, north of Stuttgart, had built all the Convertible D bodies. In 1961, roadster production was switched to the great classic-era coach-building firm of Anciens Etablissement d'Ieteren Frères S.A. in Brussels, Belgium. By then demand for the 356B had outstripped the production capacity at Reutter, and Porsche had to order additional bodies from Karosserie Wilhelm Karmann GmbH (best known for the VW Karmann Ghia). Each of the different cars bore the body plate of its individual coach builder. In total, Drauz built 386 Convertible D bodies in 1958 and 944 in 1959; 561 of the 356B roadsters in 1959 for the 1960 model year, 1,529 in 1960, and 90 in 1961. After all the changes and improvements to the sporty convertible models, Porsche was totally dismayed to discover that the original 356A Speedster, built from 1955 to 1958, was the most popular model despite the fact that it was also the car that received the complaints from its owners about its lack of features.

The Porsche crowd had always been a mixed bag, and even with the Deluxe and GT variants, there was still a strong demand, particularly from the U.S. market, for an even more luxurious Porsche. In 1959, Zuffenhausen had introduced the most opulent of all 356A Carrera models, the 1600 GS. Weighing 2,100 pounds, somewhat heavier than its predecessor, the 1959 cars were equipped with the improved 115-horsepower 692/2 four-cam plain-bearing engines.

The 1959 model year marked another turning point in Porsche history. The exclusive relationship with Max Hoffman that had begun in 1950 came to an end when Porsche took control of its exports to the United States by establishing Porsche of America Corporation. The new company imported cars through six individual distributors across the country, including Hoffman, who remained Porsche's East Coast distributor for another five years.

In 1960, Porsche's emphasis again returned to competition, with 1959 having marked the end of the luxury Carrera Grand Sport models. At the top of Porsche's new model line was the exhilarating 2-liter 2000 GS, the fastest 356 road car built by Porsche up to that time.

Porsche's total workforce had increased in size to 1,250 by 1960, and Ferry noted that "quality control was systematically improved. Every fifth worker employed in the production department was involved in supervisory tasks. For each car produced, the after-sales department kept record cards relating to the engine, gearbox, vehicle inspection, and other test data. By the end of 1960 we had delivered a total of 39,747 cars to customers."

Model changes and engineering improvements were being made almost annually and at the end of 1961, Porsche announced the new Carrera 2, powered by a 2-liter, 130-horsepower, four-cam engine. This model went on sale in 1962, and the following year the 356B series was replaced by the 356C, equipped with a further improved engine and Ate disc brakes on all four wheels.

Now in production continuously since 1948, the 356, though always evolving, was at last beginning to show its age, and discussions were taking place regarding the design of an all-new Porsche

model. Ferry wrote, "It had been clear to me for a long time that we could not go on with the 356 forever. We had to replace it. As far as a successor to the 356 was concerned, various opinions were being voiced within the company." One of those opinions was that of Ferdinand Alexander "Butzi" Porsche III, Ferry's eldest son, who had joined the company in 1957 and trained as a designer at the side of his grandfather's chief stylist, Erwin Komenda. Although Komenda had put forth a number of ideas for a successor to the 356, the aging designer was either unable or unwilling to present Ferry with a suitable replacement. Ferry then presented him with Butzi's design, which was designated the Type 7. According to Ferry, "It was really a very beautiful car, a 2 + 2, almost a four-seater." Komenda took the proposal and, in translating it from a styling concept to an engineering design, made significant changes. "I then realized that Herr Komenda was not taking any notice of my proposals and that he wanted at all costs to build the cars that he and his team designed. Moreover, he was constantly changing my son's styling to a design more in tune with his own tastes."

This was the first time Ferry realized that Komenda was a car body designer, not a stylist, and while the two disciplines were required to craft an automobile, Komenda could not see past the 356, the basis for every car Porsche had built up to this time. Ferry recalled, "We had just taken over the Reutter company, which had its own design department, so I went to see Herr Beierbach, who was at the time the managing director of Reutter, and said to him, 'Herr Beierbach, here is my son's model. Can you do the engineering drawings in such a way that the styling remains unaltered?' He said he could, and he had engineering drawings made from the model." This was to become the basis for the 911.

The future of Porsche would now rest in Butzi's hands.

CHAPTER 6

BUTZI PORSCHE'S 901/911

RE-CREATING THE PORSCHE IN ITS OWN IMAGE

THE ORIGINAL PLANS FOR A MODEL TO REPLACE the 356 were drawn up by Erwin Komenda, but Ferry Porsche felt that it was too closely tied to the 356, as was Komenda himself. Thus Ferry decided to solicit other designs, some of which came from outside the company. The first was from renowned stylist Count Albrecht Goertz, a close friend of Max Hoffman's and an associate of international designer Raymond Loewy. Goertz had created the stunning 1955 BMW 507, and his work was highly respected throughout Europe. His approach to a 356 replacement, however, was too American in design; in Ferry's words, "A beautiful Goertz, but not a Porsche."

By 1959, Butzi was also at work on his own design, which was completed as a plasticine model in October. Wanting to show a full-scale version to his father before year's end, Butzi and his small staff worked through Christmas, completing the 1:1 mock-up on December 28. Although several other proposals were on the table, Ferry liked the car that Butzi had designed, and it was from this original concept that the Type 901 prototype would evolve.

Already an accomplished designer by the age of twenty-eight (when he was appointed head of the styling department in 1961), Butzi was willing to bend if not rewrite the rules of established Porsche design in order to finalize the styling and engineering for his successor to the aging 356.

The first problem Porsche had to address with the new car was one of propriety. Must you build a new Porsche just like the old one? This had been Komenda's belief, and in many respects he had been correct. Butzi, however, approached the problem from a unique perspective. "It should be a new Porsche . . . as good or better than the old, and in the same pattern, but not necessarily the same form," he said. What exactly did that mean? One has only to compare an early 901 with a late-model 356 coupe to understand. The 901 was an out-and-out evolution of the 356 design—longer

OPPOSITE: The source Porsche: This is one of the 1963 Type 901 prototypes and the oldest 911 in existence. Dennis Frick and German Classic Cars of New Cumberland, Pennsylvania, restored the car.

and sleeker, perhaps, and certainly more powerful, but quintessentially Porsche. Butzi had accomplished what no one, even the legendary Komenda, had been able to do: re-create the Porsche in its own image.

Although changes to the engine, suspension, transmission, and interior continued even after the first prototype 901 was shown in 1963, the final body design completed by Butzi in December 1961, and known internally as the Type 644 T8, remained the foundation on which all further development of the 901 would be based.

While Porsche was developing the new model, Reutter caught everyone off guard when it announced that the company was unwilling to spend the money necessary to retool for a completely new body design. Both the elder Reutter and his son had been killed during World War II, and the company's heirs and managers, who perhaps lacked their foresight, were unwilling to risk further investment with Porsche. They had instead decided to sell the coach-building operations in Zuffenhausen, retaining only their seat manufacturing division, which became the Recaro GmbH Company.

This sudden and unexpected circumstance placed Porsche in an awkward position because Reutter's management considered its longtime neighbor and principal customer the most likely buyer. But this was a major investment, and the Porsche family considered it at some length before deciding to purchase Karosseriewerk Reutter in July 1963. This was the first real financial burden the company had taken on since the early postwar years, and it begged the question: Was this the right time to discontinue the only product it had ever produced and replace it with an entirely new one? Unlike a miscalculation by Ford or General Motors, which could sweep an unsuccessful new model under the carpet, one by a com-

pany the size of Porsche would be disastrous. As late as September 1963 there was still considerable doubt in Zuffenhausen as to whether the 356 should be replaced (the 356C actually remained in production for more than a year after the 901 was introduced), and to ensure that Porsche could gauge public and media reaction to the 901, it was shown at the Frankfurt Auto Show a full year before it was to go on sale.

Even though the response at the September motor show had been more than favorable, Porsche still felt the need to further justify its actions in print. A press release announcing the introduction of a new model to replace the venerable 356 explained the "theory" behind the design and development of the 901. "For years Ferry Porsche and his team of engineers have racked their brains as to how to keep the Porsche motto 'Driving in its purest form' both up to date and in tune with the constantly changing conditions of modern traffic." It explained that Porsche's goal in creating a successor for the 356 was to design "a car with hardly larger outside measurements than the present one, and yet one with more interior room. It should have an engine that can cope without strain with today's traffic jam . . . yet possess the performance of the Carrera—lightning acceleration to a maximum speed of over 200 km/h (120 mph). Apart from that it should have an easily accessible luggage compartment. To that should be added the roadholding of a sports car plus the comfort of the Gran Turismo for the long journey. Equally necessary was a Porsche synchronized, properly spaced, five-speed gearbox, as well as the highest quality body work, and all this within a reasonable price." A description that still suits the latest 911 models, with the possible exception of "reasonable price."

The 901 embodied more changes than the company had ever made, from the body and interior, right down to the final suspen-

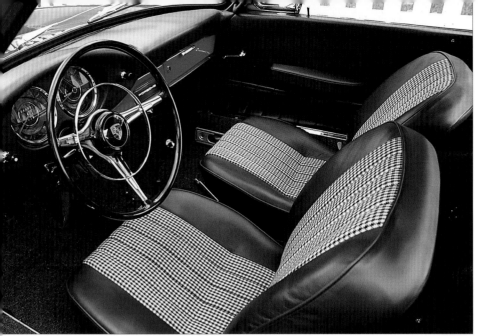

ABOVE LEFT: The interior of 13 327 was upholstered in black with houndstooth seat inserts. This was the customary upholstery for the 901/911 unless otherwise specified.

ABOVE RIGHT: From behind the wheel, this car is almost entirely different from the production 911. In place of the 911's instrument grouping are two large gauges with switches on either side. The two big dials, which may have been lifted from a BMW 503 for this prototype, demanded a higher dash and a different panel configuration. The black-and-white studio photo shows another interior design closer to that used in the final production version.

RIGHT: The 1,991-cubic-centimeter, flat-six engine of the 901/1 was designed by Hans Tomala and Ferdinand Piëch, Ferry Porsche's nephew. In 1965, Piëch would take charge of the research and development departments at Porsche. The eight main bearing engine had an oversquare design with an 80 millimeters × 66 millimeters (3.15 inches × 2.60 inches) bore × stroke. Output was rated at 130 horsepower at 6,100 revolutions per minute with 140 pounds-per-foot torque at 4,200 revolutions per minute.

sion layout and new overhead cam, six-cylinder boxer engine—the foundation of every 911 motor to the present day. The new power plant retained Porsche's established air and oil cooling system and horizontally opposed layout, but now it had overhead camshafts driven by double-row roller chains, thereby allowing the two-cam 901's 130-horsepower output to match that of the four-cam 356 Carrera 2, without the requisite mechanical complexity. This had been one of Ferry Porsche's mandates. "I said to my people that the acceleration of the Carrera is exceptional. That, I told them, the new car should have, but without the noise! It had to be much quieter." The new flat six was that and more, equal in power but less costly to manufacture. The Carrera had been a racing engine; this was a more refined engine that would prove itself in both worlds.

Porsche continued to utilize the 356's torsion bar suspension but modified its execution in the 901. Up front, MacPherson struts replaced double trailing arms, with the front torsion bars set lengthwise instead of transversely inside the A-arm, allowing more trunk space. The 901 engineering team moved the steering mechanism—now a rack-and-pinion design—toward the center of the car, utilizing an offset double-jointed shaft. The central placement of the steering box was decided upon so Porsche could easily build the car in either left-hand- or right-hand-drive configurations, the latter required for a number of markets, including Great Britain and Japan. The offset steering column also proved to be safer in the event of a severe front collision, eliminating the possibility of the steering column being pushed through into the driver's seat and, presumably, *through* the driver.

"In design there is styling, art, and other terms intermingled," said Butzi Porsche of his concept for the 901. "Design means to me that every designing engineer has the opportunity to become at some stage an artist . . . that every craftsman who can do more than what he is trained to do is an artist." Although there were several other proposals, Butzi Porsche's prototype design, known as the T7, was ultimately the foundation upon which all future design work would be based. (PORSCHE WERKFOTO)

The first 1:1 model of Butzi Porsche's T7 design was fabricated at Reutter in 1960. The foundation for the 911 had been established. (PORSCHE WERKFOTO)

The new 901 measured up as both a larger and a smaller car compared to its predecessor. The wheelbase was some 104 millimeters (4.1 inches) longer to provide additional foot room and larger rear seats—although rear accommodations were never seriously considered appropriate for anything but a short drive. The 901's greater wheelbase did have one notable advantage: longer doors that allowed easier entry and exit. The upper body was wider to increase hip and shoulder room, while the passing of the 356's "bathtub" physique allowed the 901's exterior to decrease in width by almost three inches. Yet from end to end, the new model was almost 5 inches longer.

Initially, Porsche reserved ten replacement chassis numbers beginning with the prefix 13 for preproduction cars. However, to the consternation of most Porsche authorities, the company contra-

dicted itself by listing a total of thirteen prototypes in its anniversary compilation of 911 models. The confusion may have been a result of early production cars that were also used for testing. Officially, there are only ten developmental cars with the number 13 prefix. The first was chassis 13 321, nicknamed Sturmvogel (Storm Petrel), followed by 13 322, known as Fledermaus (Bat), 13 323, nicknamed Blaumeise (Blue Titmouse), 13 324, called Zitronenfalter (Brimstone Butterfly), and 13 325, which somehow escaped the company's penchant for naming its prototypes.

Of the remaining six test cars, serial numbers 13 326, 13 327, 13 328, 13 330, 13 352, 300 001, and 300 002 (the last two being production car serial numbers), the example pictured (page 135), chassis number 13 327, built in 1963 and nicknamed Barbarossa, is the oldest and the only restored 901 known to exist.

With the Frankfurt debut of the 901 just two months away, road testing of disguised cars was being conducted in July 1963. This is the first 901 prototype photographed by Porsche while making a run between Weilimdorf and Münchingen on July 10. (PORSCHE WERKFOTO)

Butzi Porsche and his design staff posed with the first T8 Type 901 prototype in 1963. The design of the car had nearly been finalized, but there were ongoing changes that would continue until the cars went into production in 1964.

Although Porsche has always prided itself on cars that were "made by hand," nowhere is it more evident than on this 901 prototype. With the 901 there was nothing, save for minor items, that could be carried over from the 356. The chassis, engine, driveline, interior, and suspension all had to be made and assembled by hand.

The first show car, 13 325, was painted yellow and featured Porsche's traditional houndstooth fabric upholstery and vinyl trim. It premiered in Frankfurt along with the latest 356C coupe and cabriolet, also making their 1963 debut. (The 901's formal introduction was a year away, and the 356 was still in production.) The public's reaction to the 901 was a bit cool, which didn't worry Ferry, who regarded the initial apprehension as a positive sign. "At the Frankfurt Automobile Show in 1963, customers found it a 'bit too angular.' It had a significantly larger area of glass than its predecessor. Indeed everything that was new was at first considered strange by customers," said Ferry. "However, I was not actually worried by this, the reason being my own, rather individual views of this matter. It is my belief that something that appeals enormously on first acquaintance soon loses its attractiveness. On the other hand, if a certain degree of continuity is ensured, then the appeal will last." In the case of the 901/911 this was a most prophetic commentary. The basic form of the car has endured for forty years, the longest production run of any automobile design in history.

The 901 was exhibited alongside a new 356C, a car to which people were accustomed, and, recalled Ferry, their reaction to the new model was to say, "That's not a Porsche!" The world's leading automotive magazines immediately recognized the 901 for what it was. Author Richard Seiffert noted in *Auto, Motor, und Sport*, "The new sports car that will be produced in Zuffenhausen from the end of August is one of the most interesting cars in the world. It has been conceived as a car for normal road use, rather than as a GT racing car. Despite this, however, the 901 has the air of functionalism that will guarantee it enthusiastic buyers. In this respect, it is clearly quite different from the 230 SL and four-seater sports cars such as the Fiat 2300 S and the Alfa Romeo Sprint, which are both in the same price category. Price and performance compare with the Carrera 2, which it will succeed, but are significantly higher than the four-cylinder models. It is expected to be built in larger numbers than the Carrera, and it is reckoned that many Porsche customers will be willing to pay the extra to get their hands on this delightful car. This assumption will probably prove to be correct." Was it ever!

After the Frankfurt show, three additional 901 show cars were completed. According to factory records, prototype chassis 13 326, known as Quick Blue, was used by Ferdinand Piëch after it toured the 1963–64 auto shows in London, Sweden, Berlin, and Geneva. Piëch kept his car until the end of 1965, after which it was sold to a Porsche employee, Hans Mezger, and later to a private party in Stuttgart. There is no record of 13 326 after 1967. It is also believed that at least one of the four show cars was disassembled, run through the 911 production line, and sold as a new car!

Photographs of the Porsche display at the 1964 Geneva Auto Show include not only a 904 but in the background what might well be chassis 13 327 rather than chassis 13 326. Through early 1965 it was used as a test vehicle; this is on the restored car's chassis and body, which have countless patched openings where different components, hoses, and ducts were apparently routed and then rerouted by the engineering staff as they experimented with various ideas. In April 1965, ownership of 13 327 was transferred to race driver and automotive journalist

Richard von Frankenberg, who was editor of the Porsche magazine *Christophorus*. He had been with Porsche since 1950 and is perhaps best remembered, both pictorially and in Lawrence Braun's sculpture "Miracle of the Avus," for surviving a spectacular crash at the Avus Ring in 1956. Having careened over the lip of the track's north curve, von Frankenberg was thrown clear of his car moments before it crashed to the ground on the other side of the wall. He landed in the bushes and suffered only minor injuries. Fate was on his side that day. Not so seventeen years later when he was killed in a road accident.

The von Frankenberg 901 ended up in Italy and then surfaced a decade later in New York City, where it was discovered wasting away in a service garage. At the time the car was thought to be a cobbled up mixture of 911 and 356 parts, its history unknown until research by Paul Resnick revealed that the odd-looking 911 he had purchased was actually a 901 prototype. In 1984 he advertised the car in *Porsche Panorama* and sold it to its present owner, Don Meluzio, a Porsche racer and Chrysler dealer in York, Pennsylvania. The car was turned over to Porsche specialist Dennis Frick and his staff at German Classic Cars in New Cumberland, Pennsylvania, for a full restoration, a project that took several years to complete.

As he explains it, Frick had to put himself in the position of an engineer assembling a hand-built prototype. "A prototype is different from a production car," he says. "The 901 was obviously the object of extensive experimentation, and over time, several different, mutually exclusive heating and ventilation systems had been installed. When they were removed, the openings were simply patched and painted over."

Restoring the 901 to its "original" condition meant keeping these idiosyncrasies intact, virtually restoring the damage that had been done to the car during development and testing.

"Getting into this car," recalls Frick, "was like trying to assemble a puzzle when you don't know what the picture looks like!" The doorsills and seat rails were all handmade, with abandoned seat mounting holes and file marks in evidence. The body exhibited dimensional differences from side to side, "as if the guy working on the right never spoke to the guy working on the left," says Frick with an almost knowing look in his eyes.

Working on the car, he discovered that many off-the-shelf, or possibly off-the-floor, 356 parts were used for the prototype's construction. For example, a passenger assist handle from the 356C model is attached to the right A pillar. The steering wheel and horn ring were taken directly from a 356, as were the window cranks. A fresh air handle was made from a T6 hand throttle. The braking system was taken over nearly unchanged from the last of the 356 line.

One area of the 911 that exhibited a number of modifications from the 901 prototype was the exhaust system and rear valance design. On the prototype the muffler and exhaust pipes rubbed the ground when the cars were driven up a steep grade. To correct this, Porsche notched the lower panel to provide more clearance

OVERLEAF: This is the stuff of which automotive history is made. The only restored 901 preproduction prototype and the first road-going example of what was to become the legendary 911 is pictured with a 1994 Carrera 4 coupe. They are three decades apart but are clearly linked by a common design theme that has worked better than any in automotive history.

The first show car, 13 325, was painted yellow and featured Porsche's traditional houndstooth fabric upholstery and vinyl trim. It premiered in Frankfurt along with the latest 356C coupe and cabriolet, also making their 1963 debut.

for the exhaust pipes. This temporary fix worked for the show cars, but in production the exhaust system was altered to a single outlet and the valance changed from a one-piece design that incorporated the license plate panel to three individual pieces comprised of two bumperettes and a license plate insert.

Prototypes often have features that are merely for appearance; in other words, they don't work. For example, the 901 had fixed quarter windows. On the first 911 production cars they swung open for ventilation, but years later when heating and ventilation systems improved, Porsche returned to the 901's original fixed quarter window design.

Behind the wheel this is almost an entirely different car. In place of the 911's instrument grouping are two large gauges with switches positioned on either side. The two big dials demanded a higher dash and a different panel configuration. However, this was not the only design. The Frankfurt show car had an instrument array similar to the final production version of the 911, so the gauges in 13 327 may have been simply another idea that Porsche was considering. The two-gauge design was also used on Butzi Porsche's Type 695 T7 concept car. The 901 doors, although similar to production versions, had several uncommon features. For example, the vent windows had an internal pivot rather than the later frame-mounted hinges. Next to each vent window was a small hole in the doorsill cap, which was intended to be a defroster

welded together from twenty individual steel panels. Yet when you park a 901 prototype alongside a production 911, there are far more similarities than differences.

The 911 has gone through many changes since the 901 prototype, such as ever increasing engine size and power output, groundbreaking developments in fuel injection and engine management technology, turbocharging and intercooling, the development of high-performance automatic transmissions and all-wheel-drive, brakes that rank among the finest in the world, and handling improvements that would embarrass the fastest race cars of 1963. Yet at a glance, few of them are obvious. What is conspicuous, however, is the heritage and sense of history that every model carries with it—that unmistakable Porsche 911 profile.

vent. The inside door handles were heavy painted steel, hinged below the armrest and difficult to find at best—the latches were the same as those used on a period VW Karmann Ghia. Of course, all these differences are minor. The 901's basic shape hardly changed from Butzi Porsche's original design, and only slight alterations to the exterior were tried, such as a round fuel filler flap on 13 327 instead of an oval one. There were no trim strips along the rockers, and the door handles were skinnier than normal (prototype pieces made from solid brass). There were no bumper overriders up front, and even the PORSCHE script on the rear-deck lid was different, taken directly from a late model 356. The list goes on: from torsion bars used to support the trunk lid to a hand-built fuel tank

Up to the time of its introduction the new Porsche model was going to be known as the 901. How then did it become the 911? The reason for the company's famous eleventh-hour name change is one of the more interesting pieces of Porsche lore. The production version was originally known as the prototype, 901, and the lower-priced four-cylinder model, awaiting introduction in 1965, was to be named the 902.

Interestingly, the 901 model designation had nothing to do with the car's design, as is often rumored. In the early 1960s, Porsche was closely integrating its international sales and service with Volkswagen, and Porsche simply needed parts numbers that would be compatible with VWs. The next available series at Volkswagen began with 900; thus the new model was to be the 901. Not terribly romantic. And the new model would have remained the 901 had it not been for an unexpected encounter with Peugeot in September 1964 just as the new Porsche model was making its debut.

The first 901 prototype was shown at the Frankfurt International Automobile Show in September 1963. A year later another of the prototypes was exhibited at the Paris Auto Salon, and to Porsche's surprise the company was contacted by Peugeot's legal department. The French automaker's solicitors informed Porsche that Peugeot had been using three numeral designations for its passenger cars—comprised of two numbers with a zero between them—since 1929. And therefore in France 901 would be a Peugeot model designation. Under French trademark regulations they held the exclusive rights, and if Porsche wanted to sell the car in France, the name had to be changed. Since the French export market was vital to Porsche's European sales and the cars were already in production, a swift resolution was necessary, and a zero become a one. The four-cylinder 902, introduced in 1965, became the 912, although 901 and 902 were still used internally for factory designations of engines and parts numbers.

The official name change came on November 10, 1964, with chassis number 300 049. The first production 911s were not delivered until afterward even though forty-nine cars had already been built as 901s.

Racing enthusiasts might wonder, "What about the Porsche 904?" Since it was a competition car and had already been on the market, unbe-

knownst to Peugeot, for nearly a year (and one wonders how they couldn't have known), the company was willing to grant an exception. Porsche capitalized on this concession by using the middle zero for competition models through Type 909. Nothing was ever heard from Peugeot again.

By any account the 901/911 was a stunning success, continuing the traditions established by Porsche with the 356 but at the same time creating a new following: a cadre of owner/enthusiasts who have made the 911 one of the most coveted sports cars of all time.

Ferry and Butzi Porsche are seen looking over the design of a production 911 in 1968. A number of design changes had already been implemented, including more powerful engines and improved suspensions.

CHAPTER 7

THE SECOND DYNASTY

FERDINAND ALEXANDER PORSCHE, "BUTZI" TO HIS boyhood friends and family, designed the ideal sports car in 1963. The 911 was faster and easier to drive than its predecessor; it was more comfortable and, above all, not terribly complicated. Granted, it was neither as exotic as a Ferrari, a Maserati, or a Jaguar, but then it wasn't a victim of any of their shortcomings either. The new Porsche was a work of art, aesthetically and mechanically, and offered prospective owners an abundance of features, including one with which few sports cars of the 1960s were endowed: practicality. The 911 was better suited to the dual roles of sports car and grand touring car than any of its contemporaries.

Ferry Porsche had bet everything on his son's new design, and now with the 356 gone, the company's future was in the hands of automotive writers and customers who would weigh the new car against the old, a model that had in its short history become almost legendary as both road car and race car. To Porsche's relief

the world motor press, often the greatest critics of change, celebrated the 911 with accolades. *Car and Driver* wrote, "Race breeding and engineering ooze from the 911's every pore. The whole package, especially the powertrain, is designed to be more reliable and less difficult to service." The magazine concluded with glowing praise: "It's worth the price of all the old Porsches put together. More important, the 911's appeal should be considerably wider than the earlier models." Indeed it was. Similar endorsements were heard from every major American and European automotive journal, though few of the writers had any idea of the time or the turmoil that it took to create a successor to the 356. The wheels of change had been set in motion, wheels that would grind away at the camaraderie that company management and employees had enjoyed since 1948.

Despite the engineering department's painstaking efforts to build a more agile and responsive sports car, the 911's greatest ap-

OPPOSITE: On the occasion of his eighty-fifth birthday on September 19, 1994, Ferdinand "Ferry" Porsche posed with a new Porsche Carrera and the famous 1948 Gmünd roadster. (PORSCHE WERKFOTO)

With fashions and hair courtesy of 1967, this factory promotional photo shows the 911S 2.0 coupe in a more restrained pose. Since it was the Sport model in the 911 lineup, most photos of the car were at speed. (PORSCHE WERKFOTO)

peal was its styling, a fact clearly revealed by sales of the 911's lower-priced companion, the 912. When the four-cylinder model made its debut late in 1964, effectively replacing the 356C in Europe (although the cars were still available in the United States until September 1965), the 912 became Porsche's best-selling car. During 1966, the first full year in which the 911 and 912 were built together, Porsche set a new sales record of 12,820 cars, with the 912 outselling its six-cylinder counterpart by better than two to one. More than nine thousand four-cylinder 912 models were delivered into the hands of eager customers, compared to around four thousand of the pricier, high-performance 911s. By year's end combined monthly sales of more than one thousand cars had made the 911 and 912 the most popular sports cars on the market, particularly in the United States where VW and Porsche dealers could be found in almost every major city from the East Coast to the West.

Although the 911 was considered a touring car and had not initially been designed for racing (any more than the first 356 models had been), 911s quickly found their way into the hands of motor sports enthusiasts and at once acquitted themselves in Sports Car Club of America competition. In 1966 drivers steering the new Porsche coupes around the world's toughest road courses earned sports car championships in West Germany, Austria, Spain, and America. Among the accomplishments was the SCCA Class D Production trophy won by Jerry Titus in a car sponsored by Los Angeles, California, Porsche dealer Vasek Polak. Production 911s also collected their share of trophies in European hill climb events, and in 1966, a 911 finished fourteenth overall in the 24 Hours of Le Mans. Even more remarkable, the car was driven to and from the Circuit de La Sarthe on public roads. During this same period the factory works cars, the 904 Carrera GTS (also designed by

The 911 (left) was an elegantly styled sports car in 1966. It was joined in 1967 by the higher-performance 911S and by the more luxurious 911L (right) in 1968. For an additional $600 above the price of a base 911, owners received every feature of the 911S except for the high-performance engine. This 911L has the distinctive Fuchs aluminum wheels that were standard on the 911S.

Ferdinand Alexander Porsche) and 906, were triumphant in Grand Prix races and hill climbs, putting Porsche at the forefront of both amateur and professional motor sports on two continents.

With the success of the 911 coupe assured, the next step was to develop a cabriolet version. This had been a Porsche tradition dating back to the prewar Volkswagens. When the 356 was introduced in 1948, there were both coupe and cabrio models, thus the same was expected of the 911, but it wasn't going to be as easy. A true cabriolet would require a complete redesign of the 911's rear sheet metal and backlight, a new, lower windshield, and, of course, a convertible top mechanism. Such modifications were relatively simple with the hand-built 356 bodies, but with Porsche still heavily in debt from the acquisition of Reutter, the economic demands

The 911 from 1966 had a well-appointed interior. Here the car is shown with optional head bolsters.

of a major tooling change were more than the company could handle. A cabriolet simply wasn't possible, but it was necessary. Thus Ferry Porsche charged his son and the styling department with the task of finding an alternative. Butzi's innovative solution to the cabrio would become one of the company's greatest trademarks and establish yet another novel design paradigm for Porsche.

As far back as the 1930s there had been alternatives to the cabriolet: the obvious sunroof, which Porsche already offered for the 911 coupe, and sliding fabric tops, which were not the same as a convertible. Built in Germany by Webasto, they had been tried in the prewar VWs with some success and were popular on both senior and lower-priced Mercedes-Benz sedans in the 1950s, but the Webasto top, which folded back along rails built into the roof, really didn't lend itself to the lines of the 911. Such a design would have left a pile of fabric bundled over the rear window. It was neither a pretty nor a streamlined solution. In Butzi's opinion, Porsche had needed to produce a pure cabrio from the onset. Years later he remarked that "any convertible looks better with a notchback; a fastback does upset the visual balance somehow. There has never been a successful rear-engined cabriolet with a true fastback." Nevertheless, his novel solution nearly became the exception to that rule.

Ferdinand Alexander Porsche, a student of design, knew that among the various attempts at creating alternatives to traditional cabriolets and roadsters during the prewar era was a unique streamliner designed in 1938 by renowned Parisian stylist and aerodynamicist Jacques Saoutchik. Built for millionaire automotive enthusiast André Dubonnet, the aerodynamic Hispano-Suiza—powered Xenia Coupé featured a removable metal roof panel over the driver's compartment. A similar approach had also been tried on a handful of coach-built American and European cars in the

1930s, and a decade later legendary American automotive stylist Gordon Miller Buehrig proposed a parallel idea using two removable glass panels on a futuristic model called the Tasco. (Although the car was not produced, Buehrig's roof design later became the basis for the removable T-top.) These early attempts at combining the attributes of both coupe and cabrio gave Porsche the inspiration for a new and more practical design ideally suited to the structural and aesthetic demands of the 911.

At the 1965 Frankfurt motor show Porsche unveiled a new model equipped with a removable, lightweight, and collapsible roof panel that latched to the windshield header and attached at the rear to a narrow, brushed stainless steel roll bar. In addition to providing structural integrity and a rear attaching point for the removable top, the roll bar also allowed Porsche to retain the original lines of the 911 coupe with the exception of the back quarter windows. With the roof panel removed and a convertible-style plastic rear window unzipped, the car looked like a convertible with a roll bar. Porsche called the new design a Targa, and, like Carrera, it was a name rich in racing history because it was taken from the famous Targa Florio road races in Sicily.

The Porsche design, with its emphasis on the brushed stainless steel Targa bar, made the 911 the safest car of its type for

In 1969, Porsche produced the five-thousandth Type 911. It was a 911E equipped with Sportomatic. (PORSCHE WERKFOTO)

rollover protection, a factor Porsche had considered because they feared that U.S. regulations would someday eliminate convertibles without rollover protection. Porsche described the Targa in a September 1965 press release as "neither a cabriolet nor a coupe, not a hardtop nor a sedan, but rather something completely new. With this model, we not only present a new car, but a new idea: the application of a safety hoop in a production car and thereby the

Butzi Porsche in 1968 with a scale model of his 911 Targa design.

world's first safety cabriolet. . . . It is Porsche's privilege to be the first auto manufacturer in the world to offer a rollbar on a production car."

While this was still some time before the congressional safety and emissions hearings began in Washington, rumors of legislation that would run convertibles off the road were rife throughout the auto industry. Porsche was reacting responsibly but perhaps prematurely by addressing the issue of convertible safety long before it became a government mandate, which it never did. This same and mostly unsubstantiated belief brought a temporary end to the convertible market in 1976 when Cadillac built what was believed to be at the time the last American convertible, the Bicentennial Eldorado. Of course, European automakers continued to build cabrios and roadsters, giving little notice to the sky-is-falling theatrics in America.

When production began in December 1966, the Targa was made available in three versions: 911, 911S, and as an option for the lower-priced four-cylinder 912. The first production Targa was the 100,000th Porsche built and had the double honor of being delivered to the German *Polizei*, complete with a siren and a flashing blue light mounted to the Targa bar. To Porsche's surprise (and Ferdinand Alexander's delight) the Targa was far more popular than the marketing department had anticipated. The cars sold as quickly as they arrived in dealer showrooms, and in no time there were back orders and waiting periods for delivery.

In its presentation of the car, Porsche described the 911 Targa as having four top configurations: Targa Spyder, with the top removed and rear window folded; Targa Bel Air, with the top panel removed and rear window raised; Targa Voyage, with the roof in place and rear window lowered; and Targa Hardtop, with roof and rear window closed. While it was a bit contrived, there really were four different ways to arrange the top and rear window, each giving the car a distinctively different appearance.

The Targa was not without its detractors, however, and most complaints were about the plastic rear window, which when zipped down was a delight but in cold weather became quite a problem. Porsche finally advised owners not to unzip the window in cold climates. It also tended to fog easily and generally distort rear vision. A secondary concern was that it contributed nothing to the struc-

The 100,000th car to bear the Porsche name was also the first 911 Targa built for the 1968 model year. The new model was delivered to the German *Polizei* in traditional white livery with a siren and a flashing blue light mounted to the Targa bar. (PORSCHE WERKFOTO)

As production begins on the new 911 Targa, Ferry Porsche (center) discusses the car with former works driver Huschke von Hanstein (right) as Porsche's youngest son, Peter, looks on.

(PORSCHE WERKFOTO)

tural integrity of the car, and that point was not lost on the men of Zuffenhausen. In 1968 the Targa Version II was introduced; it had an optional solid glass rear window, which became standard by 1970. With the rear glass window and embedded heating elements to defrost the backlight in winter, the Targa was no longer a convertible but now a coupe with a removable roof section. Consumers welcomed the change and rewarded Porsche with record orders. By the early 1970s the Targa option accounted for more than 40 percent of Porsche production.

In 1968, Ferdinand Alexander received the greatest validation of his design for the 901/911 when the eminent French Comité International de Promotion et de Prestige honored him with the award for "the overall aesthetic conception in the creation of the Porsche body." Not only was this an illustrious tribute to Ferdinand Alexander Porsche's design, but it was the first time that the Comité had ever presented the award to an individual in the automotive industry.

With a second marketing success, all Porsche KG had to do was repeat its own history and continue to develop the 911 along

similar lines to the 356. In other words, it was time for the engineers to have their say.

Within the company there had always been two factions, the designers and the engineers, and often they did not agree. In the days of Erwin Komenda, Karl Rabe, and Ferry Porsche, the two schools of thought were more closely tied; with the 911, however, lines had been drawn from the beginning. Louise Porsche-Piëch's son Ferdinand was in charge of the 911's engineering team, and Ferry's son Ferdinand was head of design. The groundwork had thus been laid for a discord that would ultimately see Ferry Porsche banish the Porsche and Piëch families from the day-to-day operation of the company in 1972.

As had been the case with the 356, there arose a demand from consumers for a more powerful 911, and just as Porsche had bowed to the pleas of sports car enthusiasts in the 1950s by introducing the four-cam Carrera motor for the 1955 356A model line, Zuffenhausen would again offer its performance-minded clientele a sportier version. And this time it would be less difficult. The 911 engine, designed by Ferdinand Piëch and engineer Hans Tomala, was very conservative in its displacement and output. The lessons learned from the original VW-based 356 engines, which had allowed very little room for increased displacement, prompted Piëch and his team to design a horizontally opposed six-cylinder engine that was ideally suited to increases in swept volume and horsepower.

The first high-performance upgrade had come toward the end of 1966, and it was called the 911S—the "S" denoting Super, just as it had in the 356 Series. Joe Vatter, a former Porsche factory mechanic and now an independent restorer and Porsche specialist, explained, "The 911S became the flagship model. This was a high-performance version of the 901/1 engine with a different cam

profile, larger valves, better porting, larger jets on the Weber carburetors, and a higher compression ratio (9.8:1 versus 9.0:1)." The net result was an increase in output of 30 brake horsepower, enough to make the 911S a very competitive rally car in the 1960s.

Realizing that the 911S would likely be embraced by competition-minded customers, Porsche took additional steps to improve the suspension by adding a rear anti-roll bar, more costly Koni shock absorbers, ventilated disc brakes on all four wheels, and a revised five-speed transmission geared to take full advantage of the added horsepower and torque. The cars were also distinct in their use of boldly forged Fuchs aluminum wheels, which became a trademark of the 911S.

As a sports car in the hands of a skilled driver, the 911S was remarkable, but as a street car it was not the best choice; the rear end had a tendency to assume the position of the front if driven impulsively into a turn. *Road & Track* wrote, "It's easier to hang out the tail if you're in the right gear, simply because of the increased power. But the simple application of steering to the 911S at highway speeds gets the same results as in the 911, which means stick-stick-stick-oversteer! And you'd better know what you're doing in that last phase." *Car and Driver*, long known for thrashing the best performance out of a car, managed to clock zero to 60 in the 911S in a record 6.5 seconds, the quarter mile in 15.2, and a top speed of 140 miles per hour. *Road & Track* turned in a rather lengthy 8.1 seconds to 60 miles per hour and 1,320 feet in 15.7 seconds, reaching 141 miles per hour. The well-known European motoring journal *Autocar* reported 8.0 seconds to 60, 15.8 in the quarter, and a top speed of 137 miles per hour. They also applauded the car's "sparkling acceleration" and long-winded torque curve that "at about 3000 takes a deep breath and literally surges up to the next step, where the extra punch feels like an additional pair of cylinders being switched in."

ABOVE LEFT AND RIGHT: This photo of a first-series Targa, taken in 1967, shows the plastic window zipped down and the roof panel removed, creating what was essentially a convertible with a roll bar. The plastic windows did not prove to be an asset, and in 1969 the cars were offered with a fixed glass rear window and electric defroster. The model shown is a 1973 Targa with the 2.4-liter engine and Fuchs wheels. (PORSCHE WERKFOTO)

OPPOSITE AND ABOVE: West Coast Porsche distributor and race driver John von Neumann wasn't satisfied with waiting for Zuffenhausen to build a 911 cabriolet, so he collaborated with renowned Italian designer Nuccio Bertone to create a custom-bodied 911 sport convertible. The inimitable Bertone virtually rebodied the entire car, creating the rear-engine roadster that was shown on the Bertone stand at the Geneva Auto Show in March 1966. It wasn't the first or the last time that a Porsche chassis was bodied in Italy, and there was even some thought to producing a limited number of cars, but ultimately Ferry Porsche was not in favor of the idea. Said Bertone afterward, "As far as I was concerned, it was not a project that I took in order to make money. But it was a personal satisfaction that I wanted." (RANDY LEFFINGWELL)

The Porsche 911 instrument panel was one of the best designed and most functional of any sports car. This is the 911L interior from 1967.

The 911S was fast on the road course but hardly an ideal car for stop-and-go traffic, tending to foul plugs more readily than the normal 911, which itself had a consistent problem with carbon buildup if routinely driven in city traffic. Nonetheless, all three publications praised the 911S for its many virtues, making only small note of the car's shortcomings. *Road & Track* concluded, ". . . a superb GT car . . . everything a Porsche should be—and more." *Car and Driver* described the 911S as Porsche's "all-time high." In 1966 there was very little in the way of a road-going sports car that could match the 911S, at least nothing this side of a Ferrari or an E-Type Jaguar. The 911S would remain Porsche's high-performance leader until the beginning of the Rennsport era in the 1970s.

Not all Porsche owners wanted an adrenaline rush every time they got behind the wheel. And Porsche, recalling a line from its original mission statement in 1963, "the roadholding of a sports car plus the comfort of the Gran Turismo for the long journey," followed the 911S with the 911L. The "L" stood for *Luxus* (luxury), and for the additional $600 above the price of a base 911, owners received every feature of the 911S except for the high-performance engine. Zuffenhausen's pendulum also swung to the other extreme, and for those believing that less is more, Porsche offered the 911T, a lower-priced touring model with a detuned 110 horsepower engine and the basic interior and exterior features of the 911. Thus, with the 911S, 911L, and 911T, Porsche had reestablished its old three-tier marketing system of offering a sports car in each price and performance classification. In addition, the 912 coupe and 912 Targa provided even more affordable entrée to Porsche ownership in the 1960s.

Although few and far between, there is the occasional oddity in the 911's engineering history. The most peculiar was the addition of a new transmission in 1967 known as the Sportomatic. Devised by Fichtel & Sachs (which manufactured clutches for Porsche), Sportomatic was a clutchless shifter, a revival of sorts of the old semiautomatic transmissions that Detroit automakers dreamed up in the 1950s—only they didn't work. Sportomatic did, unless one had a penchant for resting a hand on the shifter. You couldn't, because applying pressure to the shifter immediately activated the vacuum servo unit that disengaged the clutch. To change up or down through the four-speed synchro one simply touched the shifter and moved it into the next gear. The only caution was to make certain your foot was off the gas before you activated the servo; otherwise, the engine would immediately over-rev. It was half the process of shifting with a clutch, but it required more concentration to coordinate the shift and gas pedal movement timing. The shift knob was marked with a P for Park, an R for Reverse, and the first through fourth gears were indicated by L, D, D3, and D4. It was noted in the instruction booklet that L was for moving at very slow speed (similar to Lo on an automatic transmission), D was for normal city driving, and D3 and D4 were for the open road, the latter being the equivalent of an overdrive gear.

While the Sportomatic worked and received favorable reviews from most automotive magazines (*Car and Driver* hated it), the idea never really caught on, especially in the United States. *Sports Car Graphic,* with no apologies to Patrick Henry, summed up the feelings of most Americans by writing, "Give me stick shift or give me death." The Sportomatic worked better than most gave it credit, however, and it was more popular in Europe. In August 1968 a 911R equipped with the Sportomatic and driven by Vic Elford, Hans Herrmann, and Jochen Neerpasch won the grueling eighty-four-hour Marathon de la Route—350 trips around the 17.58-mile Nürburgring course, proving the durability of the design. (The car was conceived by Ferdinand Piëch, and the factory built approximately twenty Porsche 911R competition models between 1967 and 1968, only one of which was equipped with the Sportomatic.) At around the same time a semiautomatic transmission of similar design was being used in Can-Am racing by Jim Hall and the Chaparral race team. Still, there were not many takers, and the Sportomatic became something of an unmentionable in Porsche owners' circles. It remained a special-order option through

May 1979 and then disappeared. A restored 911 Sportomatic is a rare find these days.

As the 1960s came to a close, Porsche had its production models ideally sorted out. For 1969 there was the 911T, developing 110 brake horsepower and offering the basic interior and trim; the 911E, replacing the 911L as the luxury version and now with an output of 140 brake horsepower; and the flagship 911S, delivering 170 horsepower. Beginning with the 1969 models, the 911E and

It was hard to distinguish a 912 from a 911 at a glance. Exterior lines were virtually identical, but from the rear the 912 emblem on the engine cover was an immediate tip-off. The 912 was powered by the 356C (1600SC) four-cylinder engine, making the car less potent on the road but far more affordable than the 911. In the first full year of production Porsche delivered 9,090 Type 912 models, roughly half of which were sold in the United States, beginning in June 1965, as a 1966 model. (PORSCHE WERKFOTO)

911S were also equipped with Bosch fuel injection, while the 911T drew its fuel from twin Weber 40 IDT carburetors. Porsche had also corrected the 911's plug fouling problems with the addition of a Bosch HKZ high-voltage capacitor ignition system. The Bosch HKZ gave both a higher spark voltage at the plug for starting and high-speed running, and a faster, steeper voltage rise at the plug electrodes to assure that less energy would be dissipated over the surface of a dirty plug.

The overall design of the 911 changed very little from 1964 to 1969. The later models had slightly flared wheel openings to cover wider brakes that had expanded the track by 0.4 inch; the 911S had larger 6-inch-wide wheels; and all 911 "B" series cars produced in 1969 rode on a slightly longer wheelbase increased by 57 millimeters (2.3 inches) to accommodate longer rear semi-trailing arms and room for suspension geometry changes on later models.

The 1969 Porsches were the most powerful road cars that Zuffenhausen had ever produced. Even the more luxurious 911E could top 130 miles per hour and clock zero to 60 in an average of 8.4 seconds. These were numbers that had previously been the domain of the 911S, which was now even faster. With improvements in suspension, performance, and increased horsepower, 1969 became a watershed year for Porsche.

While the 911S was the fastest production model one could buy, it wasn't necessarily the best Porsche for the money. That dis-

tinction, oddly enough, fell on the lowest-priced model, the 911T. The biggest difference in the 911T was the Type 901/03 engine, a specially detuned version of the 901 with reshaped pistons to reduce compression from 9.0:1 to 8.6:1 and thus allow the engine to operate with lower-octane gasoline.

In creating its entry-level 911, Porsche eliminated some interior trim features, used lighter-weight carpeting, and so forth, which coincidentally translated into less sprung weight. As a result the 110-brake-horsepower 911T, equipped with the optional five-speed gearbox, could accelerate to 60 in 8.1 seconds and reach a top

The new 2.4-liter, six-cylinder engine increased output for the 911S from 180 horsepower at 6,500 revolutions per minute in 1971 to 190 horsepower. When the 911S first debuted in 1967, output was 160 brake horsepower at 6,600 revolutions per minute; thus by 1972 Porsche had increased displacement from 1,991 cubic centimeters (2 liters) to 2,341 cubic centimeters (2.4 liters) and added an additional 30 brake horsepower to the 911S. The 1973 model had a compression ratio of 8.5:1 and Bosch mechanical fuel injection.

OPPOSITE: The driving lights, sunroof, and a rear wiper are the only options on the car. No longer the flagship of the Porsche line, the 911S was second to the all-new RS 2.7 in 1973. This was to be the last year for the original 911 body style. The beautiful long nose of the 911 had to be shortened in 1974 to accommodate the 5-miles-per-hour impact bumpers mandated by new U.S. safety standards. The bumpers changed both the front and rear appearance of the 911, marking the first significant change in the body design since 1963.

speed of 129 miles per hour, nearly a match for the more expensive 140 brake horsepower 911E. The difference between the two models was $1,200, which was not exactly chump change in 1969. Moreover, in its attempt to create a lower-priced and more fuel-efficient model, Porsche had inadvertently developed an ideal Club Racer. The 911T's performance specifications were nearly the same as the legendary 550 Spyder of the 1950s. Porsche development engineer Helmuth Bott proclaimed the 911T "the only production car in the world that can reach a top speed in excess of 200 km/h (120 mph) with an engine output of less than 120 brake horsepower." Driver Vic Elford used a 911T (although equipped with an S engine) to score his Monte Carlo Rallye victory in 1968, and driver Pauli Toivonen finished second in another lightweight 911T.

In 1970, Porsche introduced the revised "C" Series 911s, equipped with a larger displacement 2165-cubic centimeter engine and minor suspension changes to further improve steering response. Porsche ownership also became a more exclusive club in 1970 when the 912 was discontinued and replaced by the VW-Porsche 914 mid-engine model. The 911T now delivered 125 brake horsepower; the 911E delivered 155 brake horsepower; and the 911S delivered 180 brake horsepower, with a top speed in excess of 140 miles per hour.

By model year 1972, output was at an all-time high for the 911, with the E and S having gained another 10 brake horsepower and the T an additional 5 brake horsepower. The 1972 models were also distinguished by being the first equipped with an aero-dynamic chin spoiler under the front bumper. Porsche engineers had determined that the spoiler reduced front-end lift at 140 miles per hour. While that was not exactly a typical driving speed for most owners, there were still those who took their cars into competition on weekends, and others who made any open country road absent of the local constabulary their own private autobahn. Let's just say that dust never settled around the 140-miles-per-hour mark on a 911S speedometer.

As for Porsche, competition remained a major factor in the evolution of its cars, but in 1972 there was a startling upheaval at Porsche KG. It was reorganized as a joint stock company, becoming Porsche AG, with Ferry Porsche as chairman of the supervisory board. At this point the Porsche and Piëch families each held a 50 percent stake in the companies in Austria and the Federal Republic of Germany. With the formation of Porsche AG, it had been Ferry's intention to prepare the company for the next generation of the family to step into top management roles. But there was great disharmony between his and Louise Piëch's sons. Ferry wrote, "The next generation was already waiting in the wings to join a structure in which each individual did not believe that he alone was the boss. This meant that this generation was either capable of working with each other or it was not. After I ascertained that the necessary harmony and cooperation could not be created, I drew the inevitable conclusion and said, 'Then nobody's going to be boss!'

"In my view, none of the representatives of the next generation was mature enough to be trusted to get to grips with the task that lay ahead of him. Of course, each of these young people had proved his ability to a certain extent, but that alone was not enough to direct a company like ours. For that a wide range of different abilities is required. For example, I need to have an instinct that tells me whether decisions that are taken will pay off in the end. As an engineer I cannot simply indulge myself by pursuing improbable ideas that prove later to be worthless. A company cannot survive like that. I have always said, 'The greatest successes in racing can only be achieved if the production cars are marketable and do not take us into the red. If the company is not making money, I cannot get involved in racing, because I would then go bankrupt, even if I were to win every race!'

"Even Ferdinand Piëch had not really understood that. And as far as my son Ferdinand Alexander was concerned, the young man who styled the 911 and thus proved his ability in this field was not in a position at the time to manage my company, since he now had his own very successful company [Porsche Design]. But that is how it was at the time with the third Porsche generation."

It was Ferry's final decision that no member of the Piëch or Porsche families, himself included, would be involved in the direct management of the newly organized Porsche AG. And in 1972 all the members of both families withdrew from the Porsche company. Ferry remained on the supervisory board along with

his sister, Louise, and was succeeded by Ferdinand Alexander as chairman of the supervisory board in 1990. On March 27, 1998, Ferdinand Anton Ernst "Ferry" Porsche II passed away at the age of eighty-eight in Zell am See, Austria, where it had all begun half a century before.

While Americans usually opted for leather upholstery in their Porsches, in Europe the most commonly ordered upholstery featured the traditional German houndstooth seat inserts, or cotton corduroy.

CHAPTER 8

RENNSPORT PORSCHES

THE RACE-READY 911

NOTHING QUITE EQUALS THE SENSATION OF BEING pressed back hard into the driver's seat as you accelerate. Feeling that firm, linear g force has speed written all over it. For the fortunate few who purchased the 911 Carrera RS 2.7 in 1973, this was the feeling that awaited them. This was the 911 at its absolute best, a car developed for competition and powered by an air-cooled six that was capable of taking on Ferrari's twelve-cylinder Daytona and De Tomaso's V8 Ford-engined Panteras in GT competition.

The need for a car like the RS 2.7 was in many ways the result of the aforementioned Italian makes, which were threatening to win the GT class by sheer brute power. Despite the car's more agile handling, the 2.4-liter 911S needed a more competitive edge by the 1970s, and Zuffenhausen's creation of the Carrera Rennsport 2.7 was that edge honed to perfection.

In 1972 the 911S was being punished for breaking the laws of physics—the original body designed by Butzi Porsche having finally reached aerodynamic limits that the engineer's improved powertrain and suspension were capable of exceeding. With the 911S approaching speeds of 150 miles per hour, race drivers were experiencing lift at the rear, resulting in less than desirable oversteer through fast corners and challenging even the best factory drivers to keep their cars under control. The RS 2.7, then, was a carefully engineered redress—a lighter, more powerful, better balanced, and more aerodynamic version of the 911S.

The fundamentals of the RS had already been established in 1967 by Ferdinand Piëch's 911R, developed in the experimental department of the new Weissach engineering and testing facilities. Powered by an engine derived from the Carrera 6, the 911 body was made lighter and fitted with fiberglass front fenders, doors, deck lids, and bumpers. Piëch's department had built three prototypes, and another twenty were assembled at Zuffenhausen and fitted with steel bodies manufactured for Porsche by the Karl Baur company of Stuttgart. The cars, equipped with 911S shocks and

OPPOSITE: Somewhere between the road and the track was the Carrera RS 2.7 model M471. A total of 200 were built during RS 2.7 production. This car, serial number 911 3600284, was completed on December 1, 1972. It is painted in the most popular color for the 1973 Carreras: Grand Prix White with blue trim and matching Fuchs wheels. The GPW cars were also available with red or green script and color-matched wheels. Nine other standard colors and fifteen special colors at extra cost were available, as well as a match to sample colors.

anti-roll bars, 901/22 engines with Weber 46IDA 3C1 triple-throat carburetors, and Nürburgring (competition) gear ratios, were all painted white, and had lightweight interiors with Scheel bucket seats. Though some were sold to privateer racing teams, most were used by the factory team. But that was as far as the 911R project went in 1967. A proposal to build five hundred for homologation as Grand Touring cars never got past the sales department, which determined that forty cars a month would have to be sold in order to reach the required sales figures necessary for homologation. Obviously, no one at Porsche had ever spoken to Enzo Ferrari about homologation!

Five years later, following the appointment of Dr. Ernst Fuhrmann as chairman of the Porsche executive committee in March 1972, the decision was finally made to develop a racing-type 911. As Porsche's technical director in 1971, Fuhrmann had realized that the time had come to take advantage of Porsche's experience in Can-Am racing and translate that to the 911. "At the moment," said Fuhrmann in 1972, "we are ready to harvest the fruits of those years with the 908 and 917." The first car to be developed was the 1972 Carrera RS 2.7, essentially a refined version of Piëch's 911R.

As with the 911R, mass was again the first factor to be addressed. Every part of the 911 was attacked to reduce the homologated weight of the RS. The Carrera body was lightened with the use of thinner than standard sheet steel measuring 0.70 millimeter (the usual was from 1.00 to 1.25 millimeters) for the doors, roof, luggage compartment lid, front fenders, luggage compartment floor, rear seat recess in the floor pan, even the shift lever platform. Weight reduction was also achieved through the use of lighter Belgian-made Glaverbel laminated safety glass all around. An-

other 7.7 pounds was shaved by equipping the cars with Bilstein shock absorbers, marking the first time that the German-made gas-pressurized shocks would come as standard equipment.

Every conceivable facet of the Carrera's construction was scrutinized for ways to reduce weight, many of them being achieved in small increments. Most of the interior soundproofing was removed, and the regular carpet was replaced with lightweight black needle felt. Interior trim was cut down to only the essentials, and even they were simplified—flat door panels with a leather strap to operate the latches, and a small plastic handle to pull the doors closed. These were ex-Fiat 500 parts. The dashboard was the standard 911 design but with only essential instruments and no clock. The interior was stripped of every nonessential item. There was not so much as a passenger-side sun visor or glove box door. The rear +2 seats were absent, and thinly padded buckets with adjustable head restraints, rolled edges, and lightweight black cloth upholstery replaced the Recaro driver and passenger seats used in the 911S. Also missing from the Carrera RS were undercoating, doorsill trim, coat hooks, and springs to counterbalance the front deck lid. The engineers left nothing that wasn't essential to the operation of the car.

From the outside, the Carrera RS 2.7 was distinctively identified with Porsche's bold CARRERA script running the length of the sills between the wheel openings, and a *Bürzel* (German for "duck's tail") fiberglass rear-deck lid. This was fitted with rubber quick-release clamps rather than metal latches, again to cut down on weight. The real advantage, however, was the greatly reduced aerodynamic lift provided by the spoiler, which not only reduced the 911's oversteer problem but added 2 miles per hour to the car's top end—now a lively 153 miles per hour. An incidental benefit was that it also raised the pressure at the grille admitting air to the engine compartment, thus increasing airflow to the engine and lowering oil temperatures.

As with the 911R of 1967, fiberglass (polyester) was used for both the front and rear bumpers to reduce weight. Larger rear wheel arches on the Carrera also permitted 7-inch rims to be used in combination with the standard 6-inch fronts. The extended fenders widened the base from which 2 more inches at each side could be added under the provisions of the GT regulations. The track was 54 inches at the front and 54.9 inches at the rear. Porsche was now able to fit Fuchs 15-inch forged aluminum alloy "S" pat-

tern wheels on the 2.7, with either Pirelli Cinturato CN36 or Dunlop SP D4 tires, sized 185/70 × 15 for the front and a lower-profile 215/60 × 15 for the rear. The anti-roll bars were also much stiffer and were increased in diameter from the standard 15 millimeters to 18 millimeters in front and 19 millimeters at the rear. As a result, the RS 2.7 could now corner at the highest lateral g rate of any production Porsche: 0.912. None of the others could break the 0.9 g barrier.

Under the fiberglass deck lid was Porsche's improved Carrera six-cylinder engine. Since it was larger than 2.5 liters in size, Fédération Internationale de l'Automobile (FIA) rules allowed

The demands of competition finally brought about an entirely new breed of 911 in the 1973 model year, the Carrera RS 2.7. The car was offered in Sport and Touring versions, such as the model pictured here. The RS 2.7 in Touring configuration featured opening rear quarter windows, reclining Recaro front seats, and folding rear +2 seats. A rear window wiper, power windows, and even a sunroof could be ordered as options.

displacement to be increased to the next class size, which was 3 liters. The Carrera had the same stroke as the 2.4-liter Porsche sixes, 70.4 millimeters, but a larger bore, up from 84 millimeters to 90 millimeters. This was the largest bore ever used on a 911 engine up to that time and gave the RS the same piston size and rod length as the 5.4-liter, twelve-cylinder engine used in the 917/10 Can-Am cars. The six's displacement became half that of the twelve, 2,687 cubic centimeters, or, in marketing terminology, 2.7 liters.

The RS engine, designated as the Type 911/83, was essentially much like the 911S that preceded it. The compression ratio was identical, 8.5:1, and the 2.7 used the same Bosch mechanical injection, valve sizes, and timing as the 2.4-liter 911S. Output was 210 horsepower at 6,300 revolutions per minute (an increase of 20

over the S), although the engine could easily be pushed well beyond with the rev limiter set at 7,300 revolutions per minute. Maximum torque was rated at 188 pounds per foot at 5,100 revolutions per minute, and all this was achieved on regular octane fuel. Drive was carried through a 915 five-speed transaxle as used in the 911S, but with fourth and fifth ratios raised slightly. Porsche claimed acceleration times of 5.8 seconds to 60 miles per hour.

Although it was not publicly introduced until the Paris Motor Show in October 1972, Porsche had started marketing the Carrera RS 2.7 privately to prospective customers months before in the hopes of bolstering orders to expedite the car's homologation in Group 4. Following F.I.A. rules, Porsche had to build 500 examples in order to get F.I.A. sanction. As it turned out, reaction to the Carrera was beyond Porsche's greatest expectations. They had pre-sold 51 cars before the Paris debut, and within a week after the show closed had firm orders for the remaining 449 cars! The year's supply had been sold out in a matter of weeks. On November 27, 1972, the F.I.A. granted Porsche homologation number 637 for Appendix J, Group 4. Overwhelmed by the stunning sales, Porsche decided to build another 500, and when those were sold out by the following April, the factory turned out a third batch. When production of the Carrera RS 2.7 concluded, a total of 1,583 had been built, including the original homologation cars, giving Porsche a double fait accompli: Not only had Zuffenhausen exceeded its sales goal by better than three times, but the Carrera RS 2.7 could now be homologated in the Group 3 Grand Touring category as well!

Three versions of the RS 2.7 were available. The Touring model, designated as M472, incorporated 911S features including carpet, more soundproofing, opening rear windows, reclining Recaro front seats, and folding rear +2 seats. A rear window wiper,

The *Bürzel*, or "duck's tail" spoiler, greatly reduced aerodynamic lift at high speeds, helping to reduce oversteer. It also added 2 miles per hour to the 2.7's top speed, which was now a lively 153 miles per hour in the Lightweight version.

power windows, and even a sunroof could be ordered as options. Outside, the cars looked almost identical, except that the Touring had steel bumpers. The M472 carried two 6-volt batteries, one on either side of the spare tire, while the model M471, the RS *mit Sportausstattung* (with sport equipment) employed a single 12-volt battery located on the left side. A total of 200 Sport (lightweight) cars and 1,308 RS Touring cars were built during RS 2.7 production.

The Lightweight model, although intended for club racing and amateur motor sports, could also be driven on the street but with a great sacrifice of comfort and a lack of convenience. Race driver and motor journalist Paul Frère wrote of the 2.7 Sport model, "If you drive at city traffic speeds on a rough road, you may wonder if there are any springs fitted."

In either form, the Carrera RS 2.7 was a formidable car. The Touring version, weighing 2,398 pounds, some 250 more than the

With three out of four tires touching the ground, Hurley Haywood pilots his Carrera RSR through a right-hander heading to a first place in Group 5 at Daytona in 1973. Along with driver Peter Gregg, Haywood and the RSR repeated their performance at Sebring.

Challenging Camaros and Corvettes, among others, Peter Gregg and Hurley Haywood drove a 911 RSR 2.8, car number 59, in Group 5 competition at the 1973 Daytona 24 Hours. The car finished first and repeated its performance at Sebring.

Sport, and one second slower off the line to 60, was still capable of reaching nearly 150 miles per hour. In competition, the Lightweight Carrera 2.7 RS was faster and more agile, but the real competitor was the third version, the M491. Built to order at Porsche's Werk I in Zuffenhausen, this became the factory's full racing model, and it was known as the Carrera RSR, or *Rennausstattung*.

The name "Carrera" itself had been used by Porsche to denote high-performance models since the introduction of the 356A four-cam in the fall of 1955. The literal translation of *carrera* is "race," and the name is taken from the Carrera PanAmericana Mexican road races held in the late 1940s and early 1950s. In 1953 and again in 1954, Porsche 550 Spyders won the 1500cc class, in what many considered at the time, along with the Mille Miglia in Italy, the toughest road race in the world. The back-to-back victories in Mexico forever linked the Carrera name with Porsche.

Driving an RSR was an experience. "This isn't like driving a regular 911 or even a 911 RS," says former race driver Bruce Canepa. "When you get on the RSR, it nails you right into the seat!" The car also nailed most of its competitors for two consecutive seasons. The Carrera RSR 3.0 that Canepa once owned was

the factory works car driven by John Fitzpatrick, Toine Hezemans, and Gijs van Lennep in 1974 and 1975. Supported by the Porsche factory and sponsored by Gelo (Georg Loos Racing), the car was driven by Fitzpatrick to the F.I.A. GT Cup title in 1974, to class victories at Spa, the Nürburgring, Dijon, the Norisring, Imola, and to a stunning first in class and fifth overall finish at Le Mans in 1975.

The 1974 Carrera 3.0 RSR can best be defined as an evolutionary car in that its design and engineering evolved over a number of years through the advancement of RS and RSR types, rooted as far back as the 911R and progressing through the 2.7-liter RS and 2.8-liter RSR series.

The 1974 Carrera 3.0 RSR competition cars—essentially full race versions of the limited production 3.0 RS models—were assembled by the Porsche Competition Department and sold as *ready to race*. For 1974 the factory produced the Carrera 3.0 RS models, which were homologated in Group 3 as an "evolution" of the Group 3 Carrera RS 2.7. The Type 911 3.0 RSRs produced by the Competition Department were built directly to racing specifications for competition in Group 4, Special Grand Touring.

The conversion from 3.0 RS to RSR was made easier by the fact that the RS was almost a fully race-prepped car itself, equipped with the racing crankshaft, the very costly Type 917 brakes with four-piston calipers, 300-millimeter (11.8-inch) diameter perforated and ventilated discs, and twin master cylinders—17-millimeter diameter for the front brakes and 22-millimeter for the rear—providing an adjustment for front/rear pressure ratio. The five-speed transmission had an 80 percent limited slip differential and an oil pump, complete with cooling serpentine in the right front fender and a large front-mounted engine oil cooler.

The RSR modifications mainly involved bringing the engine up to racing specification, fitting a sintered metal-lined clutch disc, widening the front and rear fenders to fit the wide magnesium racing wheels, and changing the front suspension struts to provide a lower ride height.

For racing, the Type 911/77 engine of the 1974 Carrera RS was converted to the Type 911/75 of the RSR—a full 3 liters, identical to the 1973 factory prototypes that had been the first of the Porsche sixes to achieve the magic 300-horsepower mark. This seems remarkable today when you consider that the 2003 Porsche Turbo delivers 444 horsepower and is a production street car!

Bobby Unser leads Peter Revson in the 1974 IROC race at Riverside, California.

RSR engines had aluminum pistons, cylinders, and cylinder heads; higher lift camshafts; slide throttles; and a breakerless capacity discharge twin-ignition system. The RSR-tuned engines had a bore × stroke of 95 millimeters (3.75 inches) × 70.4 millimeters (2.8 inches) and displacement of 2,992 cubic centimeters, so their compression ratio was raised to 10.3:1. Output was nominally 320 horsepower at 8,000 revolutions per minute, but ranged 10 horsepower above and below that estimate, depending on the individual engines.

The Competition Department supplied all the essentials in the stripped-down racing cockpit of the Carrera. The interior was furnished with a special Recaro racing seat with a high squab and headrest, full harness restraint, built-in roll bar, and a fire extinguishing system. The driver faced a stock 911-style instrument panel equipped with a 10,000-revolutions-per-minute tachometer and a 300 kilometers-per-hour speedometer. The cars were fitted with center lock hubs carrying racing pattern wheels of 10.5-inch and 14-inch front and rear widths covered by almost comic-book-proportion fenders made of fiberglass.

The overwide fenders gave the RSR 3.0 an incredibly aggressive stance. At the rear, the flares were blended into the body but punctured at both their leading and trailing surfaces by air vents to cool the rear brakes. The wider front fenders were smoothly flared into the nose panels, but at their rear edges, just at the door cut line, they simply stopped, leaving a huge rear-facing opening to vent air. This break with conventional fender design looked, and was, so functional that other builders of modified production cars immediately adopted it.

The racing modifications—interior, engine, suspension, body work, wheels, and tires—added a hefty $6,000 to the price of a 1974 Carrera RS 3.0, which at that time was already the highest priced Porsche 911 ever at $25,000. Max Hoffman would have fainted dead away.

As for the stature of the Carrera RSR in the eyes of the racing community, Mark Donohue summed it up quite nicely after testing an RSR prototype at the Paul Ricard Circuit in France. Donohue, who was never long on words, said, "The Carrera is, without a doubt, the very best off-the-shelf production race car available at any price."

On Donohue's advice, Roger Penske ordered fifteen Carreras to use for the 1974 International Race of Champions (IROC). Mechanically, the cars were a combination of the RS and RSR models, but they were built to look more like production 911s and thus were more readily identifiable to spectators as Porsche road cars. Each was tested on Porsche's Weissach skid pad and tuned to give comparable performance before being shipped to Penske. All the engines were set up to deliver around 316 horsepower. If there was any advantage a driver could gain in the IROC series, it was in knowing how to drive a 911. As luck would have it, at the end of the season it was Donohue who won the IROC title, besting a field that included such racing luminaries as Emerson Fittipaldi, Denis Hulme, A. J. Foyt, George Follmer, Peter Revson, David Pearson, Bobby Allison, Richard Petty, Bobby Unser, Roger McCluskey, and Gordon Johncock. Not bad company. The biggest winner of all, however, was PORSCHE, its name boldly spelled out on each of the brilliantly painted cars and seen by millions of motor sports fans on ABC's *Wide World of Sports*, which broadcast the final race in the series from Daytona. No amount of paid advertising could ever have equaled the exposure that Porsche received from the IROC series.

Throughout Europe and all across America the RS and RSR were almost unbeatable for two consecutive seasons, and even well

OPPOSITE: The 3.0 had a wider body based on the newer G-model. The 3.0 RS used thinner sheet metal and was equipped with 8-inch wheels at the front and 9-inch wheels at the rear. The racing cars were equipped with a 917 Turbo braking system to scrub off the speed generated by the full-race version of the 3.0, which delivered 330 horsepower.

Chassis number 911 460 9040, former race driver Bruce Canepa's RSR 3.0, is one of only thirty-seven built in 1974. This was the factory car driven by John Fitzpatrick to the 1974 F.I.A. Cup for G.T. cars and to a first in class and fifth overall finish at Le Mans in 1975. The RSR 3.0s produced by the Competition Department were built directly to racing specifications for Group 4, Special Grand Touring. The GEORG LOOS name across the top of the windshield was a common sight on factory cars. After the 1975 season, the car was retired and remained at the Porsche factory until 1982. Approximately twenty of the original cars are still in existence.

into the late '70s the cars were still being raced successfully. From 1973 to 1976, Carrera RS and RSR models won titles in virtually every type of road race and hill climb championship held in the United States and Europe.

By the mid-1970s, racing technology was about to bring another change to the 911. The Carrera RS and RSR would become the last factory competition cars equipped with normally aspirated en-gines. On the horizon was a new car, a new 911, the Turbo Carrera.

Turbo-generated energy is free horsepower, and while that's a fairly generalized explanation, it is basically true. A turbocharger works off wasted energy in the exhaust gas stream, which is rerouted to spin the turbine, powering a compressor that draws in air, compresses it, and then forces it into the cylinders. Combined with a higher fuel injection rate, specific output from an engine can be significantly increased—and better than doubled in some instances. It is a simple principle that has been around since Swiss engineer Alfred Büchi patented the turbocharger in 1905 to increase power output from diesel engines. The turbo's greatest contribution to automotive technology, however, was for motor racing.

In the early 1970s, Porsche's twelve-cylinder 917 Can-Am cars were unleashing 1,200 horsepower, and it was during this period that the formula was born for the Porsche 911 Turbo. A road car with a turbocharged boxer engine could easily surpass the highest performance of the race-bred Carrera 3.0 RSR, which at its best was turning out 350 horsepower.

Designing a turbocharged engine for the flat-six boxer motor did present a multitude of problems, however, not the least of which was a means of regulating the boost pressure. This had not been an obstacle on the 917 Can-Am cars; the boost was always at the maximum. For a production road car there would have to be a means of controlling boost pressure, or there would be blown 911 engines in record numbers. Control was achieved with the addition of a device called a wastegate to divert exhaust gases away from the turbine at a predetermined level, thus preventing boost pressure from going beyond a specific pounds per square inch (psi), or atmosphere. The exhaust-driven turbine wheel developed speeds of up to 90,000 revolutions per minute, precompressing air to a density of 11.4 psi, and attaining an air-fuel mixture that was truly an automotive alchemist's dream. For the first 911 Turbos the limit was set at 12 psi (0.8 atmosphere).

Porsche engineers also had to overcome turbo oiling problems and high temperatures, but by 1973 they had sorted out all the technical difficulties and built the first turbocharged 911 Carrera RSR racing engines. A year later the turbo was ready for production, and the first model, designated Type 930, made its debut that

fall at the Paris auto salon. The car was introduced first in Europe and then in the U.S. market in 1976 as the 911 Turbo Carrera, a car for which Americans were willing to mortgage their souls to buy. In 1976 the 911 Turbo sold for more than $26,000, making it the most expensive nonracing 911 up to that time. And there were no discounts at dealerships, lots of waiting, and very little argument about color or options. When the keys were handed over, it

One of Porsche's greatest marketing achievements in the United States was to provide the cars for the 1974 IROC series. On the advice of race driver Mark Donohue, Roger Penske ordered fifteen Carreras to use for the 1974 International Race of Champions. The cars were a hybrid of the RS and RSR, and were built to look more like production 911s. They had flared rear fenders and a front end similar to the RSR as well as the duck's tail deck lid. A dozen of the cars are seen here at the Porsche factory late in 1973 before being readied for shipment to the United States. (PORSCHE WERKFOTO)

On the car hauler en route to the shipping dock, the first eight of fifteen Porsches built for the 1974 IROC Series are ready for their trip to the United States.

The 245 brake horsepower Turbo Carrera was more than another Porsche; it was what one magazine described as "the ultimate extension of the 911." In many ways it was exactly that—the road car Zuffenhausen's performance-minded clientele had been demanding since the turbocharged RSR first appeared in competition. But heaven help the inexperienced who thought this was just a faster, more exclusive 911 model!

When the Turbo first hit America, owners who were unfamiliar with a situation that race drivers like to call "trailing throttle oversteer" found themselves destined for very costly visits to the body shop and higher insurance premiums. In any given corner, near or at the limit, often referred to by automotive journalists as the "polar moment of inertia" (I personally refer to it as "the edge of wetness"), the immediate instinct of an inexperienced driver was to back off the throttle—a serious breach of Turbo etiquette. This caused longitudinal forces to reverse in the rear suspension, at which point the power-on weight was reduced and the back end of the car would lift, allowing the wheels to toe out and immediately induce acute oversteer. Since the Turbo Carrera's basic power-on behavior (rear end forced down) was terminal understeer, once you were committed, the proper method was to stay on the throttle, correct with steering input, and let the car do what it was engineered to do. This is more

appeared that the wait and the expense had been well worth it. This was unlike any previous 911, and there was no mistaking the Turbo Carrera for any other Porsche model. Most came with the word TURBO swept back over widely flared rear fenders in letters eight inches high, Pirelli 215/60VR-15 tires, and Porsche's now famous "Whale Tail."

OPPOSITE: In 1976, those desiring a U.S. version of the Porsche 930 Turbo got their wish when the car was offered for sale stateside as the 911 Turbo Carrera. For $26,000, a price that could make anyone's wallet throb in 1976, the handful of Americans who took delivery of the first U.S. specification cars got a rousing 245-brake-horsepower, turbocharged engine delivering unprecedented performance. They also got a car that demanded professional driving skills to handle properly.

There was no mistaking the 1976 Porsche 911 Turbo Carrera for any other model. Most came with the word TURBO swept back over widely flared rear fenders in letters 8 inches high.

difficult in reality than it is to write about, and the alternative was usually a lesson paid for by check. The car's quirky handling characteristics were predictable, and in the hands of an experienced driver, a virtue. The problem was that most Turbo owners were wealthy guys who thought they were Hurley Haywood or Mark Donohue. To properly handle the car at the limit, they needed to be one or the other.

In designing the Turbo, the engineers at the Weissach technical center had utilized a suspension more closely tied to that of the RSR than a production 911, and there were precious few owners who had the skills to take its full measure. Those who did reveled in the Turbo's race-car-like performance. Those who did not did one of three things: They drove with caution after seeing the grim reaper in their rearview mirror, went to a driving school and learned how to handle the car, or continued to drive it until their luck ran out.

Tucked beneath the whale tail was the most potent engine Porsche had offered its customers, a 3.0-liter, sohc-opposed six developing 234 to 245 horsepower at 5,500 revolutions per minute and 246 pounds per foot of torque at 4,500 revolutions per minute. Compression ratio for the turbo engines was reduced to 6.5:1, absolutely vital in the Turbo, which had an effective compression ratio of 11.5:1 on full boost. Equipped with Bosch K-Jetronic fuel

injection and a Kühnle, Kopp & Kausch (KKK) turbocharger, the Carrera could clock zero to 60 in 6.7 seconds, the quarter mile in 15.08 at 99.5 miles per hour, and reach a top speed of over 150 miles per hour.

Unlike the cammy 911S models, there was no sudden surge of power when the throttle was floored. At first it seemed as though nothing was happening, and then you were suddenly pressed into the seat as the exhaust note changed from a husky rasp to a robust bellow and the car began to gather speed at an almost alarming rate. It was not the jolt that owners had anticipated but, rather, a relentless application of power that continued up to the 6,950 revolutions-per-minute rev limit. The momentary lapse in throttle response was known as turbo lag—the time it takes the turbine to build speed, or "spool up," a popular term in automotive magazines. With a lower compression ratio and the inherent lag characteristics, the Turbo Carrera was only eight-tenths of a second faster than a normally aspirated 911 from zero to 60. On the other hand, once it got rolling, it was nearly 10 miles per hour faster in the quarter mile!

Snicking the all-new type 930 four-speed shifter (the 911S used the five-speed) through the pattern was almost euphoric as engine tone and speed increased with every gear change. In a matter of fifteen seconds the Turbo was at over 100 miles per hour, and it was easy to get caught up in the car's straight-line acceleration. For most Turbo Carrera owners, 1976 was the year of driving dangerously, before they learned to control either the car or their enthusiasm.

For the 1976 model year (September 1975 to August 1976) Porsche produced a total of 1,201 Turbos, 519 of which were sold in the United States. For the 1977 model year, 1,772 were built, with 716 destined for American garages. In 1978 the Turbo

Carrera name was dropped following the introduction of the new 3.3-liter Turbo.

In the mid-1970s, when the F.I.A. began deemphasizing prototype racing cars in favor of production-based machines, Porsche was ideally positioned to take advantage of the change. Despite their high state of tune, the turbocharged 934 and 935 race cars were fundamentally based on the 911, making them eligible to compete in the World Championship of Makes (WCM). These were 930 Turbos modified for F.I.A. competition in Group 4 and Group 5 (the 4 and 5 indicating the group for which each had been homologated). There was also a mid-engine 936 Spyder for Group 6 competition, which had no requirements for production-based body work. The 934 qualified for Group 4, Grand Touring, by virtue of the production level achieved by the 930 Turbo (and 911 Turbo Carrera); Group 4 was essentially production 930 Turbos modified at the factory for competition.

The 935 was a significantly modified 930, designed to compete in the Special Production Car category, which was open to modified cars from Groups 1 through 4. As noted by Porsche historian Tobias Aichele, "The Types 934 and 935, developed in Weissach, were built in Zuffenhausen under the direction of Elmar Willrett. From the outset, the 934 was intended as a customer race car. The fact that the factory itself entered both 934 and 935 models in competition is due to a change in the rules, which were influenced by various international interests. Porsche adapted to the changes, prepared only one works 935 for the 1976 season (historian Karl Ludvigsen states that two 935 race cars were prepared by the factory for the 1976 season), and won the world championship for the fourth time, repeating its 1969, 1970, and 1971 success but this time with a production-based car instead of a sports prototype."

In 1978, Zuffenhausen upped the ante with the new SC 3.0 Turbo. It had a blistering 300 brake horsepower from a revised flat six with a swept volume of 2,994 cubic centimeters. (PORSCHE WERKFOTO)

While the 934 was close to a street car in appearance, very reminiscent of the Carrera RS 2.7, the 935 was a rolling test bed for ever-improving technology, and as Group 5 cars became ever more competitive, Porsche and Martini, its racing partner, began to modify the 935 until only the basic silhouette of the 911 remained.

With the now famous 935 slant nose reshaping the 911's prow and spoilers towering above the rear deck lid, the cars gradually moved further and further away from the 911 configuration until they were almost a parody of the production cars. They were also the inspiration for countless knock-offs, both in competition and for the street. Even Porsche contributed to the model's proliferation by offering kits of parts that allowed the conversion from 934 to 934/5.

The 935 slant nose came about as the result of a variance in the F.I.A. rules for Group 5. As noted by Ludvigsen in *Excellence Was Expected*, the rules stated that "the original outside shape of the bodywork should be retained." The rules also stated, however,

that "the material and shape of the wings (fenders) are free." "Free" meant that Porsche could redesign the fenders to improve the car's aerodynamics. Ludvigsen wrote: "The Porsche engineers seized on the specific permission granted in the second sentence to cut off the tops of the fenders completely, headlights and all. This helped reduce aerodynamic drag and also improved visibility by reducing the area of the front of the car in profile. Vents in the fender surfaces relieved pressure in the wheel wells. The headlights were moved behind transparent covers in the front spoiler of the new nose, which cut 0.4 seconds from the best lap time at the Paul Richard track."

Beneath the rear-deck lid was the 2,808-cubic-centimeter Type 935 engine, packing water-cooled four-valve heads, intercooling (later adapted for the new 3.3-liter production 911 Turbos introduced in 1978), and an output variously rated from 590 net brake horsepower at 7,800 revolutions per minute to better than 600 horsepower. With a boost of 23 psi from the KKK turbocharger, usable only for short periods, output was rated as high as 630 horsepower.

In its final configuration the 935 was the most powerful 911 derivative built up to that time. In competition trim a 935 tested by *Road & Track* in 1976 had turned zero to 60 in 3.3 seconds, the quarter mile in 8.9, and a top test speed of 150 miles per hour, achieved from a standing start, in just 11 seconds! In 1979 a 935, driven by Klaus Ludwig and the Whittington brothers, brought Porsche an overall victory in the celebrated twenty-four-hour day-into-night marathon at Le Mans.

The Porsche 935 was the dominant endurance racer of the decade, clinching the WCM manufacturer's laurels every year from 1976 through 1980 and winning the over-2000cc category in the last season of the series in 1981. With drivers Peter Gregg,

In 1978 came another advance in Porsche engine technology, the intercooler. The device, mounted at the top of the engine, reduced intake air temperatures, allowing smaller turbochargers, higher boost pressures, and an increase in specific output to 300 brake horsepower. (PORSCHE WERKFOTO)

Klaus Ludwig, John Fitzpatrick, Danny Ongias, George Follmer, Al Holbert, and Hurley Haywood taking these cars to repeated victories, their domination of GT racing was so absolute that at one time the question wasn't whether Porsche would win but, rather, which Porsche.

Even after Porsche ceased further development of the 935, privateer racers continued to win championship titles with factory-built cars (approximately ten were sold to private teams), most notably Kremer Brothers, which also modified 930s into the 935 K3 and K4 models, both of which were put into limited production by Kremer.

In the brief period from 1976 to 1981, the 935 earned its place in the pantheon of great sports cars.

The idea that racing improves the breed is more than a sales pitch. In 1978 there was another advance in Porsche technology, the intercooler, which reduced intake air temperatures, allowing smaller turbochargers, higher boost pressures, and an increase in specific output to 300 brake horsepower. It appeared for the first time on the production 3.3-liter Turbo, but a year after its introduction, the 3.3 Turbo was withdrawn from the American market due to the energy crunch that began in late 1979. Several years would pass before the car was officially sold again in the United States. In Europe the 3.3 remained in production as the 930, and the great "gray market Turbos," cars allegedly certified by private importers to meet U.S. emissions and safety standards, kept a good number of them on American roads despite import restrictions.

The factory's 930 and 935 *flachtbau* (flat nose) cars had also attracted a great deal of attention over the years, and these, too, became available at a price. By the early 1980s aftermarket tuners became heavily involved with the manufacturing of 930 flat nose conversions for production 911 Turbos as well as for other 911

models. These posers became highly popular, and the flat nose Turbo is still one of the most desirable 911 models on the road.

Among the best-known examples in the United States were those produced by Alan Johnson Racing. Johnson was a Porsche racer and dealer in southern California who had been racing 911s since 1967, the year in which his red C Production Class 911 coupe came out on top in the National Championship runoff at Daytona. Earlier in the year he had also placed ninth overall and first in the GT category at Sebring. Johnson won the SCCA Class C Production title again in 1968 and was a five-time National Champion by the time he retired and opened his race shop in 1975. The Alan Johnson 930S Turbos are still regarded among the best high-performance road cars ever built outside of the Porsche factory.

From duck tail to whale tale, the Turbo models demanded greater down force at the rear as speeds exceeded 150 miles per hour. The larger rear wing design also created a natural environment for air to be drawn into the grille and intercooler as it rolled off the aerodynamic roof and backlight.
(PORSCHE WERKFOTO)

CHAPTER 9

THE 911 ROAD CARS

THE AIR-COOLED COUPES AND CABRIOS

WHILE PORSCHE HAD MORE THAN ABUNDANTLY addressed the demands for higher-performance cars, it had yet to produce the long-awaited 911 cabriolet. The Targa had provided Porsche with a solution for eighteen years, but the time had finally come to build the one model missing since 1964.

The cabriolet model introduced in 1983 was not entirely a Porsche design, at least not from the windshield up; independent designer Gerhard Schröder created the patented convertible top mechanism for Porsche. Rather than a conventional fabric folding top, the cabriolet utilized a unique series of stamped steel panels—one in front and one in back, connected by the folding mechanism. The steel panels provided a solid surface on which to attach the convertible fabric, significantly reducing wind noise and adding some rollover protection with the top raised.

The first models had manually operated tops, but Porsche and Schröder were already at work on a fully automatic one even before the first cabriolet was introduced. The electric top offered a simple transformation from open to closed, and vice versa, without any intervention from the driver aside from pressing a button. Electric motors released the header locks and activated thirteen moving bows and the top frame, concealed within the padded headliner; in a matter of twenty seconds the whole operation was complete. To everyone's surprise the pressed steel substructure of the convertible was so rigid in the closed position that when a 911 cabriolet was tested in the wind tunnel, it revealed a lower Cd (coefficient of drag) than the 911 coupe.

Even though Porsche now had two open cars, both continued to sell. Targa enthusiasts remained true to their favorite model, while others drawn by the allure of a true convertible Porsche flocked to the new cabriolet. The cabriolet could also be ordered with a removable hardtop, giving the model a profile almost identical to that of the 911 coupe.

As the Targa and cabriolet continued to increase in popularity, there arose yet another demand from Porsche buyers for

OPPOSITE: The 1970 model year was another pivotal change in Porsche history. The four-cylinder companion model 912 was discontinued and a new, mid-engine Targa-style model, the 914 (center), was added to the Porsche line. (PORSCHE WERKFOTO)

This attention-grabbing photo from 1974 was intended to show off the new front and rear bumper designs necessary to meet U.S. safety standards. This marked the beginning of the 911's second decade and the first major change in body styling. Unlike most European automakers attempting to comply with U.S. crash bumper standards, Porsche managed to handsomely integrate the 5-mile-per-hour buffers into the design of all their cars. (PORSCHE WERKFOTO)

that was missing was a modern-day version of Porsche's most famous 356 model: the Speedster.

By fulfilling the wishes of sports car enthusiasts Porsche completed the circle, rekindling the last 356 tradition in 1987 with the debut of the 911 Speedster. The thinking behind the new Speedster, intended by design to recapture the unique character of the original, was to create a modern version without compromising the 911 in the process. As it turned out, there was just enough of the 356 in the new speedster to set it apart from other 911 models. As in the original, the windshield was lower and more steeply raked, laid back five degrees farther than the standard 911's, and with the top up, the car had a very trim profile, repeating the 356 Speedster's shallow stance. But this was no simple roadster reincarnate. Aside from the lower windshield and unlined manual top, for all intents and purposes you were behind the wheel of a cabriolet and surrounded by Porsche's traditional 911 instrument panel, bottom-pivot pedals (a truly homogenous link to the original '54 Speedster), and multi-adjustable, power-operated, leather-faced seats. A Porsche 911 by any other name.

The most distinctive and telling clue to the 911 Speedster's identity, since the factory chose not to reissue the original car's

turbocharged versions of both models. After some hesitation Porsche management decided that if customers wanted turbo cabriolets and Targas, then Porsche would build them. Beginning in 1986 the 3.3-liter turbo was available as a coupe, Targa, or cabriolet. Porsche now had three significant cars on the road at once. All

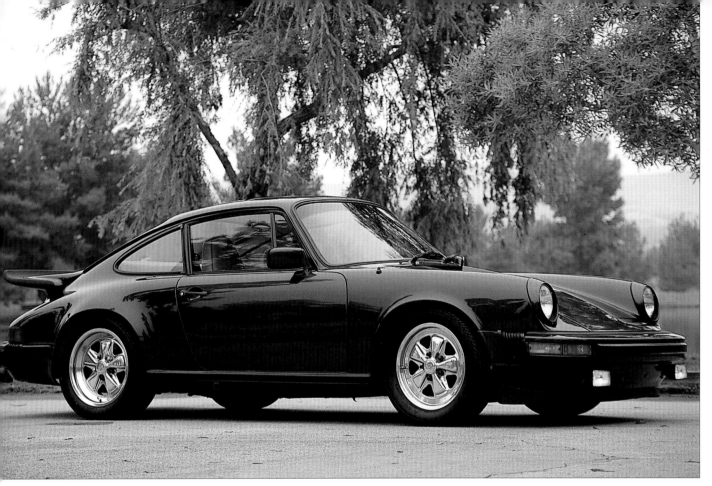

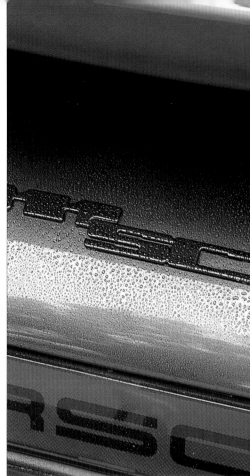

The 1980 Porsche 911SC Weissach was a special limited-edition model to honor the engineers at Porsche's development center. Sales literature for the 911SC model proclaimed it "one of the most exclusive production cars you can own. The Limited Edition Weissach Coupe has been produced to honor the men of Weissach who have made this series what it is." The Weissach was limited to four hundred examples, half of which were painted a distinctive metallic black and the others metallic platinum. Although equipped with a normally aspirated engine, they came with the Turbo whale tale. All four hundred were sold in the United States.

stylized script, was the unique rear tonneau design. Arching over the back of the two-seater, the one-piece cover gave the appearance of dual head fairings while completely concealing the convertible top mechanism. Hinged from the rear, the cover lifted and the top unfolded from beneath. As simple as this may sound, de-

ploying the cloth or folding it back was best done seasonally, according to owners of early 911 Speedsters. The operation of the 911 Speedster top was a far cry from the original 356, which required all of a few seconds to reach back, grab hold of the header bow, pull the top up, and secure it to the windshield frame with two simple latches. The reverse procedure took even less time if you cared little for the condition of the plastic rear window. You simply unlatched the top and threw it back.

The 911 Speedsters were modern, high-performance cars equipped with the 3.2-liter, fuel-injected six that dropped 214 brake horsepower to the ground at 5,900 revolutions per minute through a five-speed manual. The 911s shot from zero to 60 in a scant six seconds and could easily tease the 150-miles-per-hour mark.

The 911 Speedsters featured Turbo-style fenders and utilized Turbo-based underpinnings with struts in front and trailing arms in the rear. And while still given to rude awakenings when driven into a turn out of shape, the 911 Speedster exceeded the limits of the 356 Speedster's swing axle hindquarters so far that no reasonable comparison can be drawn between the two. When you get right down to it, they were like distant cousins of noble parentage who had little more in common than a name.

A limited-edition model, only 2,100 Speedsters were built before the first model went out of production at the end of 1989. The Speedster's popularity vastly exceeded the production run, and for two years afterward they sold used for more than they did when they were new.

The 1983 model year was comprised of three cars: the 911SC coupe, the Targa, and the long-awaited cabrio, marking the return of a convertible model to the Porsche line for the first time since the 356C in 1965.

With the 964 series on the road in 1990, plans were under way to revive the Speedster as a Carrera model. The third-generation Speedster made its debut at the Paris Salon in October 1992, and once again Porsche had a hit on its hands. Initially sold with only the standard narrow-body Carrera cabriolet fender lines, by mid-year the Carrera Speedsters were also being offered in Europe with the wide Turbo fenders at an additional cost.

The 1993 Speedsters were vastly improved over the first series, with a more easily operated manual top, Carrera RS seat shells painted in body color, and leather upholstery specifically designed

The turbo "look" was more popular than the car itself, and the 1986 cabriolet was available with the wide turbo fenders, sans turbo engine, powered instead by a 3.2-liter normally aspirated six-cylinder engine. This example is midnight blue with special-order champagne leather and polished Fuchs wheels.

179

Porsche interiors were still almost always black up through the 1980s; however, for an additional charge and a rather lengthy wait, the Special Works Department would provide customer-chosen color combinations, such as this beige leather cataloged as champagne.

By the late 1980s the appearance of the horizontally opposed, flat six-cylinder engine had changed considerably from the first 911 models. Horsepower and displacement of the normally aspirated Porsches had been increased from 1,991 cubic centimeters and 130 brake horsepower in 1965 to 3,164 cubic centimeters and 231 brake horsepower by 1986.

for the Speedster model. The new interiors also had other unusual features for Porsche: body-colored instrument panel accents, shift lever, and parking brake handle (all usually a Special Works Department order). The Carrera Speedster was again produced as a limited edition, this time totaling only 930 cars.

Two Carrera Speedster models were offered for a brief production run in the 1994 model year, and this was the second version equipped with Porsche's new Tiptronic transmission. The two-seaters did not reappear in 1995, and the 1997 Boxster has

since taken its place as the Porsche Speedster for the next century.

In 1989 the new 964 platform had been introduced, along with the all-wheel-drive Carrera 4, giving the venerable 911 yet another new lease on life. The 964 program was an evolution of the 1987–88 Porsche 959 all-wheel-drive turbo competition cars, of which only three hundred were built.

In 1993 Porsche introduced the third-generation turbo motor, a 3.6-liter that developed 355 brake horsepower at 5,500 revolutions per minute. The new engine not only increased horsepower but also torque, up to 383 pounds per foot at 4,200 revolutions per minute. Top speed was also elevated to an adrenaline-pumping 174 miles per hour.

The 3.6 was improved throughout and equipped with larger brakes and new 18-inch wheels, derived from the Carrera Cup cars, which gave a clear view of the brilliant red four-piston aluminum brake calipers. Although the 3.6 was the best Turbo model Porsche had yet built, its time would be limited: just one model year, from October 5, 1992, through the end of production in December 1993, at which time Porsche concluded manufacturing of all other 911 models to reinvent itself once again for the car's thirtieth anniversary in 1994.

Zuffenhausen celebrated the 911's third decade with the introduction of the Type 993 Carrera, an altogether different car but instantly recognizable as a 911. Butzi Porsche remarked in 1994, "[The new Carrera] is an absolutely worthy and masterfully made successor to all previous 911s."

To celebrate the thirtieth anniversary of the 911, Porsche produced a limited-edition Carrera 4 coupe with

Turbo fender flares and 17-inch wheels. The edition of, appropriately, 911 cars was produced in a special violet metallic color with rubicon gray interior upholstery and subtle detail accents such as a silver-colored metal plate on the rear package shelf that bore the sequential number of the car in the *30 Jahre* commemorative series. A semi-matte silver emblem below the 911 insignia on the rear-deck lid also read *30 Jahre*.

The factory-built 911 flat-nose competition models, such as this 1987 Turbo 3.3-liter Flachtbau, inspired a number of custom-bodied models in the late 1980s and early 1990s.
(PORSCHE WERKFOTO)

Other significant Porsche benchmarks have also been noted with special models such as the 1988 series produced in Blue Diamond Metallic to celebrate the sale of the 250,000th 911. Color-matched Fuchs wheels, silver gray carpeting, and silver-blue leather upholstery with Ferry Porsche's signature stitched into the headrests set off these commemorative models. A total of 875 were produced, in coupe, cabriolet, and Targa versions.

Since the America roadster, Porsche has produced limited-edition models intended for sports car club racing. One of the rarest was the 911 Club Sport, which was produced twice, once in 1987 as a lightweight (stripped) base 911 sold in Great Britain, Germany, and the United States, and again in 1996 as the 911 Carrera RS Clubsport, equipped with a 3,746-cubic-centimeter, 300-brake-horsepower engine, with special front spoiler, flared rear fenders, and rear spoiler. The factory also produced a road version of the 911 GT 2 in 1995. Neither the Clubsport nor the GT 2 models were sold in the United States.

In 1993 and 1994 there was the 911 RS America, introduced as a club racer and the lowest-priced 911 model of the year at $54,800, more than $10,000 lower than the Carrera 2. Porsche was once again commemorating its past, only this time with a car that could be sold in the United States.

The RS America traced its roots to the Carrera RS 2.7 of 1973, which by the early 1990s had become one of the most sought-after Porsche models of all time.

In its introduction of the RS America, Porsche noted that "the original Porsche 911 Carrera RS led to the RSR, a special racing model that won the 24 Hours of Daytona and the 12 Hours of

From wide in 1989 to wider in 1994, Porsche offered the Speedster with the turbo fenders to make the car more aggressive in appearance. Note that the European version is badged as a Carrera. The cars were never badged as Speedsters, even though that was the model designation. (PORSCHE WERKFOTO)

OPPOSITE: In 1989, Porsche brought its product line full circle with the addition of a Carrera Speedster model. The car was basically a 911 cabriolet with a rear tonneau, manual fabric top, and lower windshield. But it had the cachet of the original 356A. Pictured is a 1989 Speedster and a black 356A originally owned and raced by actor Steve McQueen.

OPPOSITE AND RIGHT: The entire 911 model line was carried over into 1987, and the only notable change was the addition of the 911 Carrera Club Sport (Sport Package M 637). Designed for SCCA and Porsche Club competition, this was a stripped-down racing version that shaved 110 pounds from the standard Carrera and tipped the scales at 2,555 pounds. The Club Sport had a higher engine rev limit, sport shocks, 7 and 8 J × 17 wheels, stiffer engine mounts, and the turbo rear wing.

Even though the Club Sport was a Lightweight, Porsche managed not to sacrifice any of the interior aesthetics of the luxury 911 interior.

Sebring in 1973. In the process, the RSR earned Porsche the IMSA [International Motor Sports Association] Drivers Championship as well as the Manufacturers Championship. The RS formed the starting point of Porsche's decade-long domination of production-based GT racing with the RSR, 934, and 935."

It was with this historical imperative in mind that Porsche designed the RS America to emulate the first 911 Carrera models. The cars were equipped with corduroy Recaro bucket seats, and the rear fold-down seats were replaced with a flat parcel shelf that had two lockable storage bins (thus becoming a legitimate 2-seater like the 911 Speedster). Most of the sound insulation from the RS America was eliminated, as were armrests and storage panels; even the door latches were released by nylon pull straps. Basically it was a modern version of the Carrera RS 2.7 Lightweight.

The cars were powered by the normally aspirated 3.6-liter engine, which, combined with the RS America's lighter weight, was able to reach higher levels of performance than the Carrera 2. It was the fastest accelerating non-turbo model, capable of zero to 60 in 5.4 seconds and a top test track speed of 162 miles per hour.

Intended for club racing, the America was not available with air-conditioning. The RS came standard with larger, wider 17-inch wheels and tires, more aggressive spring and shock absorber tuning, a larger front stabilizer bar, and nonassisted rack and pinion steering. It was a club racer in the fullest sense.

By 1996 the Turbo Carrera had become the very image of the sought-after but unobtainable (and illegal in the United States except for racing) all-wheel-drive, turbocharged 959. The body lines were a little sweeter, rounded at the rear in an almost 928 theme, with the front taking on more of the angular crispness around the headlights and fenders characterized by the 959.

With the fifth generation, the 911 Turbo reached a new level of development, with the 3.6-liter aluminum alloy, boxer engine delivering 400 brake horsepower and 400 pounds-per-foot torque through a six-speed transaxle, full-time all-wheel-drive, limited slip differential, and automatic brake differential (ABD) traction control. The 1997 Turbo S refined performance even further by increasing horsepower to 424, making it the most powerful road car offered by Porsche up to that time.

The 1998 model year marked the end of a thirty-five-year era in Porsche history—the last 911 models powered by an air-cooled flat-six boxer engine, with the exception of the 911 Targa, which was carried over into the 1999 model year. In that respect alone, the 1998 coupes and cabriolets may become the most collectible 911s of the late twentieth century. The last of anything is always afforded special prominence among enthusiasts.

The air-cooled 911 ended its career almost when it started in coupe, Targa, and cabriolet versions, albeit in a far more contemporary idiom with available all-wheel-drive for both the coupe and cabriolet models.

Porsche's on-again, off-again affair with the turbo was off once more as the twin-turbocharged and intercooled Carrera all-wheel-drive Turbo and Turbo S (1996 and 1997) were dropped from Zuffenhausen's elite 1998 lineup of Carrera models. In preparation for the all-new 996 series, the turbos were the first models to be phased out.

Porsche celebrated its fiftieth anniversary in 1998 with the best built and most technologically advanced cars in its history and an international reputation that was built on the framework of the original 911, an automobile that has not only withstood the test of time but through its unparalleled longevity established standards that no other automaker has ever approached.

There were five distinct body styles for the 1998 Porsche 911

OPPOSITE: The Porsche 911's thirtieth anniversary display featured a new Type 993 model and a 1964 coupe. Ferry Porsche and Ferdinand Alexander posed with the cars in 1993. (PORSCHE WERKFOTO)

30 years Porsche 911 · 30 Jahre Porsche 911 · 30 années Porsche 911

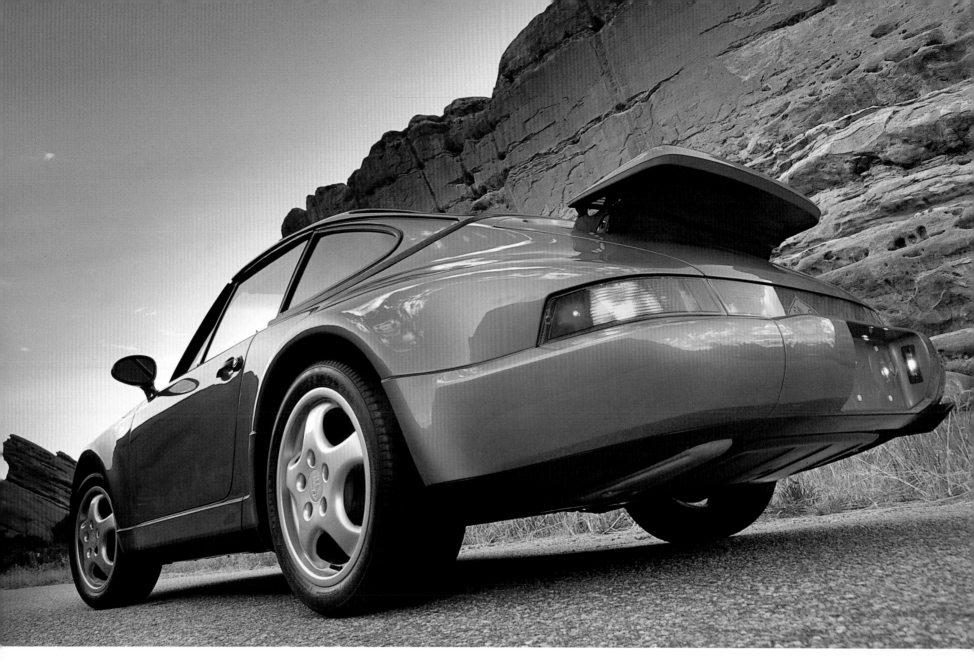

The commemorative 1992 RS America was a reprise of the Lightweight design and featured a 260-brake-horsepower normally aspirated 3,600-cubic-centimeter engine. The rear wing (shown extended) was part of the engine cover and deployed automatically at high speeds or could be manually raised and lowered from a control on the console.

stable: the Carrera S coupe widebody with turbo-style fender treatment; the Carrera cabriolet, which used the standard 911 body shell; the Carrera 4S coupe, which combined the widebody look with the Porsche all-wheel-drive powertrain; the Carrera 4 cabriolet, incorporating all-wheel drive and a convertible body style; and the glass-topped Carrera Targa introduced in 1996.

The Carrera S coupe, which made its debut in March 1997 at the New York International Auto Show, incorporated the wide front and rear body work of the 911 turbo and 911 Carrera 4S, with a split rear spoiler grille, "Cup Design" 17-inch alloy wheels, steel gray interior trim, black leather instrument panel and door trim, and Carrera S identification on the rear engine cover. This became the entry-level 911, with all these features at no increase in price compared to the 1997 Carrera coupe.

For the air-cooled boxer engine's finale, all 911 models featured Porsche's latest normally aspirated 3.6-liter, air-cooled, horizontally opposed, six-cylinder, 282-brake-horsepower boxer engine. Redesigned in 1995, the venerable Porsche engine had a 9 percent increase in power without any fuel economy penalty, at the same time meeting stringent international emission standards. The additional increase in horsepower, with a substantial boost in the engine's mid-range torque curve, was achieved by the incorporation of Porsche's patented Varioram induction system.

Varioram optimized the engine's volumetric efficiency for high torque output, resulting in quick throttle response and strong acceleration. This was accomplished through the use of variable-length intake pipes and separate, differently tuned air intake systems for medium and high engine speeds, thus optimizing torque and power output characteristics across the usable engine revolutions-per-minute range. The improved engine used inlet valves that were larger—50 millimeters compared to 49 millimeters—and

exhaust valves that were 43.5 millimeters instead of 42.5 millimeters. The camshafts had modified valve timing, and an optimized ignition system was also employed.

The Varioram system's intake manifold operated with long intake pipes at moderate engine speeds. Cylinder filling was improved by resonance in the individual intake pipes, resulting in a significant increase in torque at moderate engine speeds across a relatively wide revolutions-per-minute range.

A set of sliding sleeves, which form part of the long intake pipes, uncovered apertures located approximately at their centers, at engine speeds over 5,000 revolutions per minute. This reduced the effective length of the intake pipes and established a connection with the resonance compartments. The alternating intake cycles in the left-hand and right-hand cylinder banks forced the air column in the intake manifold to oscillate, or resonate, the first achieving optimum torque at the top end of the engine speed range, while resonance charging achieved optimum effect over a narrower revolutions-per-minute range.

The Varioram resonance system was designed to change over quickly. From 5,800 revolutions per minute up, a resonance flap opened, exposing another resonance cross-section between the resonance compartments of the two cylinder banks. The intake manifold's resonant frequency was then optimized for very high engine speeds. Combining ram effect charging and resonance charging, a combination unique to the Varioram intake manifold, high torque was produced across the entire engine speed range. Torque was improved by 18 percent at mid-range engine speeds between 2,500 and 4,500 revolutions per minute. A peak output of 229 pounds per foot of torque was achieved at 3,500 revolutions per minute compared with 193 pounds per foot on the earlier engine design. The torque gain was reflected in the acceleration time

LEFT AND BELOW: In 1993, Porsche produced the 911 Carrera 2 3.6 Speedster. The new model was a vast improvement over the first series; it had a more easily operated manual top, Carrera RS seat shells painted in body color, and leather upholstery specifically designed for the Speedster model. The new interiors also had another unusual feature for Porsche: body-colored instrument panel accents, shift lever, and parking brake handle. Again produced as a limited edition, only 930 were built. (PORSCHE WERKFOTO)

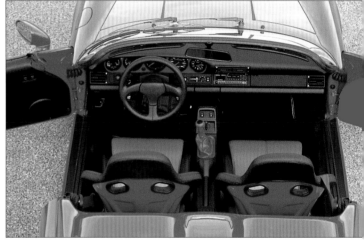

from 50 miles per hour to 75 miles per hour in fifth gear, which was reduced by about 18 percent. With Varioram in place, it became possible to drive in a higher gear and with lower engine speeds with no loss in engine flexibility.

Engine output with Varioram increased from 270 horsepower to 282 horsepower, and maximum torque from 243 pounds per foot to 250 pounds per foot. The high specific output and ex-

ceptional pulling power of the 3.6-liter Varioram engine made the best of everyday driving and had the added benefit of lower fuel consumption. This was the final step in making the 911 a practical car for both daily driving and taking advantage of an open stretch of highway.

A monitoring system for all components with exhaust emission control relevance was another feature of all 1998 Porsche 911

The 1994 model year provided Porsche enthusiasts with a great diversity of models. Pictured are the Turbo 3.6; Speedster; 30 Jahre 911; and Carrera 2 cabriolet. (PORSCHE WERKFOTO)

engines. Anytime the car was driven, the OBD II (onboard diagnostics, second generation) system measured the efficiency of the catalytic converter, identified misfiring, and monitored the fuel system, fuel tank venting, secondary-air injection, oxygen sensors, and other components and systems that affected exhaust emissions.

Delivering output to the rear wheels, Porsche offered two transmissions for the 911 series: a standard six-speed manual and the patented Tiptronic S automatic with computer-programmed shifting and steering-wheel-mounted remote shift for spirited manual gear selection. Based on Formula One–style racing transmissions, the Tiptronic steering wheel toggles allowed for quickly activated gear changes without the need of a clutch or removing your foot from the accelerator. Hands stayed on the wheel and eyes on the road.

In addition to the 911 models, Porsche had a new Boxster, introduced in early 1997, with its 2.5-liter water-cooled boxer engine and five-speed manual or Tiptronic S transmission. In both convertible and optional hardtop configurations, the Boxster pointed the way to the 911's future as the foundation for the all-new 911 series for 1999.

For the 1998 model year, the new Boxster roadster offered standard front and side air bags but was otherwise unchanged from the 1997 model.

The latest air-cooled Porsche convertible, the 911 Carrera 4 cabriolet, offered the advantages of all-wheel-drive. Key features included the 3.6-liter, flat six, 282-horsepower engine, six-speed manual transmission, all-wheel-drive, high-performance all-disc brakes with ABS (antilock braking system), high-performance tires on alloy wheels, welded unitized body of double-sided galvanized steel, aluminum suspension components, speed-dependent extendable rear spoiler, second-generation side-impact protection, heated windshield washer nozzles, fog lamps incorporated into the front spoiler, and modular polyellipsoid headlamps with a headlamp washer system. Litronic gas-discharge headlamps, which are twice as powerful as halogen headlamps while using 30 percent less electrical current, were optional.

Modifications to the six-speed manual transmission made the Porsche 911 Carrera 4 cabriolet more enjoyable to drive in everyday conditions. Dual-cone synchronizers for first and second gears, along with ball-bearing sleeves that reduced friction and enhanced shift precision, were features of the manual gearbox that made shifting action more precise and driving a 911 an even more enjoyable experience.

The six-speed transmission weighed virtually the same as the previous five-speed, and weight savings coupled with operating efficiencies were design parameters throughout development of the Porsche Carrera 4 cabriolet. As a result the Tiptronic S automatic transmission was not offered on the Carrera 4 cabriolet.

OPPOSITE: The color that was the most difficult to get for the 1994 model year was pearlessence, a silver-white metallic that turned heads a half mile away. The Turbo Carrera was now equipped with the new 3.6-liter engine (introduced in 1993) that developed 355 brake horsepower at 5,500 revolutions per minute and 383 pounds per foot of torque at 4,200 revolutions per minute. The 3.6-liter Turbo was equipped with larger brakes and new 18-inch wheels, which provided a view of the brilliant red four-piston aluminum brake calipers. At 174 miles per hour, the Turbo Carrera 3.6 was the fastest and most powerful production car Porsche had yet produced.

The same all-wheel-drive system used on the 1997 Porsche 911 turbo was used on the 1998 Carrera 4 cabriolet. At 111 pounds the system was half the weight of the earlier Carrera 4 all-wheel-drive system and 33 percent more efficient in operation. A maintenance-free viscous center clutch controlled power distribution between the front and rear wheels. Torque split between the rear wheels was regulated by a conventional rear-locking differential. The viscous clutch and rear differential worked together to divert engine torque to the wheels with the most traction.

Making the 1998 models some of the world's most advanced sports cars was Porsche's automatic brake differential (ABD) system, which augmented rear differential action. In practice, if one rear wheel began spinning, the locking differential would transmit the power to the other wheel that still had traction. And if this wasn't sufficient to restore traction, then ABD, using input from the antilock brake system sensors, applied braking power to the slipping wheel to help initiate traction. The ABD system functioned at speeds up to 43 miles per hour.

The 1996 Carrera 4 Turbo had reached a milestone, not only in styling but in performance, delivering an adrenaline rush with every shift and making the jump from zero to 60 miles per hour in 4.4 seconds, less time than it takes to say it. The 3,600-cubic-centimeter turbocharged and intercooled engine was pumping out 408 brake horsepower at only 5,750 revolutions per minute and 400 pounds per foot torque at 4,500 revolutions per minute. These were figures that would have outshone a factory race car a decade earlier! It was also one of the best handling and manageable sports cars ever built.

The three-way combination of locking differential, ABD, and all-wheel-drive provided greater directional stability and offered maximum traction on less than ideal road surfaces. All-wheel-drive also reduces weight transfer differences, which can affect stability, by allowing the maximum of the Carrera 4 cabriolet's weight to be used at all times to help maintain traction. This ideal arrangement made the 1998 models the best handling and most predictable cars in the Porsche's then fifty-year history.

The Carrera 4 cabriolet front suspension was an evolution of the MacPherson-type strut, coil spring, and stabilizer bar unit from past 911 models that provided increased stability, excellent handling, and ride comfort. Due to design changes made to most suspension components, the suspension system tipped the scales at some 6.6 pounds less than its predecessor, thus improving driving characteristics by reducing unsprung weight.

Porsche's Lightweight-Stable-Agile (LSA) multi-link, subframe-mounted rear suspension system replaced the semi-trailing arms and struts of previous 911 models. Four lateral links in two horizontal planes, which appear like upper and lower A-arms, provided precise wheel control. A refined version of the Weissach suspension pioneered on the Porsche 928 helped improve stability by using the outside rear wheel toe-in during cornering. Stability, regardless of side forces, and precise tracking were the system's virtues. The LSA package, in addition to the four links, included dual gas shock absorbers, coil springs, and a rear-mounted forged aluminum subframe.

Porsche cars have made their reputation on their braking as well as their acceleration and cornering, and the 1998 Carrera 4 cabriolet carried on that tradition. The Carrera 4 cabriolet and all other 911 variants used large-diameter, internally vented and

Porsche had achieved the final evolution of Ferdinand Alexander Porsche's original 911 design with the Type 993 Carrera 4 Turbo. The full-time four-wheel-drive system made the 911 the most manageable, predictable, and forgiving high-performance sports car of the twentieth century.

The 3.6-liter, 911 turbo engine featured dual-exhaust turbochargers. The swept volume of the six-cylinder, horizontally opposed air-cooled engine was 3,600 cubic centimeters with a 3.94-inch (100 mm) × 3.01-inch (76.4 mm) bore × stroke. Compression ratio was 8.0:1 and output at 400 (408) brake horsepower delivered at 5,750 revolutions per minute.

cross-drilled rotors, four-piston calipers, and asbestos-free brake pads, augmented by the Bosch ABS 5 antilock braking system.

The Carrera 4 cabriolet came equipped with 17-inch pressure-cast alloy wheels (7J by 17 inches in the front and 9J by 17 inches in the rear) fitted with steel-belted radial 205/50 ZR-17 tires up front and 255/40 ZR-17 rear tires.

Designed for those drivers desiring Porsche's legendary acceleration, braking, and handling performance, combined with the joys of open-air motoring in a traditional rear-wheel-drive configuration, the Porsche 911 Carrera cabriolet combined the structural strength of a 911 coupe with a high-performance convertible top system. This model was available with either the six-speed manual or the four-speed Tiptronic S automatic transmission.

The cabriolet came equipped with 16-inch pressure-cast alloy wheels (7J by 16 inches in the front and 9J by 16 inches in the

rear) fitted with steel-belted radial 205/55 ZR-16 tires up front and 245/45 ZR-16 rear tires. Targa-style 17-inch pressure-cast alloy wheels and Turbo-look 18-inch pressure-cast alloy wheels, both with wheel locks, were optional on the cabriolet for 1998.

The familiar 911 silhouette was evident in the 1998 Carrera S and incorporated all the aerodynamic and safety refinements made to the 911. The Carrera S had all the same key features as the cabriolet.

At the heart of the 1998 Porsche models was the Tiptronic S control unit, which featured five different adaptive shift programs, each applied according to the needs of the driver, with a range extending from economy to performance. The Tiptronic S electronic transmission made decisions in choosing the right gear based on vehicle and driver behavior. If the driver suddenly took his or her foot off the accelerator, the Tiptronic S system sensed the car was no longer under power and prevented the transmission from shifting up, keeping the current gear engaged. Brake application likewise made the transmission shift down at an appropriate road speed. Built-in grade detection prevented the transmission from upshifting too soon on uphill and downhill grades. If the wheels were to spin on a low-traction surface, the Tiptronic S would upshift earlier, providing engine torque management and enhanced driving stability.

Tiptronic S allowed a driver to participate in shifting decisions, choosing the four gears as appropriate. Transmission control on the 911 Carrera S included the choice of manual or automatic mode depending on the position of the selector lever. Once selection of the manual mode was made, shifting was done either by using the upshift and downshift buttons on the steering wheel, as on Formula One racing cars, or by using the floor shifter, pushing forward for a higher gear or pulling back for a lower gear.

The Carrera S came equipped with special "Cup Design" 17-inch pressure-cast alloy wheels incorporating colored Porsche crest wheel caps (7J by 17 inches in the front and 9J by 17 inches in the rear) fitted with steel-belted radial 205/50 ZR-17 tires up front and 255/40 ZR-17 rear tires. Targa-style 17-inch pressure-cast alloy wheels and hollow-spoke 18-inch pressure-cast alloy wheels, both with wheel locks, were optional on the Carrera S.

Special Carrera S interior equipment included black leather and steel gray interior trim, steel gray doorsill panels, instrument rings, shift lever knob, hand brake lever and push knob, a textured black leather dashboard center and door panels, along with dual front airbags, three-point restraints for driver and passengers, automatic temperature control air-conditioning, power windows, electronic sunroof, central locking and alarm system with immobilizer and remote entry system, heated external rearview mirrors, individually folding rear-seat backs, leather-covered steering wheel, interior lights with delayed shutoff, cruise control, cassette and coin holder, and door trim panels with covered armrest bins and open map pockets.

The Becker six-speaker AM/FM cassette audio system was also standard on the Carrera S. Available options were the Tiptronic S automatic transmission, full-power leather sport seats, Litronic high-intensity-discharge headlamps, sport

chassis (with larger front and rear stabilizer bars, stiffer springs, and specially tuned front and rear shock absorbers), a rear-seat delete package, infrared security system, and limited-slip differential with automatic brake differential (ABD).

The 1998 Carrera 4S combined the widebody exterior design of the famed 911 Turbo and the Turbo's all-wheel-drive system with the normally aspirated 911 engine and six-speed manual transmission. As an all-wheel-drive model the Tiptronic S automatic transmission was again not available on the Carrera 4S.

The 911 Targa, now with a sliding glass roof, was the last air-cooled model produced and was carried over into the 1999 model year because of its unique and popular design. Offered with the Tiptronic S transmission, it was the most practical 911 model ever produced.

The 1997 Porsche turbo was the last of the air-cooled turbos. Fast, well engineered, and ridiculously expensive—$110,000—it wasn't the Porsche for everyone, but it was the greatest air-cooled 911 ever built. The end of an era—and the beginning of another.

Porsche 911 Turbo. The Carrera 4S, like the legendary Turbo, was fitted with a front air dam featuring large air intakes to provide additional cooling air for the engine and auxiliary equipment. Rather than the Turbo tail, the Carrera 4S used the speed-dependent, extendable rear spoiler identical to other 911 models.

The same all-wheel-drive system used on the 1997 Porsche 911 Turbo was used on the 1998 Carrera 4S coupe. The three-way combination of locking differential, ABD, and all-wheel drive provided the C4S with greater directional stability and maximum traction.

Interior features of the Carrera 4S were the same as the C4 cabriolet. Electronic sunroof, central locking and alarm system with immobilizer, and remote entry system were also standard features.

Included with the Carrera 4S were Turbo-look 18-inch pressure-cast alloy wheels and the same power-assisted, internally vented four-piston disc brakes used on the 911 Turbo. The Carrera 4S six-speed manual gearbox was optimized for smooth, light, and precise shifting.

The side rocker panels and wider rear fenders of the Carrera 4S were adapted from the widebody design used on the 1997

A six-speaker AM/FM cassette audio system manufactured by Becker was standard on the Carrera 4S. Options included full-power leather sport seats, Litronic high-intensity-discharge headlamps, sport chassis (with larger front and rear stabilizer bars, stiffer springs, and specially tuned front and rear shock absorbers), a rear-seat delete package, infrared security system, and limited-slip differential with automatic brake differential (ABD).

OPPOSITE: The 1997 Porsche model line. (PORSCHE WERKFOTO)

On July 15, 1996, Ferry Porsche presented the one-millionth Porsche 911 built to the German police. At eighty-six years of age, Ferry Porsche had seen the company bearing his family name rise from its humble beginnings in Gmünd, Austria, in 1948 to become one of the world's best-known and most revered sports car manufacturers. Like his father, Ferry, too, had seen his life's work realized.

The final model of the final air-cooled 911 series was the revised Targa, introduced in 1996 and featuring a unique electric sliding glass roof system with sun visor and separate wind deflector, in place of the original removable Targa roof design. Nearly the entire roof over the passenger compartment slid down and back to its stowed position under the rear window at the push of a button, providing an open-air feeling much greater than that of the original 911 Targa.

While the original Targa differed from other 911 models, from below the window line the 1996 and 1999 Targas shared their body and platform with the 911 Carrera cabriolet, including additional body and chassis reinforcements for increased structural rigidity. The roof module, which resembled the coupe roof in profile, consisted of two-layer laminated safety glass, a sun visor, a wind deflector, a rear window, and an aluminum frame.

The Targa was designed to provide several advantages over the original design, including minimal noise, maximum operating convenience, and no undesirable drafts or turbulence in the passenger compartment with the roof open. The Targa's roof contour offered nearly the same amount of headroom in the rear seats as the coupe, even with the roof open, and slightly more front seat headroom than the coupe when the roof was closed. The interior noise level was quieter inside the open-top Targa than in a Carrera cabriolet or a coupe with a sliding sunroof, and the Targa roof could be opened or closed while the car was moving.

The 1998 and 1999 Targas came equipped with their own special Targa-style 17-inch pressure-cast alloy wheels (7J by 17 inches in the front and 9J by 17 inches in the rear) fitted with steel-belted radial 205/50 ZR-17 tires up front and 255/40 ZR-17 rear tires.

The Targas were available with either a six-speed manual or the four-speed Tiptronic S automatic transmission, along with full-power leather sport seats, Litronic high-intensity-discharge headlamps, a rear-seat delete package, infrared security system, and limited-slip differential with automatic brake differential (ABD).

Of all the 911 models, the Targa represented the highest tier of design evolution. On the horizon was the road to a new century and for Porsche the end of an era that had begun with the first air-cooled models after World War II. As 1999 rolled around, Porsche's future was about to change, as was the way in which their cars would be powered.

The Targa was to be the last air-cooled model to remain in the line as the company prepared to launch its next generation of 911s, the very first to utilize liquid-cooled engines.

The air-cooled era was over.

CHAPTER 10

DRIVING ON ALL FOURS

EVOLUTION OF PORSCHE ALL-WHEEL-DRIVE

N 2003, PORSCHE CELEBRATED THE TWENTIETH anniversary of its first all-wheel-drive model, or the 101st anniversary, depending on which all-wheel-drive Porsche you're talking about!

Ferdinand Porsche pioneered the concept of providing power to all four wheels, known as *allrad* in German, more than a century ago with a vehicle driven by four electric wheel-hub motors. *Auto Motor und Sport*'s Reinhard Seiffert, in Porsche's *Christophorus* book *Carrera 4—Porsche Allrad 1900–1990*, noted that Ferdinand Porsche's name "not only appears at the very beginning of all-wheel-drive history, he remained concerned with drive problems throughout his life. Nobody during the first half of our century designed and realized more four- and all-wheel-drive vehicles than this engineer from Maffersdorf in Bohemia."

Ferdinand Porsche's car with four wheels and four electric motors earned double honors as both the first all-wheel and four-wheel-drive vehicle. The first example was delivered to a customer in 1902. Four years later, at Austro-Daimler, Porsche designed an all-wheel-drive truck. The original idea, however, had not been to create a vehicle with better traction or handling but, rather, to provide more power with an electric motor for each wheel. Unfortunately, the electric car, like the steam car, both of which were popular at the turn of the century, would soon be forced from the road by improvements in the internal combustion engine. But Porsche's all-wheel-drive concept was not so easily dismissed.

Porsche continued to develop all-wheel-drive vehicles, and in 1934 his chief designer, Karl Rabe, laid out the plans for an all-wheel-drive variation of the NSU Volkswagen that was under development. Rabe's design showed a drive shaft from the rear-mounted engine to a front axle differential. This was the blueprint that would lay the groundwork for all future designs, the greatest benefactor of which was to be the German military. Every all-wheel-drive VW built for military purposes during World War II and every Type 166 VW amphibian was based on Karl Rabe's de-

OPPOSITE: The Three Musketeers, Porsche's off-road 959 Paris-Dakar race car, a production 959 for homologation, and a Group B race car at the Weissach Development Center test track in 1986. (PORSCHE WERKFOTO)

Porsche's emerging four-wheel-drive technology was utilized on the company's design for a Mercedes-Benz streamliner, or Rekord-wagen, in 1939. The T 80 was not a true four-wheel-drive car because it had three axles, only two of which—the front and rear—were driven.

used primarily by officers. The versatile staff cars were known as the Kommandeurwagen.

Porsche's all-wheel-drive models from World War II played no small role in the company's postwar resurrection in Gmünd, Carinthia. After the guns fell silent, Ferry Porsche's 1947 design for the four-wheel-drive Cisitalia grand prix car (the profits from which had been used to buy Ferdinand Porsche's and Anton Piëch's freedom from imprisonment by the French) proved again the sporting applications of all-wheel-drive. But, alas, it was the military once again, this time for the peaceful use of the Federal Republic of Germany, that brought forth the next develop-

sign that utilized selective front-wheel drive, thus disengaging the rear wheels rather than the front wheels for open road driving. The selective drive also included a locking differential (transverse lockup) in the front axle, since after fording a river or lake the amphibians usually reached shore with one wheel only. This differential lock had to be disengaged for road use, however.

In addition to building the amphibious VWs, Porsche also produced 667 all-wheel-drive Volkswagen sedans, which were

ment of Porsche all-wheel-drive technology. This was the Porsche Jagdwagen, introduced in 1955 and based on the engine and chassis design of the 356 sports car, combined with the wartime Kommandeurwagen all-wheel-drive system. Conceived for the German border patrol, the sporty Jagdwagen proved too costly for the military, and only civilian versions were built. Thus, with no further military or racing contracts in the 1950s, Porsche KG saw no need to pursue the continued development of its all-wheel-drive technology and allowed more than two decades to pass before the company took up the idea again.

Motor sports, Porsche's historically rooted raison d'être, breathed new life into Zuffenhausen's long-dormant all-wheel-drive experience in the early 1980s after Audi had gone rallying with the Quattro. The innovative all-wheel-drive sports model had been pioneered by Ferdinand Porsche's grandson, Ferdinand Piëch, who had moved over to Audi in 1972 following the Porsche and Piëch families' banishment from the company by Ferry Porsche. The highly successful Quattro rally cars prompted the Porsche engineers at Weissach to develop a 911 along similar lines, and thus was born the Type 959.

In his 1993 book *Porsche Legends*, author Randy Leffingwell noted that renowned race driver Jacky Ickx was one of the first to suggest developing an all-wheel-drive 911 to race in the famed Paris-Dakar Rallye, which Ickx had won five times. Leffingwell wrote, "This race, unlike the rallies that Ferdinand Piëch's Audi Quattro was winning, had been a specialty-vehicle event since its beginning. However, Ickx, with plenty of seat time in the durable Porsche 956, wondered if the race could be won in a four-wheel-drive sports car."

Professor Helmuth Bott, who spearheaded the 959 program at Porsche beginning in 1983, noted that with the new technology they were developing for the 959 the objective was "to show the people, without changing the concept, this car, the 911, is capable of completely different things." Tony Lapine, who had begun his career as a General Motors stylist in 1952, was the head of Porsche's design studio during the 959's development, and he, too, recognized the importance of the car and its potential impact on future Porsche models. After more than thirteen years in Detroit,

In almost final form and equipped with an electronically controlled, multi-disk clutch in place of the center differential and two-stage turbocharging for the engine, a Type 959 was entered in the Pharaohs Rallye in Egypt. There, against tough competition, the car prevailed. The 959 broke new ground in the use of automotive computer technology for the engine, suspension, and driveline. The car's powerful engine, all-wheel-drive design, and high ground clearance gave it the edge to win one of the world's toughest off-road races. (PORSCHE WERKFOTO)

Lapine had moved to GM's Opel division in Rüsselsheim, Germany, and after four years took a position with Porsche. He had a very Americanized sense of style but was quick to recognize the propriety of the 911 design. "There was a design legacy," he said. "From Komenda, from Butzi? Certainly. Definitely. Absolutely. I understood my job as being the custodian of the tradition. I may improve on it, but I may not change it. Changing is easy; improving on it is harder, much harder." Porsche cars were expected to last in the marketplace for a model run of twenty years. Leffingwell noted in his interview with Lapine, "[He] laughed as he thought of the contrasts. 'In America, I could do a new car every three years. If I make a mistake this time, I can correct it quickly. And yet for Porsche it was reasonably easy. You had the main characteristics from your tradition.'" The 959 was an evolution of the 911 design, dissimilar but unmistakable, although mechanically quite a different automobile.

With its all-wheel-drive system and substantially higher ground clearance, a 959 prototype, known as the Type 953, won the grueling 7,500-mile Paris-Dakar Rallye in January 1984 with Belgian driver René Metge. That car, however, did not have the later turbocharged engine but instead a normally aspirated 911 engine. Nevertheless, Porsche's victory in the Paris-Dakar was an unprecedented achievement. *Auto Motor und Sport*'s Reinhard Seiffert wrote: "It was the first time a sports car could win this extremely difficult rallye, taking several weeks, where only off-road vehicles and motorcycles had started previously." Porsche team manager Roland Kussmaul remarked that "never before have such

high-technology cars been taken into the burning desert. In such country, it would lead a normal car to total destruction. In the desert, it was our daily bread!"

In the autumn of that same year a 959, in almost final form and equipped with an electronically controlled, multi-disk clutch in place of the center differential and two-stage turbocharging for the engine, was entered in the Pharaohs Rallye in Egypt. There, against tough competition, the 959 prevailed. Said Bott, "We went to the desert because it was the only race at the time where all the regulations were free, unlimited. You could do anything. And what we had to test . . . not only was it mechanical, but so much [of it was] electronics." The 959 broke new ground in the use of automotive computer technology for the engine, suspension, and driveline. In the 1986 Paris-Dakar race, covering 8,750 miles, Metge finished first in a new Porsche 959, with Ickx coming in second and Kussmaul sixth. A one-two finish in the desert and first, second, and sixth overall out of five hundred starters and only 80 finishers! Vindication for Porsche.

The second version of the 959 was a mechanical marvel. It was also more than a car for racing in the desert. It marked the beginning of a new era in Porsche history.

Acknowledged as one of the greatest sports cars of the twentieth century, the limited-production 959 was a model designed for competition and European roads, and not certified for sale in the United States. The cars were not allowed into the country except for racing or display in a museum. That isn't to say that a few road miles weren't accumulated by a handful of 959s that crossed the

OPPOSITE: In 1986 it was back to the desert and another attempt at the Paris-Dakar with the improved 959. Covering 8,750 miles, René Metge, driving the Rothmans Porsche 959, finished first, with Jackie Ickx coming in second. With a one-two finish in the desert, it was first and second out of five hundred starters and only eighty finishers. (PORSCHE WERKFOTO)

with a new generation of production Porsche sports car: the all-wheel-drive Carrera 4.

Speed is tangible. You can feel it, see it, test it. How fast can the car go? What limits can it reach? How fast can I go? What are my limits? For the better part of the twentieth century that limit was usually attained in production automobiles around 120 miles per hour. And at that, for most cars and most drivers, traveling at two miles per minute was testing the very mettle of their abilities. For a select few automobiles that boundary was extended into the rarefied reaches of 150 miles per hour; and for

Atlantic in the late 1980s, but the 959 was never legally allowed on American roads back then, and only two hundred were built. The intrepid Porsche 959 race cars, however, were to be reborn in 1989

an even more exclusive handful in the 1980s and 1990s, velocities approached 200 miles per hour. Agreed, there is a certain absurdity to driving a road car (as opposed to a race car) capable of reaching

ABOVE AND OPPOSITE: Tony Lapine, who had begun his career as a General Motors stylist in 1952, was the head of Porsche's design studio during the 959's development. "There was a design legacy," he said. "I understood my job as being the custodian of the tradition. I may improve on it, but I may not change it." The 959 was an evolution of the 911 design, dissimilar but unmistakable. (PORSCHE WERKFOTO)

200 miles per hour, but perhaps the rationale for owners and enthusiasts is that one does not have to commit the act but simply know that it can be done.

However, in 1989, on an open road in the south of France, the speedometer needle on the Porsche Carrera 4 that I was testing was playing with the 160-mile-per-hour line. The engine was turning at maximum revs. The exhaust note was as melodious in the cold morning air as the call of Ulysses' Sirens, matched only in tone and intensity by the howl of air rushing over the car's rooftop and deflecting off the side mirrors. At that clip the world passed by in a torrent of wind and color. Yet, at two and a half times the limit we're allowed to drive on American highways, there was an uncanny sense of security behind the familiar wheel of the Porsche Carrera 4. The car could have gone faster, but I couldn't.

It was here that the old and the new had come together in perfect harmony—a synergy between man and machine that must be maintained to preserve the 911's traditional values, values critically important to the purist loyalists of the Zuffenhausen breed. With its introduction in 1989 the Carrera 4 became the Porsche 911 personified.

RIGHT AND OPPOSITE: As a limited-production sports car, the 959 was essentially a race car for the road. The design by Lapine captured the very essence of Ferdinand Alexander Porsche's 911 design, yet it evolved into a completely new car. Aesthetically and mechanically it would influence the future of all 911 designs beginning in 1986. (PORSCHE WERKFOTO)

However similar to previous 911s the Carrera 4 appeared on the outside—traditional windshield, doors, roof line, fenders, and trunk lid—beneath that familiar veneer lived a fully independent coil-spring suspension, antilock brake system, power-assisted rack-and-pinion steering, and four-wheel-drive system generations ahead of anything Porsche engineers could have imagined in 1964. As much as it may visually resemble 911s, 85 percent of the Carrera 4's components had no ties to the past. Their closest relative was the rare 959, and even that legendary car paled in comparison.

There was more than a hint of what lies beneath the Carrera 4's comely exterior if one considered the design characteristics gleaned from Porsche's quarter-million-dollar all-wheel-drive 959 competition cars. At both ends the bumpers were similar in appearance, the front with the 959's functional air intakes. At the rear the 959's overstated whale tail had been replaced by a subtle, integrally mounted wing, which appeared from the

This devotion to the "only true Porsches"—those with their air-cooled engines tucked neatly in the rear—was rewarded by the Carrera 4, a car that represented over a quarter century of development but was still curiously as much the same as it was different from the first 911 models of 1964.

engine cover to apply the necessary downforce at speeds above 48 miles per hour, a design still used on all current-day Porsches. Underneath, the Carrera 4 was virtually sealed by a full-length belly pan, as was the 959, a practice employed to reduce the amount of noise emanating from the car and the admission of road noise into

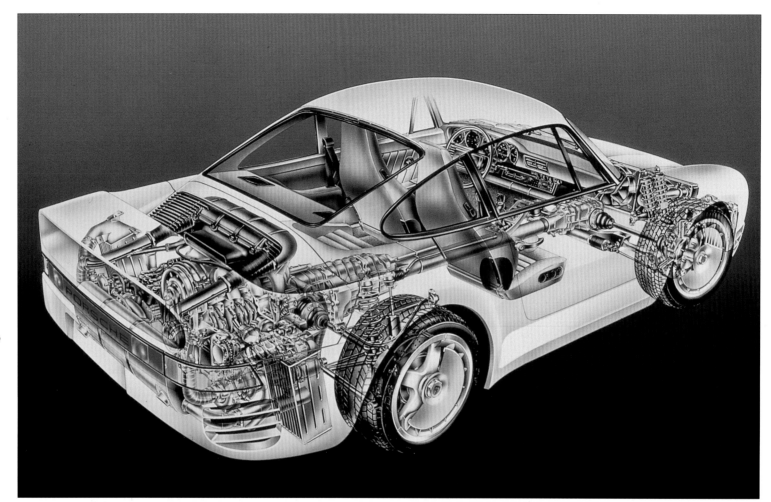

The 959 was both a mechanical and an electrical marvel, combining computer and electronic controlled suspension components to operate the all-wheel-drive system. As a Group B race car and then as the Type 961 race version of the 959 it was used in competition at the Le Mans and Daytona endurance contests.

the passenger compartment, as well as contributing to the car's aerodynamics.

At its worst the 1989 Carrera 4 was the best Porsche ever. At its best it was one of the most thoroughly competent road-going sports cars in the world—comfortable, easy to drive, and practical enough to undertake even mundane day-to-day motoring tasks.

From behind the wheel there were the first of many changes to come, yet it still seemed as though there had been very few. The all-new chassis and all-wheel-drive system introduced in 1989 repositioned the shift lever so that it fell more readily at hand, and yet even the most modern Porsche interior is no more than a luxurious redress of the original.

Under the rear wing and deck lid was Porsche's most sophisticated air-cooled engine. The limited production 959s produced 450 brake horsepower. (PORSCHE WERKFOTO)

The 3.6-liter engine produced the same air-cooled, six-cylinder rumble from behind. Tease the throttle and the whine is music to a Porsche owner's ears. Play it. Push the pedal, and the Carrera 4 consumed zero to 60 in 5.5 seconds. At the upper reaches of 150 miles per hour, the driver could sense that the four driven wheels were firmly in touch with the road, that the power-assist steering was ever so precise, and that the antilock disc brakes could scrub off speed with unfaltering reliability in an instant. Confidence. That is what the Carrera 4 gave its driver.

At the heart of the Carrera 4 was an all-wheel-drive system that, surprisingly, was not derived from the 959 but utilized an entirely new and less costly design. It divided torque through a mechanical center differential, delivering 31 percent of the drive force to the front wheels and 69 percent to the rear under normal driving conditions. When needed, the system automatically directed more power to the wheels offering the best traction. During our test in France we couldn't tell when it was working except for the indicator light on the dash.

While the C4 Porsche hadn't exactly rewritten the laws of physics with its all-wheel-drive system, let's say a few of its precepts had been adjusted. Cruising along tree-lined country roads on the outskirts of Saint Paul de Vence, I pressed the car into corners at speeds that would have explored the dreaded and perilous 911 oversteer, requiring deft counter-steer, often followed by a solemn oath never to do it again. Knowing this, it was at first confounding to drive a 911 with neutral handling that, when pushed harder into a turn, developed a slight tendency toward understeer. Though contrary to past experience, it was nonetheless so. The Carrera 4 did not feel like a 911 in the classic sense, but so much the better.

With this improved level of responsiveness came an element of what we'll call Carrera euphoria, beckoning you to press the car deeper into turns. To our surprise and relief, if you err (as we did) and lift in a curve (a normal, often regrettable reaction when you realize there isn't enough road), everything worked as Porsche's engineers had promised me. The dynamically controlled all-wheel-drive system instantly redistributed torque to keep the car in shape. The Carrera 4 held the line, and I swore that terrible oath.

While the changes that set the Carrera 4 apart from its 911 heritage were subtle at best, Porsche's most advanced design improvements were mostly unseen unless one slid underneath the car and looked up. But then you would see nothing, as on the bottom side of a 959.

The most important part of aerodynamics is minimizing resistance to the flow of air over the body of the car. But equally important, though seldom addressed, is the resistance to airflow from beneath. Thus, the Carrera 4 became the first production Porsche to offer a full-length belly pan, the underside almost totally enclosed by plastic and metal panels. A full pan, bordered on either side by molded plastic panels, encapsulated the engine itself. The exhaust system was also fully enclosed. Except for the wheels and outer perimeter of the suspension, everything was concealed. While reducing the exposed area, the panels also retained heat, so the functional air intakes in the front of the bumper were used to direct air through the sealed undercarriage and assist in cooling the transmission, engine, and antilock brake system.

In their overall application the undercarriage panels served several purposes: Foremost are the obvious aerodynamic gains provided by a smooth, unobstructed surface—in theory, a race-car-proven ground-effects design. The enclosure was also designed to reduce the level of noise emanating from the engine compartment in compliance with European regulations, making the Carrera 4 noticeably quieter than previous 911s. In turn, this reduced exterior road noise entering the passenger compartment, providing an uncommonly quiet interior environment. Not too quiet, of course: You still got a proper mixture of engine, transmission, and exhaust sound, but fewer bumps and thumps were felt from the pavement below.

With the Carrera 4, Porsche managed to establish a new generation of cars with enhanced aerodynamics, handling, and performance, at the same time avoiding an attack on holy 911 standards. The Porsche had evolved once more.

Back in 1989 Carrera 4 technology was available only on the 911 coupe. Since then the all-wheel-drive system had been ex-

With one car Porsche again redefined the 911. It was the Carrera 4, the production evolution of the legendary 959 Group B car. Although similar in appearance to previous 911 models, 85 percent of the Carrera 4's components had no ties to the earlier 911 designs. Beneath the familiar veneer of windshield, doors, roof line, fenders, and trunk lid was a revised independent coil-spring suspension design, antilock brakes, power-assisted rack-and-pinion steering, and four-wheel-drive system that were generations ahead of anything Porsche had to offer a year before the Carrera 4's introduction.

tended throughout the Porsche line, and in 1996 the Turbo was added, creating the most powerful and best-handling 911 in the company's history. It was followed in 1997 by the very limited Turbo S model with special S features and a 424 brake horsepower, twin-turbocharged, and twin-intercooled engine.

The enhanced 3.6-liter boxer delivered a chest-swelling load of power to the car's 18-inch "Technology" polished-look wheels, and did so in what seemed like milliseconds. The Turbo S didn't deliver breathtaking acceleration; it was gasping acceleration in every gear and at every speed. Going from first to second set you

The 993 series brought about the final evolution of the 911 shape with more sweeping fender lines and integrated headlights, taillights, and bumpers. The 1996 Turbo pictured was the ultimate extension of the 911 design, equipped with second-generation Carrera 4 all-wheel-drive technology and a 400-brake-horsepower, twin-turbocharged, and intercooled engine.

back in the seat after a moment's lag, and second to third at full song—with the bellow of the engine filling the cockpit—was a perfect accompaniment to the ever-increasing g force. For the first several seconds it was almost Wagnerian grandeur: trumpets blaring *Flight of the Valkyries* as an aggressive 400-pounds-per-foot torque, dispensed through the six-speed gearbox, reeled in the distance with such haste that it was almost alarming. So much power was unleashed from the twin-turbocharged 3.6 that the car dashed from zero to 60 in just a click over four seconds, and with little more than a delayed shift to third at full throttle, 100 miles per hour was a mere five

The last word in Turbo models was the S, the final version of the 911 Turbo, introduced as a limited edition in 1997. With special interior and exterior styling, a 425-brake-horsepower engine, and a staggering $150,000 price tag, it bid farewell to the air-cooled turbo.

The 1997 Turbo S sported the most luxurious interior ever offered on a 911. The limited-edition model featured special interior colors, including brick, which aptly describes the earthen hue of the Turbo S upholstery. The new dashboard design still echoed the original 911 layout, and even the ignition key remained to the left of the steering wheel, as it had since 1964.

beats away. This car got fast so fast that you needed to watch even the most innocent indulgence of speed, or you were into triple digits. Needless to say, the Turbo S was not for the timid or the underinsured. It made the 911 Turbo of 1975 seem like a pedal car.

The greatest problem with the older 911 Turbos was the inability of drivers to manage power and handling. The original Turbo model of 1975 proved to be more than a handful for most owners, and the number of damaged cars within the first year validated Porsche's suspicion that giving customers what they wanted—a street version of a factory race car—wasn't necessarily a good idea. Subsequent Turbo 911s have softened the edge, but what it took to make this car viable for the road was the C4's all-wheel-drive. As sure-footed as the Carrera 4, the Turbo S had a decided advantage in brute power. What the C4 Turbo served up as standard fare would have been considered a factory race car just a few years before. The Turbo S utilized the same AWD system from the 993 Carrera 4, but at only 111 pounds this system was half the weight of the earlier 964 C4 and 33 percent more efficient in operation, with the

viscous center clutch controlling power distribution to all four wheels as needed to maintain ideal traction. The system provided the Turbo S with perfectly neutral handling and turn-in that felt as though the car was mounted on rails. All the ills of the past were gone. This was a marriage made with technology that all but defied the laws of road physics.

For $150,000 this car so far exceeded our expectations as to rival the Lamborghini Diablo VT, priced at over $100,000 more, and to vanquish all Ferraris short of the half-million-dollar F50. Too much praise? Call it infatuation with perfection. Porsche had ended the air-cooled 911's career on a high note by taking the design as far as it could possibly go.

The Porsche 911 Turbo of 1997 featured the same engine and drivetrain design theory as the 959 but in a less expensive and, in the opinion of some, better looking production version designed to be driven daily on North American roads.

To be fair, the 911 Turbo, aside from speed and agility, was no different from any other 911 model, with the exception of the larger Turbo tail. The interior was the same traditional Porsche design, nicely tailored in leather, but no more or less distinctive. In fact, no one noticed this car unless you blew past them at 120 miles per hour, which in most states is unpopular with the local constabulary. Then again, being unobtrusive is more in vogue these days, and the Carrera 4 Turbo delivered on its promise of unmatched performance in such a way that most casual observers never knew what had passed them.

Had they known, they would have recognized it as the end of an era: the last all-wheel-drive, turbocharged, air-cooled 911. The original 901/911 design had reached the end of the road.

The last of the air-cooled 911 Turbos, the 1997 Turbo S was equipped with a stylish deck lid spoiler treatment unique to the Turbo body.

CHAPTER 11

A MOVE TO THE MIDDLE

THE PRESUMPTION THAT THE ONLY TRUE PORSCHE is a rear-engined, air-cooled Porsche has been put to the test many times in the company's history. Point in fact: The very first Porsche built in 1948 was a mid-engine design, as were many of Zuffenhausen's legendary sports racers such as the 550 Spyder and the 718 RSK. Thus it came as no surprise when a mid-engine production car entered the Porsche lineup in 1970. That the new 914 model wasn't built by Porsche left more than a few diehard enthusiasts shaking their heads in disbelief; it was a Volkswagen! This, too, should have come as no surprise. The Porsche 356 began life as a sports car built around VW components, and it remained so well into the early 1950s.

The relationship between Porsche and VW dated back to their origins; they were two companies bound by history and marriage. If Porsche ever required the assistance of another automaker, Volkswagen certainly would have been the first choice; yet many Porsche elitists, forgetting the marque's humble roots, failed to recognize the ingenious evolution of the new 914 sports model from the original mid-engine Gmünd Porsche. It was a category of snobbery unique to the 914.

"The 914 arose from the realization that we needed to broaden our program at a less costly level but that we couldn't do it alone," wrote Ferry. Indeed, just as Enzo Ferrari had turned to Fiat to produce the mid-engine Dino, Ferry Porsche had enlisted the aid of his longtime friend Heinz Nordhoff at VW in order to effectively expand the Porsche model line. It was Nordhoff who had come to Porsche's aid in 1948 with an agreement to provide the parts necessary from Wolfsburg for the manufacture of the 356. In addition, he had approved the arrangement for VW to sell and service Porsche sports cars through its dealer network, helping launch Porsche on the road to success.

In the mid-1950s, Nordhoff himself had encouraged VW's production of a sports model, the Karmann Ghia, designed in Italy by Carrozzeria Ghia and based for the most part on the

OPPOSITE: Nicknamed the Bumblebee, the 1974 Typ 914 2.0 Special Edition cars commemorated Porsche's significant--and repeated--Can-Am championships. These cars used 2.0-liter flat-fours that developed 100 brake horsepower. (RANDY LEFFINGWELL)

The five-speed transmission gave the Typ 914 2.0 a top speed of 118 miles per hour (190 kilometers). Full instrumentation was one of the features of the Special Edition package.
(RANDY LEFFINGWELL)

afford the price of a Porsche 911. The 914 then was the answer to both Volkswagen's and Porsche's problems. One car for two companies!

Though produced for only six years, the 914 became one of the most successful models ever sold by Porsche. While that may seem hard to believe, it's a fact. Despite less than encouraging reviews by the automotive press, debate over the car's mixed parentage, which cast a pall on the 914's image among Porsche purists, and its unusual styling, between 1970 and 1976 more than 118,000 of the mid-engine two-seaters were delivered! In Europe the 914 eclipsed the Opel GT to become the most popular German sports car.

That the 914 was popular in the United States can be attributed almost completely to its base price of only $3,495 and its recognition as a Porsche model. In Europe, however, the car was sold as a VW-Porsche. The coachwork for the cars was produced by Karmann, the same firm that had built the VW Karmann Ghia, known in some circles as the "poor man's Porsche." How nearly right they were. In Europe the 914 was intended to replace the 1500 Karmann Ghia.

Although it was the product of a joint venture entered into by Porsche and VW, neither firm was responsible for the 914's peculiar styling. Ferry Porsche and Heinz Nordhoff had decided that the new car could not look like an existing Porsche model, or resemble an older one, specifically the mid-engine 904, which had become the second signature car of Butzi Porsche's styling career. And certainly there could be no visual resemblance to a Volkswagen! In the face of such limitations, the body design for the 914 was developed outside of the VW and Porsche styling studios, under contract to Gugelot Design GmbH in Ulm, some 50 miles southeast of Porsche's Stuttgart headquarters.

styling of the 1953 Chrysler-Ghia Specials built under the direction of Chrysler chief stylist Virgil Exner. Over the years the sporty little Karmann Ghias had whetted the appetites of VW owners looking for something a bit more exciting but unable to

One of the most successful industrial design houses in Germany, Gugelot had never designed an automobile, and although some would say it was quite obvious from the appearance of the 914, the mid-engine two-seater was an extremely innovative and well-engineered sports car that evolved into one of the best-handling Porsches ever built.

Asked to economize production costs, Gugelot conceived a design that called for a simple, no-frills approach with flush fender lines, a recessed rear window, sharply raked windshield, recessed door latches (which became infamous for catching fingers), elongated running lights capping the upright front fenders, and distinctive blacked-out rocker panel and valence treatments. The most intriguing feature of the Gugelot design, however, was the "adaptation" of the Porsche Targa roof. Like the 911, the 914 had a removable roof panel that attached to the windshield header and Targa bar, the latter also accommodating the rear window, which was recessed into the structure. The easily removed roof panel was designed to stow in the *rear* trunk. That distinction was necessary since the mid-engine design permitted a *front* trunk as well. One thing the 914 wasn't short on was luggage space.

VW's newly designed 1679cc Type 411E (*Einspritzer*) fuel-injected four-cylinder engine powered both the European and export 914 models. With an output of 85 brake horsepower at 4,900 revolutions per minute, it had exactly the same bore and stroke, 90 mm × 66 mm, as the old VW-based Porsche Type 547/5 four-cam racing engine used in 1957. The addition of a VW-Bosch–designed fuel injection system also allowed the 914 export models to meet both federal and California exhaust emissions standards. Remember, this was at a time when there were forty-nine-state cars and California cars, something that drove domestic automakers crazy when California's more stringent emissions standards burdened an already troubled U.S. auto industry. Import automakers had to deal with the same problem, but Porsche managed to circumvent the dilemma by building a car that first met California standards, thereby automatically passing the federal requirements. (American automakers found this solution more problematic because certain engines simply could not meet California standards.)

The 914 models built for the home market were distinguished by the Wolfsburg (VW) emblem in the center of the steering wheel and were affixed with VW-Porsche badges. While that worked well in Europe, for American export the cars were sold through the new Porsche+Audi Division dealerships established in 1969 and jointly owned by Porsche and Volkswagen.* In the United States the 914 was considered a Porsche, thus it bore the company coat of arms in the center of the steering wheel and the PORSCHE name in chrome letters across the engine grille aft of the rear window. The Porsche crest, however, was conspicuously absent from the hoods of both European and export models. Many owners later added the Porsche crest to their cars. (The same was true of the Dino, which did not originally bear the Ferrari emblem, although many do today.)

The car was not well received by the American automotive press in 1970, which tended to view the new model as a poseur, a Porsche that wasn't a Porsche. The least praise came from the editors of *Car and Driver*, who wrote: "The 914 is a compact but

---

*A similar marketing plan was created in Germany under VW-Porsche GmbH and was again jointly owned by Porsche and Volkswagen.

spacious mid-engine sports car—a well-conceived machine." This was the literary lull before the storm. *Car and Driver* continued, "Brace yourselves, Porsche fanatics. That is the outer boundary of its excellence. The name Porsche is automatically associated with performance, mechanical refinement and quality workmanship—all assets of which the 914 is conspicuously bankrupt. It's about half the cost of a 911S—and about half as good as a 911S."

Although the four-cylinder 914 hadn't exactly been welcomed with open arms, the biggest criticism concerned performance, and thus Porsche saw the opportunity to build a sportier version by also equipping the car with a 911 engine. The result was the 914/6, which by virtue of its engine and assembly was actually a Porsche and not a VW. The 914/4 was built completely at Karmann utilizing VW components, whereas the 914/6 was finished at Porsche on the 911 assembly lines. Karmann delivered completed 914/6 bodies to the Zuffenhausen assembly hall, where they were fitted with the same 2-liter, six-cylinder, single overhead cam engine with twin triple-throat Weber carburetors used in the 1968–69 model 911T. The 914/6 was also equipped with larger brakes, ventilated 11.12-inch front discs and 11.26-inch solid rear discs, and 165 HR 15 tires

OPPOSITE AND ABOVE: The 914 and 914/6 created an entirely new genre of Porsche. Although in Europe the hybrid model was a Volkswagen, in the United States, Porsche's largest market, the VW-built 914 was sold as a Porsche. The 914/6 and 914/6 GT (pictured) were actually completed at the Zuffenhausen work hall and regarded as Porsche models.

mounted on five-lug-nut Porsche hubs. Mahle die-cast magnesium wheels were offered as an option, but more common, at least on models sold in the United States, were Fuchs forged aluminum wheels identical to those on the 911E.

ABOVE LEFT: The 914's interior was simple, functional, and basic in the way that the 356 Speedster's interior had been. Note the Porsche crest embossed in the center of the steering wheel. On European 914s the emblem was the Volkswagen coat of arms.

ABOVE RIGHT: The unusual body styling for the 914, created by Gugelot Design GmbH, featured pop-up headlights and elongated running lights capping the upright front fenders. The 914 was innovative if not a bit peculiar looking. As an entry-level model, it brought many new members to the Porsche family.

BELOW LEFT AND RIGHT: Beneath the engine grille, which had PORSCHE evenly spaced across its width, was the 125-horsepower, two-liter, six-cylinder, single overhead cam engine with twin triple-throat Weber carburetors. This was the same engine that Porsche had used in the 1968–69 model 911T.

While faster acceleration was the foremost objective of the 914/6, a quicker run from zero to 60 wasn't all that the 125-horsepower 914/6 offered owners. With its lower, wider stance and lower center of gravity, the mid-engine model enjoyed a 6 to 8 percent advantage in cornering over a comparable Porsche 911. On the skid pad the 914/6 recorded 0.9 g lateral acceleration, while the best a stock 911 could manage was 0.85 g. A 911S with racing tires could reach 0.93 g before breaking loose, but the 914/6 with the same tires could pull a remarkable 1.0 g! Treading on the territory of F.I.A. competition cars, the 914/6 turned into one of the best handling models ever produced and a favorite in Porsche Club, Sports Car Club of America, and International Motor Sports Association (IMSA) racing circles.

Ironically, what had started out as a significantly lower-priced model ended up costing Porsche KG more per body than the 911; thus the sticker price for the 914/6 was nearly the same as the 911T. *Road & Track* wrote in its review of the 914/6, "We'd probably pay the extra $431 for a 4-speed 911T, with its handsomer body, better detailing, extra years of development, slightly higher performance and +2 seating." Fortunately, the majority of reviews were far more favorable, as was the response to the 914/6, which helped *Motor Trend*'s editors decide on the Porsche 914 as the Import Car of the Year for 1970. In evaluating what *Motor Trend* christened "the first modern sports car for the masses," the 914 and 914/6 received accolades for their handling and braking. "The car is so stable, so flat in cornering, that you want to go quicker and quicker each time until you either exceed the machine's limit or your own, and usually the latter occurs first." The *Motor Trend* staff recorded a zero to 60 time of 12.4 seconds for the 914; 8.4 seconds for the 914/6; and quarter-mile times

Ferry Porsche (by car) was greeted by his engineers at Zuffenhausen with a very special 914, fitted with an eight-cylinder engine. The idea was considered for production, as was a 914/6 with the 911S engine, but only a handful of prototypes were ever built.

of 18.25 seconds and 16.06 seconds, respectively. In addition to the 1970 Import Car of the Year award, Porsche scored another triumph in the 914's debut year by winning the GT category and finishing sixth overall at Le Mans with a 914/6 GT. The following year the 914/6 of Peter Gregg and Hurley Haywood became the Under-2.5 Champion in IMSA's GT Series, with Gregg and Haywood winning their class in all six IMSA races and finishing first overall at Danville, Bridgehampton, and Summit Point.

After a few improvements to the 914's interior, even *Road & Track* was singing a different tune by 1972: "The 914 takes care of two people extremely well, with a high comfort level resulting from the combination of roomy interior, good seats, low noise level at cruising speeds and first-class weather protection from the convenient lift-off roof panel. There's nothing new to say about the handling and braking, which are excellent and give the 914 claim to the Porsche name. It's a car for the really enthusiastic driver." And enthusiastic they were. Porsche 914/4 owners were renowned for flogging their cars at every opportunity, mostly because the little two-seaters could take it, and being rewarded with an average of 22.5 miles per gallon and a cruising range of over 350 miles before refilling the 16.4-gallon fuel tank.

While the 914/6 was a natural out-of-the-box racer, for the general public the cars were viewed with a jaundiced eye. As *Road & Track* had noted, priced at only $431 less than a Porsche 911T, the base car was a hard sell in the United States. The retail price in 1970 was $5,999 on the East Coast and $6,099 on the West Coast, an average of $2,400 more than the four-cylinder 914! That was a lot to shell out for two more cylinders and a Porsche pedigree, but for some it was reason enough.

Following Porsche's string of victories with the 914/6, the company added the 914/6 GT version along with the M471 competition option group (which allowed anyone to make a 914/6 into a GT). This was a simply brilliant marketing ploy by Porsche+ Audi to reinforce the sportier image and the substantially higher price of the 914/6. By the mid-seventies, GT-styled 914s began to appear en masse—some real, some not. Adding to the confusion, Porsche produced a limited number of 914/6 bodies with flared front and

With his father behind the wheel, Ferdinand Alexander Porsche (center) regards the lines of the experimental 914/8 in September 1969. (PORSCHE WERKFOTO)

rear fenders, wider tires, and Fuchs wheels. The factory flared fender bodies, which were not to be confused with the 914/6 GT or M471 optioned cars, were intended for competition. Homologated for Group 4 competition, the 914 had finally earned the right to bear the Porsche name.

Fred Garretson, who with his race driver brother Bob re-engineered the Porsche 934s and 935s for Dick Barbour, Bobby Rahal, Brian Redman, Rolf Stommelen, and Paul Newman, noted, "The 914/6 GT was a pure performance car. It weighed around 1,500 pounds, and with the 911T 2-liter six-cylinder engine, it had rousing acceleration."

If the 914/6 had any shortcomings, outside of its unusual styling, Garretson says it was the car's shift mechanism. "The five-speed box didn't have the same crisp, almost hands-free detents that it had in the 911. Because of the way the mechanism was assembled in the 914/6, the stick felt sloppy, and it was easy to miss a shift." With about 3 inches of play in every direction, the 914's gearbox was the subject of continual criticism by the motoring press. The most scathing critique by one publication noted that "the shifter seems to be mostly neutral, i.e., you can find it in every gear."

The 914's gearbox was essentially the standard 911 transaxle turned end for end, with the ring gear moved to the other side of the differential carrier so that the car would go in the proper direction. (Otherwise, you would have had five speeds in reverse!)

In the U.S., Porsche + Audi referred to these as 914/6R models. Each came with the "R Competition Option Group." With widened steel fenders to accommodate 15x7 wheels in front and 15x8 Fuchs alloy wheels in back, oil cooling, 100-liter fuel tank, racing seats, "specific suspension," a "changeable gear transmission," performance exhaust, and the 911S braking system, Porsche charged $15,568 for this car. (RANDY LEFFINGWELL)

The 2-liter 911T engine, with an 80 mm × 66 mm bore and stroke and 8.6:1 compression ratio, was the least powerful and lowest-priced flat six available in 1968 and 1969. "It suffered from poor chain tensioners and did not have chain oilers like the newer 2.2-liter 911 engines," noted Garretson. It did clearly distinguish the old from the new, however. And if you wanted the new 2.2-liter Porsche engine, you still had to purchase a 911.

Garretson believes the standard four-cylinder 914 was one of the most underrated cars ever put on the road. "Granted, it wasn't a powerhouse, but it was probably one of the best handling automobiles that you could drive." The 914/6, though destined for greatness among racing enthusiasts, was not a great success commercially. The high cost of the specially built bodies, which was dictated to Karmann by VW in an effort to recoup tooling expenses over a shorter time, made the car virtually unmarketable for Porsche. After less than three model years, profits were so bleak that the 914/6 simply disappeared from the model line after 1972. The GT look, however, continued on throughout the 914's production run, thanks to a vigorous aftermarket that produced GT-style conversions, which led to many of the standard six-cylinder cars being modified to race in GTU and SCCA classes. "A lot of them were crashed and others just rotted away," says Garretson. Among the more than 118,000 Porsche and VW-Porsche 914s produced, only 3,360 were 914/6 models. Garretson estimates that fewer than half of them are left on the road today.

With the demise of the 914/6, the 914/4 was further improved for the 1973 model year with the addition of an optional 2-liter engine. With a 94 mm × 72 mm bore and stroke, displacement was increased to 1,971 cubic centimeters. The changes increased output to 100 horsepower on European models and, to meet U.S. unleaded fuel and emissions standards, 95 horsepower for the export models, which were certified for all fifty states. The base 1.7-liter four had to be detuned to meet California standards and developed an anemic 69 horsepower at 5,000 revolutions per minute. Porsche also remedied the 914's sloppy shifter with a new gearbox, the Type 914/12. Brakes, which were traditionally superior, were also further improved, and new aluminum alloy wheels forged by Fuchs were standard on the 2-liter cars; it was an additional $202 for the 1.7-liter base model 914.

Beginning with the 1973 models, Porsche changed the bumpers from chrome to matte black to better coordinate with the rubber trim and the original black rocker panels and aprons, although in the U.S. market, chrome bumpers remained standard on the more expensive 2-liter models and optional on the 1.7. Priced at $5,199, the 2-liter model, which was badged as the 914 2.0 beginning in 1974, was greeted by Porsche enthusiasts with open arms and wallets. *Car and Driver* wrote, "The 914 2.0 is a peppy sports car. Datsun 240Zs, Alfas and the Jensen-Healey might still have an edge in acceleration but the Porsche offers something in addition, it feels good to its driver. When you toe the pedal and grab another ratio in the 5-speed transmission you definitely reel in the pave-

ment." *Car and Driver* reported a zero to 60 time of 9 seconds, shaving 2.3 seconds off the 1.7 liter's best time and nearly matching the test results from the 1970 914/6.

In 1974 the base engine gained a little more displacement, increasing to 1.8 liters, and to meet new safety standards all models had black bumpers with black bumper guards. For 1974 the 914 recorded one of its best years with 21,370 sales, the second highest in the car's production history. New color schemes and trim were making the 914 more noticeable on the road. In Germany, Porsche AG bought out VW's interest in the manufacturing of the car, giving Zuffenhausen full marketing control, although in Europe the cars were still sold as the VW-Porsche. VW considered itself fortunate to be out of the joint venture, and perhaps its timing had been good. In order to meet increasingly stringent U.S. safety regulations, another redesign of the 914's bumper system was necessary for the 1975 model year. The new look was ungainly at best, with large rubber bumpers covering a box-section steel beam beneath. The 914 might have been safer by U.S. standards, but it looked bulky.

The 914's engines needed revisions as well to satisfy new emissions standards, and the 2-liter engine sacrificed both horsepower and torque to meet the federal mandates. Output was lowered to 84 brake horsepower at 4,900 revolutions per minute and torque fell to 97 pounds per foot at 4,000 revolutions per minute. With prices going up and performance going down, by the end of the 1975 model year the fate of the 914 was sealed. The 1976 models would be the last, and when production came to an end, a total of 118,976 cars had been built over six years: 115,596 in the 914 series, 3,360 six-cylinder 914/6s, and 20 experimental 916 models with more powerful six-cylinder engines, which Porsche had considered for production in 1972.

PORSCHE RACING HISTORY

FROM SCCA TO LE MANS

I have raced Porsches for over thirty years, both in Europe and the United States, and have been a part of the wonderful evolution of race cars over that period of time. My first drive for Porsche was with Peter Gregg and the Brumos race team at the 1973 Daytona 24 Hours. We won and went on to win again at the 12 Hours of Sebring a few weeks later. That started a long relationship with Porsche that has resulted in five championships, five Daytona 24-Hour wins, three victories at Le Mans, and two 12-Hour Sebring wins.

The cars that I have driven to achieve these successes have been many. The evolution begins with the 914/6 and runs through the 911 RS, 911 RSR, 934, 935, 917/10, 936, 956, 962, and 911 GT 1.

I am proud to have been a part of Porsche's past and look forward to being a part of its dynamic new future.

—HURLEY HAYWOOD

Author's note: Haywood made his final start in the 2012 Daytona 500 with his Porsche GT 3, finishing third in the GT class. Today, he is Chief Driving Instructor for the Porsche Sport Driving School.

PORSCHE HAS ACCUMULATED MORE OUTRIGHT VIC-
tories and class wins in World Championship sports car events,
hill climbs, and international rallies than any other automobile
manufacturer in history. It can be said that racing is in Porsche's
blood, but it was there long before the 356 and 911. It was there as
far back as the turn of the last century when Ferry Porsche's father
designed his first racing car, the Lohner-Porsche, built in 1900.

As chief engineer for Daimler-Benz in the 1920s, Ferdinand
Porsche designed the incomparable Mercedes-Benz SS and SSK,
and with such legendary drivers as Rudolf Caracciola, Christian
Werner, Otto Merz, Manfred von Brauchitsch, Adolf Rosenberger, and Hans Stuck, he brought Daimler-Benz its earliest
international victories. In one of Porsche's competition SS Mercedes, Caracciola surpassed 120 miles per hour in the 1927 Belgian
Speed Trial and won the first race ever held at the Nürburgring.

After resigning from Daimler-Benz AG in 1928, and establishing his own design and engineering firm in Stuttgart, Ferdinand Porsche, his son Ferry, and a staff of talented designers,
engineers, and craftsmen created the most successful German racing cars of the 1930s.

In 1934, Porsche's Auto Union Grand Prix car, powered by a
sixteen-cylinder engine mounted behind the driver, became the
firm's benchmark design. When the fuselage-shaped cars made
their first appearance, drivers Hans Stuck, the Prince of Leiningen, and August Momberger set three world records on the Avus
course, reaching a top speed of 180 miles per hour and averaging
134.93 miles per hour. In its first year the sixteen-cylinder Auto
Union race cars were victorious in the German Grand Prix at the
Nürburgring, the Swiss Grand Prix at the Bremgarten circuit in
Bern, and the Czech Grand Prix at the Masarykring in Brno.

For the Porsche family,
racing was in their blood
from the very beginning.
In 1922, Ferdinand Porsche
(leaning on the hood)
designed the little 1.5-liter
Austro-Daimler Sascha
sports cars. Neubauer
raced one in the 1922
Targa Florio in Sicily.
This is a second example
raced in 1922 in the
Targa Florio, driven by
Alexander Graf Kolowrat.
(PORSCHE WERKFOTO)

From the time that Ferry Porsche began to work at his father's side in the 1930s, he was enmeshed in the world of motor sports and surrounded by legendary drivers and the finest engineers and designers in Germany. In such an environment, Ferry also honed his skills behind the wheel, road testing the notoriously difficult to handle Auto Unions at competition speeds, and though he could have matured into a championship driver, Ferry's heart was in creating cars for others to race. But he was never far from the driver's seat.

Throughout the greatest years of Porsche racing, from the earliest competitions in the 1950s to the races at Le Mans, Nürburgring, Avus, and in America at Sebring and Daytona, Ferry Porsche was there in the pits, stopwatch around his neck, watching, encouraging—and figuring out ways to make his cars better. And every year they were.

The racing history of Porsche AG began with the first car built, Porsche No. 1, the 1948 mid-engine Gmünd roadster. This sporty two-seater was based on the principles of Porsche designs from the 1930s, including the sixteen-cylinder Auto Union and prototype VW Type 64 60K10.

Once in production, the VW-based rear-engine Gmünd coupes and cabriolets were raced enthusiastically by their owners, but

In 1934, Porsche's Stuttgart design and engineering studio created the sixteen-cylinder Auto Union race car. With its engine positioned behind the driver, it was an indication of things to come.
(PORSCHE WERKFOTO)

Ferry Porsche (third from left) reviews the design of a new engine in 1965. His younger son, Peter, looks on at the far right as Bertil von Schweden closely examines the design. Ferdinand Alexander Porsche (with beard) can be seen in the background. (PORSCHE WERKFOTO)

sports. By the end of 1951, Porsches had won their class in the Swedish Rally, Alpine Rally, Travemünde Rally, and Tour de France, and in the United States, American driver Briggs Swift Cunningham won the race at Palm Beach Shores.

Porsche's record in international road rallies, hill climbs, and endurance races includes hundreds of overall and class wins in the first fifty-four years of the company's racing history: A record sixteen outright victories and nearly one hundred class wins at Le Mans between 1951 and 2002; a record twenty-one victories in the Daytona 24 Hours from 1968 to 2003; a record seventeen wins in the Sebring 12 Hours from 1968 to 2002; a record eleven triumphs in Sicily's grueling Targa Florio from 1956 to 1973; eleven wins in the Nüburgring 1000km from 1967 to 1984;

Ferry Porsche saw something more in the basic design of the 356: The car needed only a few modifications to become a serious competitor. A trio of Gmünd coupes were prepared for the 1951 Vingt-Quatre Heures du Mans, the most important sports car race in Europe. Each car was fitted with full fender skirts to further reduce aerodynamic drag, larger capacity fuel tanks, finely tuned engines, and sturdier suspensions. Two of them, however, were written off prior to the race; the third, also damaged, was repaired in time for the start, and twenty-four hours later it finished first in class and twentieth overall. It was Porsche's first major racing victory and the beginning of a legacy unsurpassed in the history of motor

seven at the Spa-Francorchamps 1000km between 1969 and 1986; six at Monza from 1969 to 1985; and the two most important international sports/endurance championships in the world: the IMSA Camel GTP/GTX Championship, won nine out of ten years between 1978 and 1988, and the World Championship of International Endurance Racing, where Porsche recorded a remarkable thirteen victories between 1969 and 1986. Porsche also has thirty class wins in the new American Le Mans series from 1999 to 2003, the most of any auto manufacturer.

It would take an entire book to cover in detail more than half a century of Porsche racing, but the highlights, the great races, and the great cars are very much a part of the 356 and 911 story, and the evolution of the Porsche sports car over the last fifty-five years.

"To Ferry Porsche," said sports car historian Doug Nye, "racing was the great banner waver that would provide customs for his company, for his design bureau, and for his own talent, and that became inbred effectively within the Porsche family, and by the Porsche family I mean the wider group of engineers that they gathered around them." The people who made up Porsche, the company, were interested in every form of auto racing, from hill climbs, sprint races, and road rallies to the quixotic backdrops of Le Mans and Daytona.

Legendary race drivers like Phil Hill, Stirling Moss, Dan Gurney, Hurley Haywood, Jacky Ickx, Derek Bell, Peter Gregg, Vic Elford, Brian Redman, Mark Donohue, and Al Holbert came to Porsche during their careers to be on the factory team, to slide behind the wheel of the most advanced sports and race cars of their day, to drive, to win.

Along with Ferry, the guiding hand behind Porsche's early competition efforts was former race driver Huschke von Hanstein, the man responsible for the operations and indeed much of the company's early success. He was to Porsche what Alfred Neubauer was to Daimler-Benz: the maestro. And how beautifully he conducted that orchestra.

Although the 356 had been successful in most competitions, by the early 1950s Porsche and von Hanstein realized that to be really competitive they were going to need cars built specifically for racing, cars requiring none of the compromises necessary for the road. And thus was born the first purpose-built Porsche race car, the 550 Spyder. Von Hanstein was responsible for having more than one hundred examples in the 550 series produced and delivered to customers around the world.

Porsche's first purpose-built race car was the Type 550 Spyder. Factory driver Hans Herrmann drove this 1953 example to victory in the 1954 Carrera PanAmericana. After the race, the Carrera name became part of the Porsche lexicon.
(PORSCHE WERKFOTO)

The 550 Spyder became an instant hit in America. Here the legendary Ken Miles is seen in competition with a 1954 model in February 1957. (PORSCHE WERKFOTO)

later wrote that it was one of his greatest races. Moss was amazed at the car's performance and capabilities, as were Porsche's competitors. But there was much more to come from Zuffenhausen in the 1960s.

Ferry Porsche's eldest son, Ferdinand Alexander, had become the head of the styling department and, working in concert with the factory engineers, had designed what many regard as the most beautiful racing Porsche ever built, the 904 Carrera GTS. Often considered Ferdinand Alexander Porsche's signature car, more so than the 911, the 904 was a phenomenon. With a very short time available to develop the car for the 1964 season, the 904 went from concept to completion in an unprecedented six months!

The basis of the 904's design was a pressed-steel chassis onto which a lightweight fiberglass body was bonded. Mounted midship was Porsche's venerable four-cam, four-cylinder engine dispensing 185 brake horsepower through a five-speed gearbox. The cars were homologated into Group 3, meaning that one hundred examples had to be built, but selling the 904 wasn't a problem. It was affordably priced and also quite suitable as a road car. One of the first went to Stirling Moss.

The design of the Carrera GTS allowed a variety of engines to be utilized for competition, and Porsche built cars with the four-cam four, the new horizontally opposed six designed for the 911, and an eight-cylinder racing engine; but the four-cam, four-cylinder version was the most popular.

The 904 was succeeded in 1966 by the 906, a car built specifically for racing and wholly unsuitable for the road. The company's first dedicated race car, the 906 was the work of Ferdinand Porsche's grandson, Ferdinand Piëch. Like the 904, the 906 immediately cut a wide swath through the competition, scoring three major victories in 1966 with firsts in the Targa Florio, at Le Mans,

In the hands of Porsche factory drivers, the 550 Spyders were a stunning success both in Europe and abroad. In 1954, Hans Hermann won his class in the grueling Carrera PanAmericana road race in Mexico, forever linking the Carrera name to Porsche. Stirling Moss, who drove a 718 RSK in the 1958 Buenos Aires 1000km,

The 1960 Type 356B Carrera GTL, also known as the Abarth-Carrera, bodied in Italy by Zagato, was a more streamlined variant of the 356 Carrera. The more aerodynamic lines proved themselves at Le Mans when the Abarth version ran faster than the Reutter-bodied Carrera, clocking 138 miles per hour down the Mulsanne Straight. With a lower overall height and lower center of gravity, the Abarths seemed to handle better as well. From the rear, the deck lid was heavily louvered to allow the Type 692/3A engine to breathe.

and at the Circuit of Mugello. That same year American Sam Posey drove a 904 to victory at the Watkins Glen 500, and 911s won the German and Osterreichische rallies. There were also class wins at Daytona, Sebring, Monza, Hockenheim, Zandvoort, and the SCCA Sports Racing Championships in Class C Production and Class D Production. In all, 1966 was a very good year for the Porsche 904, 906, and 911.

The 906 evolved into the 910 in 1967 and was another stunning success on the world's racing circuits, along with the new 911S, which won four major races, finishing one, two, three in the Solitude Rally, and first in the Tulip Rally, Osterreichring, and Geneva Rally. In addition were class wins at Monte Carlo, Daytona, Sebring, Monza, Spa, Nürburgring, Le Mans, Rheims, BOAC, and Hockenheim. From the perspective of other racers, Porsche was almost unconquerable. Even Enzo Ferrari had to shake his head in wonderment. The 910 was similar to the 906, which was based on the 904; each successive version showed improvements in handling and performance. Carried over to the 910 was the basic frame design of the 906, a tubular structure of welded steel in which the tubes were used to carry oil to and from the front-mounted cooler. New running gear was the

OPPOSITE: Four ways to have gone Porsche racing in the late 1950s and early 1960s. Pictured in the foreground is a 1958 Model 718 RSK Spyder, and clockwise: a 1960 Type 356 GT coupe, 1964 Type 904 Carrera GTS, and a 1961 Porsche Abarth-Carrera 356 coupe.

ABOVE LEFT: Ferdinand Alexander Porsche admires a new 904 Carrera GTS, regarded as his signature design, at the Zuffenhausen assembly facility. (PORSCHE WERKFOTO)

BELOW LEFT: In production at Porsche for the 1964 season, homologation required that one hundred examples be built. Here the 904 is seen during construction, awaiting delivery. (PORSCHE WERKFOTO)

Two generations of legendary Porsche sports cars, the 718 RSK and the Porsche 904 Carrera GTS.

910's greatest improvement, with wheel diameters down from 15 to 13 inches and rim widths increased to 8 inches in the front and 9.5 inches in the rear. For the first time a Porsche race car was fitted with magnesium wheels.

An offshoot of the 910 was the 907, which was fitted with a more aerodynamic body. This is somewhat of an understatement considering the impact that the innovative new design would have on racing. The 907 in both short- and longtail versions and the new 908, powered by a horizontally opposed eight-cylinder engine, delivered a one-two punch in 1968, winning every major race for the year: the Daytona 24 Hours with three 907s finishing in order, the Sebring 12 Hours with a one, two finish, first in the Targa Florio;

and with the 908s, a one, two rout at the Nürburgring 1000km and one, two in the Austrian GP. The 911 and 911T capped off the season for Porsche with a first in the Swedish Rally and a one, two finish in the Monte Carlo Rally, the first time ever that a Porsche won the event outright.

The 908 became one of Porsche's most successful and longest-lived race cars, continuing on into the 1969, 1970 (908/2 and 908/3), and 1971 seasons. The 908 was a brand-new car with a brand-new engine, essentially the 911 flat six with two additional cylinders. Output was 335 brake horsepower, but by the end of the first season it had been increased by roughly another 35 brake horsepower. The chassis used the proven tubular space frame from the 907, and the fiberglass body was also styled along similar lines to the longtail. The cars were capable of reaching 200 miles per hour on the long straights, and in four seasons 908 series cars won nearly a dozen races outright, including first through third place sweeps at Brands Hatch, the Targa Florio, and Watkins Glen in 1969, and at the Nürburgring 1000km in 1971.

Porsche won the World Championship of Makes in 1969 with the 908, and concluded the 1970 season winning the World Championship of Makes for the second consecutive year, the World Rally Championship, and the World GT Trophy. Porsche was firmly entrenched as the dominant marque in rallying and endurance racing.

The 908s were retired after the 1971 season and replaced by the 917K, which had been introduced to the racing world in 1970. It scored outright victories at the Daytona 24 Hours, a one, two, three sweep at Brands Hatch, and firsts at Monza, Le Mans, Watkins Glen, and Osterreichring. (Porsche first introduced the Type 917 in 1969, but the design needed some shaking out and reappeared the following year as the 917K.) It has been said that

the 917K marked a turning point in endurance racing. Doug Nye noted, "In all motor racing history there are very, very few pinnacle cars, and in endurance racing, one of the ultimate all-time pinnacle cars is the Porsche 917 series."

For the 917, Porsche took the flat eight from the 908 and added four more cylinders to create a horizontally opposed twelve-cylinder engine displacing 4.5 liters and initially developing 580 brake horsepower at 8,400 revolutions per minute. The engine was increased to a swept volume of 4.9 liters late in 1969, adding another 10 brake horsepower to the cars at the beginning of the 1970 season. By the end of the year, output was closer to 600 brake horsepower. And another increase to 5 liters in 1971 brought the 917's flat twelve up to 630 brake horsepower at 8,300 revolutions per minute.

The 917s, fitted with varying body styles, were campaigned by Porsche, the John Wyer team, and Gulf Oil Company for three seasons, after which they were banned by the F.I.A., which changed the rules to eliminate the cars from the Manufacturers' Championship. Karl Ludvigsen wrote in *Porsche: Excellence Was Expected*, "At the end of the 1971 season Porsche summed up the results of the three years of intense and costly competition for the Manufacturers' Championship in which the 917 played such a dominant role."

The 917 established Porsche as the undisputed leader in world endurance racing, accounting for fifteen of the twenty-four championship events won by Porsche over the 1969–71 seasons. The other wins were contributed by versions of the 908. Fifteen drivers helped Porsche win the three championships; Jo Siffert shared ten victories, and Pedro Rodriguez and Brian Redman each contributed eight. In Porsche's three championship years, they were victorious each year at Monza, Spa, the Nürburgring, and Zeltweg.

With drivers Gijs van Lennep and Ben Pon, the Type 906 pictured, chassis number 906134, won the 2-liter class at the 1966 Nürburgring, finished first overall at Zandvoort, and in 1967, with Pon and Vic Elford, finished first in the sports car category and seventh overall at Le Mans.

Statistically, the winning Porsches in twenty-four races covered about 24,490 miles in some eight and two-thirds days, for an average speed of 116 miles per hour. "This was only 400 miles short of a full lap of the earth," noted Ludvigsen.

In three years Porsche and the 917s, of which thirty-seven were built, had written an unforgettable chapter in the history of endurance racing. But there was still more to come.

The United States was Porsche's largest market, yet the company's major racing presence was in Europe. In 1972, Ferry Porsche decided to remedy that situation. The company launched a Can-Am racing program, bringing to North America the same intensely focused effort that had brought them three consecutive Manufacturers' Championships in Europe. The 917 was about to get a new lease on life as the 917/10 Turbo, a 1,000 brake horsepower dreadnought that was the most powerful road racing car in history.

In 1972 the 917/10 was almost unbeatable. Porsche won the Road Atlanta, Mid-Ohio, Road America, Edmonton, Laguna Seca, and Riverside Can-Am races, with drivers George Follmer and Mark Donohue. Peter Gregg and Hurley Haywood teamed up to win the Daytona 6 Hours in a 911S, and Porsche ended the year with the Can-Am championship, winning six of eight races; the Interserie Championship; the European GT Trophy; the F.I.A. Cup for GT cars; and eight national championships.

Porsche followed its winning 1972 year with an even more powerful 917 model, the 5.4-liter 917/30, which Follmer and Donohue drove to a second Can-Am championship in 1973. The car's twin-turbocharged flat twelve-cylinder engine produced 1,100 brake horsepower! Nothing outside of a top fuel dragster or land speed record car had more horsepower. To prove the point, on August 9, 1975, Mark Donohue set a closed-circuit record average

ABOVE: The 906 was powered by a flat six mounted amidships and delivering between 220 and 225 brake horsepower. The engine, clutch, and transmission were derived from the production Porsche 911.

BELOW: The view that only Porsche team drivers Willy Mairesse, Herbert Müller, Gerhard Koch, and Jochen Neerspach had of the 906 in 1966. They all had first overall finishes in the Targa Florio and the Circuit of Mugello.

speed of 221.12 miles per hour on the banked oval track at Tal-ladega. Donohue's record stood for fifteen years.

When the factory-supported 917 program was concluded in 1973, one year after the departure of the Porsche and Piëch families from the company, the 917 had become one of the most successful race cars in the history of motor sports. Ferry had achieved his goal of making the cars as well known on American racetracks as they were in Europe.

There really was no substitute for a Porsche.

Although the 911 series competition cars are fully covered in Chapter Eight, they bear mentioning once again because of the significant role they played in the story of Porsche racing, a tale that began to change after the 1972 racing season.

Just as the Porsche factory race cars were gaining in power and performance, so, too, were the 911 models, which were being successfully campaigned by the company and privateers in road rallies, hill climbs, and various sports cars racing series around the world. In 1972, however, Porsche's highest performance model, the 911S, hit the wall, aerodynamically speaking. The original body designed by Ferdinand Alexander Porsche had finally reached aerodynamic limits that the engines designed by his cousin Ferdinand Piëch were capable of exceeding. With the 911S approaching speeds of 150 miles per hour, race drivers were experiencing lift at the rear, resulting in less than desirable oversteer through fast corners, and challenging even the best factory drivers to keep their cars under control.

What Porsche needed was a modified 911 body to better suit the engines and suspensions being developed for competition. The result was the RS 2.7, a carefully engineered redress—a lighter, more powerful, better-balanced, and more aerodynamic version of the 911S.

Ferdinand Piëch's 911R, developed in the experimental department of the new Weissach engineering and testing facilities in 1967, had already established the foundation for the RS 2.7, but it took five years, until the appointment of Dr. Ernst Fuhrmann as chairman of the Porsche executive committee in March 1972, before the decision was made to develop a racing-type 911.

As Porsche's technical director in 1971, Fuhrmann realized that the time had come to take advantage of Porsche's experience in Can-Am racing and translate that to the 911. "At the moment," said Fuhrmann in 1972, "we are ready to harvest the fruits of those years with the 908 and 917." The first car to be developed was the 1972 Carrera RS 2.7, essentially a refined version of Piëch's 911R.

An even more powerful model, the RSR, followed the RS 2.7. Built to order at Porsche's Werk I in Zuffenhausen, this became the factory's full racing model, the Carrera *Rennausstattung*.

In its first full year of production, 1973, with factory drivers Petermax Müller, Gijs van Lennep, Peter Gregg, and Hurley Haywood, the Carrera RSRs were the outright victors in the Targa Florio and Daytona 24 Hours and at Sebring.

The factory works cars campaigned by John Fitzpatrick, Toine Hezemans, and Gijs van Lennep won again in 1974 and 1975. Supported by the Porsche factory and sponsored by Gelo (Georg Loos Racing), the RSR was driven by Fitzpatrick to the F.I.A. G.T. Cup title in 1974, to class victories at Spa, the Nürburgring, Dijon, the Norisring, Imola, and to a stunning first in class and a fifth overall finish at Le Mans in 1975.

The 1974 Carrera 3.0 RSR can best be defined as an evolutionary car; its design and engineering evolved over a number of years through the advancement of RS and RSR types, rooted as far back as the 911R, and progressing through the 2.7-liter RS and

CLOCKWISE FROM LEFT: The evolution of the 911 competition car began with the 911S but quickly matured into the Carrera RS 2.7 and 3.0 RSR, the latter being a flat-out race car available directly from Porsche. For 1974 the factory produced 108 Carrera 3.0 RS models homologated in Group 3 and 37 of the Type 911 3.0 RSR models pictured for Group 4 competition.

For the World Championship of Makes in 1976, Porsche developed an all-new 911-based race car, the 935, powered by a turbocharged flat-six engine delivering over 500 brake horsepower. Body work for the 935 was completely new and had a long slanted front end, wider fenders, and a high rear wing.

Porsche race cars had traveled a lot of miles by the time the Type 956 was introduced in 1982. When looking at this spectacular car, it is hard to believe it is now more than a decade old. The 956 Porsches won Le Mans in 1982, 1983, 1984, and 1985.

OPPOSITE AND ABOVE: While Porsche was establishing unbreakable records in endurance racing, there was plenty of activity on the 911 production line with specially built competition cars such as the 1989 Porsche 911 C4 Lightweight. The customer racing department in Weissach produced only twenty copies of the hand-built Lightweight model, priced at roughly $150,000 apiece.

ABOVE RIGHT: In 1976, Porsche could claim a dual World Championship for Production Sports Cars and for Race Sports Cars. Pictured are the 1976 Type 935 Turbo, with the winning Type 936 from Le Mans with (left to right) Manfred Schurti, Rolf Stommelen, race manager Manfred Jantke, Jochen Mass, and Jacky Ickx.

BELOW RIGHT: A successful trio of Porsches: the 911 2.0 "Monte" of 1965, with which Porsche celebrated the car's successful sporting premiere in the 1965 Monte Carlo Rally; the famous 1978 Model 935 "Moby Dick," which became the most successful vehicle in the era of the near standard race sports car, with victories in the World Championship of Makes in 1976 and 1977; and the 961 coupe of 1987, a circuit version of the Porsche 959 that raced at Le Mans and Daytona.

2.8-liter RSR series. The amazing thing is that no matter how different the 2.7 and 3.0 were, they were still 911s. From 1973 to 1976, Carrera RS and RSR models won titles in virtually every type of road race and hill climb championship held in the United States and Europe.

For the World Championship of Makes in 1976, Porsche developed an all-new 911-based race car, the 935, powered by a

The 956 was one of Porsche's most "stylish" racing cars, establishing a look that evolved into the 962 version shown. (PORSCHE WERKFOTO)

turbocharged flat six engine delivering over 500 brake horsepower. Body work for the 935 was completely new, with a long, slanted front end, wider fenders, and a high rear wing. The aerodynamics of the car combined with the more powerful turbocharged engine gave Porsche just the edge it needed to win the World Championship of Makes title in 1976.

Another development of the racing program was the 936, which Porsche had designed for Le Mans, again with the desired results, winning the Vingt-Quatre Heures du Mans with drivers Jacky Ickx and Jochen Mass. The pair also won the 1976 races at Circuit de Mugello and Dijon in the 935.

In 1981, Ickx and Derek Bell drove another purpose-built Porsche race car, with a twin-turbocharged and intercooled flat six of 2.65 liters, giving Porsche yet another victory at Le Mans. In 1983, Porsche won the 24 Hours again with the all-new monocoque body 956, driven by Vern Schuppan.

The 956 Porsches won in 1982, 1983, 1984, and 1985, after which they were retired in favor of the new 962 model, which won Le Mans twice more in 1986 and 1987. At this point you can imagine that other automakers were growing weary of seeing Porsches in the winner's circle after seven consecutive years!

In International Motor Sports Association (IMSA) competition, Porsche teamed with American race driver Al Holbert, and the Porsche team won the IMSA Camel GTP/GTX Championship nine out of ten years between 1978 and 1988.

With the exception of the Indianapolis 500, Porsche had won

OPPOSITE: The 956 models were replaced by the 962, which won two more Le Mans titles for Porsche in 1986 and 1987, bringing Porsche's consecutive winning streak at the Circuit de La Sarthe to seven.

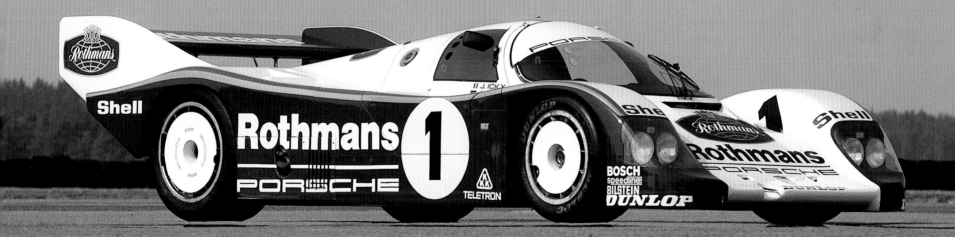

championships in every type of motor sports competition in the world, including the grueling 7,500-mile Paris-Dakar Rallye in January 1984, with René Metge steering the all-wheel-drive 953 through the African desert. In the 1986 Paris-Dakar race, covering 8,750 miles, Metge finished first in the new all-wheel-drive Porsche 959, with Jacky Ickx coming in second. Porsche built two hundred of the 200-mile-per-hour, 450-horsepower 959 models, the most expensive and exclusive road car produced by the company up to that time.

In the early 1990s, Porsche returned to GT racing with the 911 Carrera and to the Circuit de La Sarthe to compete in the new GT category. Converted 962 models provided the basis for the GT entries, which not only won their class but finished first overall in the 1994 Le Mans day-into-night marathon.

By 1996, Porsche had won the French 24 Hours thirteen times. In the GT-1 category, Porsche entered two brand-new cars and another pair in the prototype category, winning the race for the fourteenth time with a first-through-fourth-place sweep.

The following year, water-cooled and updated GT-1 cars were back on the starting grid, but both were knocked out of the race—one crashed and the other caught on fire. Yet Porsche prevailed with a third entry, the 1996 prototype, which won for the company its fifteenth outright victory at Le Mans. In 2002, Porsche won again for an unprecedented sixteenth time, the most of any automaker in the history of the race.

With the air-cooled era coming to a close, Porsche's future on the race tracks of the world has remained one of multiple triumphs, right up to the 2015 victory at LeMans—the company's seventeeth win at the Circuit de La Sarthe, proving that air and water do mix. But it is the heritage of the air-cooled competition cars upon which Porsche's fortunes were built, and today these fabled cars are still campaigned in sports car club and vintage races the world over, perpetuating a lineage that traces back to Ferdinand Porsche's first competition cars. Both on road and on track, for more than a century, the Porsche name has stood for uncompromising performance, quality, and engineering. As it was in 1900, when Ferdinand Porsche built the first car to bear the family name, a Porsche is designed to achieve one goal and one only—to be the best.

OPPOSITE: The 1983 Porsche 911 SC RS was another limited-production model produced at Weissach. Again, only twenty were built for amateur motor sports and equipped with 935 cylinder heads, more radical cams, and other race-tested equipment. Intended for serious competition, the SC RS delivered 225 brake horsepower and was capable of a top speed of 158 miles per hour. The cars were also equipped with 911 Turbo disc brakes. For Group B racing the SC RS had aluminum front fenders, front deck lid and doors, plastic bumpers and front air dam, and thinner window glass; it weighed only 2,115 pounds.

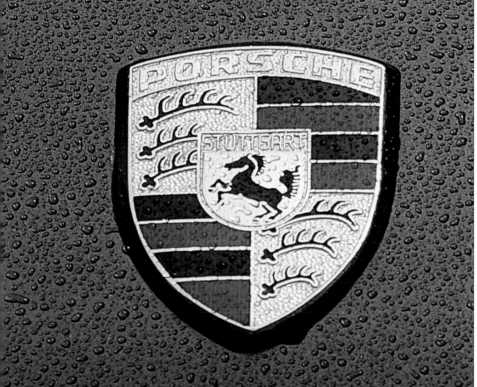
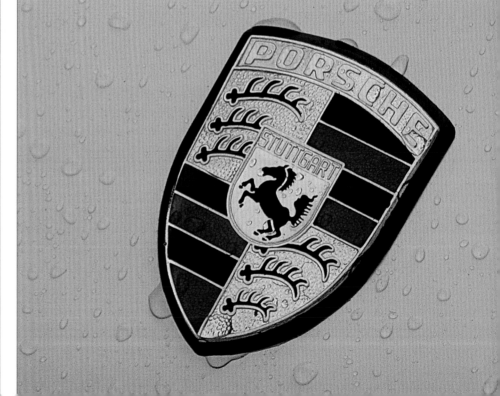

CHAPTER 13

PORSCHE IN PRINT

THE HISTORY OF PORSCHE ADVERTISING AND POSTER ART

THIS CHAPTER presents but a small cross-section of the prime collectibles associated with Porsche and its cars. There are literally thousands of pieces of collectibles—from the extremely expensive to the absolutely free, from large to small, covering more than one hundred years of history, and all Porsche. Porsche collectibles run the full range of factory-printed materials, including racing commemorative posters, showroom display posters, sales brochures, technical literature, and owner's manuals; factory gift and advertising items; factory awards and trophies; toys and models—some of them sold by the factory; and magazines devoted to the marque. This chapter concentrates on collectibles originally issued by the factory and items most popular among collectors.

—PRESCOTT KELLY[*]

[*]The items shown in this chapter are from the Prescott Kelly collection. Mr. Kelly is a contributing editor at *Porsche Panorama*, the magazine of the Porsche Club of America, specializing in research articles on famous historic Porsche race cars and drivers. He also writes a monthly column on Porsche collectibles for *The 356 Registry Magazine*. He vintage-races a 1972 Porsche 911 2.5-liter FIA coupe (ex–Peter Gregg and Jacques Bienvenue) and owns four show car 356s and early 911s.

FROM THE PRIMITIVE BEGINNINGS IN GMÜND, ONLY sales brochures and the owner's manuals emerged as future collectibles. With the move back to Stuttgart in 1950, however, things quickly became more interesting. Almost as soon as the quirky little 356 began to register class wins in rallies and road races, the factory started issuing posters to commemorate those victories. Springing from Ferdinand Porsche's earliest years with Lohner-Porsche, on to Austro-Daimler, then with the Daimler-Benz SSK-SSKLs, and finally the Auto Union Silver Arrows, the fledgling Porsche firm understood the publicity value of racing competition successes.

In June 1951, Porsche had its first important international race victory, a 1,100-cubic-centimeter class win at Le Mans in the silver "356SL" Gmünd coupe with spatted wheel openings, driven by Auguste Veuillet and Edmond Mouche. To celebrate that victory, Porsche forged a long-term partnership that would prove extremely beneficial for the factory—and collectors. Richard von Frankenberg, a motor sports journalist and able racing driver, began to do public relations and advertising work for Porsche. (Later, of course, he would go on to drive impressively for Porsche, especially at Le Mans, where he registered class wins in 1953, 1955, and 1956.)

TO GO WITH HIS WRITING, von Frankenberg recruited graphic artist Erich Strenger to execute artwork. Their first collaboration was this beautiful poster of a red coupe with the number 46 of the Le Mans car—but obviously not the silver color. By the time the poster was ready, the moment for the Le Mans class win had probably passed, and the poster was subsequently issued in three variants. One was plain, with no overprint; the second commemorated Porsche's September 1951 world speed records set

at Monthléry; and "Porsche announces new successes" is the third overprint—Briggs Cunningham's class victory in the December 1951 Palm Beach Road Races, and the Picard/Nizza class win in Morocco.

ERICH STRENGER quickly became art director for all of the factory's printed materials, including posters, sales brochures, and the factory magazine, *Christophorus*. In addition to his painting, he also did a lot of inspired photography for Porsche. Most of Strenger's early art is very collectible—not just among Porsche aficionados but among general ephemera collectors as well. Among the most sought after is this poster, the first true Le Mans commemorative, coming after Jon Claes and Paul Stasse took

prototype 550.12 to a class win in the June 1954 running of the Sarthe classic. Its wonderful coloring, depiction of the historic Dunlop Tire Bridge, and interpretative image of the Spyder make it very collectible.

(BELOW) PORSCHE ISSUED POSTERS for both the 1953 and 1954 Carrera PanAmericana road races. In an interesting

interpretation of what denotes the "new world," both posters featured large depictions of pre-Columbian art positioned above the silver Spyders. This is the 1954 version, commemorating Hans Herrmann's first in class and third overall finish—a result that led to the factory's use of the word "Carrera" on significant race and high-performance cars in the 1950s, 60s, and early 70s. Later, the name was applied to production street cars, where its use continues.

(RIGHT) A LAST NOTEWORTHY 1954 poster was set on the brick banking at Avus with a 356 coupe leading a silver Spyder. The overprint celebrated five German Championships won by Porsche. As is true of many Porsche racing victory commemorative posters, this one mentioned sponsors Dunlop and Castrol. Factory posters that depict 356s attract extra attention because of that model's fanatical following, making them even more difficult to obtain. Most of these early posters were relatively small in size at about 16.5 inches by 24 inches.

(FAR RIGHT) BY 1956, Erich Strenger had evolved his style into an even more painterly, interpretative technique. Two highly prized images exemplified this style. The first was this image of a red Spyder in front of a yellow 356 coupe, speeding past an imaginative interpretation of spectator stands. It is probably the single most sought-after Porsche poster—because of its artistic merit and the combined depiction of a Spyder and a 356. It exists in several overprints. In addition to the one shown here for the 1956 Le Mans, with copy harking back to the string of class victories since 1950, other commemorations that used this artwork were 1957's Le Mans and Rheims in combination, the 1957 Mille Miglia, and the 1957 Senegal Grand Prix.

PORSCHE FREQUENTLY ISSUED these early posters in several languages, always in German and most often in French and English as well. Later, some posters were issued in only the language of the race's host country, very notably the 1970s and 1980s Can-Am, Interserie, and IMSA posters.

Strenger executed the second 1956 poster of note to commemorate Huschke von Hanstein's first in class and third overall finish at the Swiss Hill Climb. For this event, the factory overprinted a red-and-white Swiss cross next to the silver Spyder, set against a background of extremely colorful mountains. Porsche used this image a second time—but without the Swiss Cross—for the 1957 Swiss Hill Climb, won overall by Wolfgang von Tripps in another Spyder. It appeared a last time to commemorate the Jean Behra/Scarlatti and Huschke von Hanstein/Cucci class victories in 1958's forty-second running of the Targa Florio. These 1956 posters are larger than the earlier posters, which were 24 inches by 33 inches, the size dominant from the mid-1950s into the mid-1960s.

TO CELEBRATE SIGNIFICANT CLASS WINS at the 1958 Sebring 12 Hours race, Strenger executed a different type of painting. It did not depict a car, but instead a close-up of a helmeted, begoggled driver against a bright red background. No driver was named; it would be 1968 before a real driver was featured and the 1980s before it was commonplace.

THROUGH THE REMAINDER of the 1950s and into the 1960s, Porsche increasingly turned to photographs for their posters. One of the last great Strenger paintings came in 1964 for the Type 904's overall and class victories in four events. This poster is huge, about 33 inches by 46.5 inches. On a wall it dominates the room—and frequently the conversation.

IN THE PHOTOGRAPHIC ERA, one of the most desirable posters is this depiction of the winning 910 at the Nürburgring in 1967, driven by Joe Buzzetta and Udo Schutz. The reason for its popularity is obvious: a 910 in full flight is an appealing image. Although this poster came after print quantities began to increase, it is nonetheless very difficult to find and brings prices close to those for the older 356 Spyder–era pieces.

THIS 1968 TARGA FLORIO victory poster is believed to be Porsche's very first to depict only the driver and no race car; the driver is Vic Elford, an Englishman. In 1960, Wolfgang von Tripps was featured for his European Hillclimb Championship, and in late 1968, Gerhard Mitter was featured for his European Hillclimb Championship, but in both cases the drivers were shown in their cars.

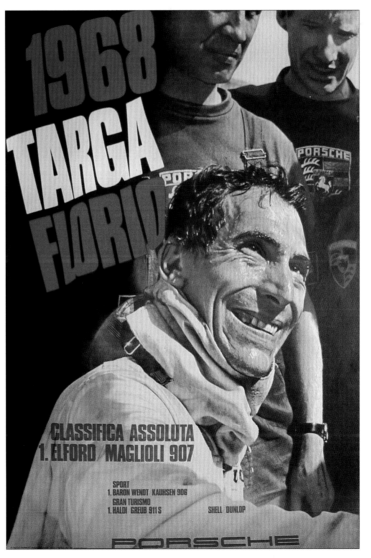

THE 1969–70 WORLD CHAMPIONSHIP racing seasons generated a lot of interesting posters. One such is this follow-up to the Elford poster, in this case with a well-known movie star who also happened to be a terrific motorcycle racer and race car driver. Because both Porsche and movie fans seek out this image, it is hard to acquire today—and expensive when you do.

THIS FOUR-COLOR PHOTOGRAPHIC depiction is of the Jo Siffert and Brian Redman 908-3 at the fifty-fourth running of the Targa Florio in 1970. Note that the distinctive red-and-white Swiss cross painted on the helmet is the tip-off that Siffert was driving. The terrific action image and the enduring popularity of Brian Redman, especially in the United States, make this a highly sought-after poster.

THIS POSTER has a great story behind it, although it could well be apocryphal. Porsche had issued posters for all of its consecutive Monte Carlo Rally victories, 1965 through 1970. During the 1971 running, the Alpine-Renault team was in the lead over the Porsche 914 GTs. The Alpine team chided their opponents that Porsche wouldn't be issuing a poster that year, unless they wanted to be real sportsmen and congratulate Alpine-Renault. So that is what Porsche did, making this the only Porsche non-victory rac-ing poster. Because the factory most likely limited the print run on this poster, and because it is one of only three factory racing posters to feature the 914, it is quite collectible today.

THE CAN-AM ERA is one of the highlights in Porsche history because the 917-10 and the 917-30 dominated the series in 1972 and 1973. Porsche issued a poster for every single one of those victories, and they are very collectible—and fortunately also readily available and therefore inexpensive. All of the Can-Am posters, except the 1972 Final Standings, use black-and-white photographs of the cars, most frequently with several bright background colors. Occasionally the black-and-white photo is "toned." That is what Porsche did on this stylized 1972 Riverside poster. Among collectors, the California races at Riverside and Laguna Seca are the most desirable.

A RELATIVELY RARE Can-Am image was this black-and-white photo, believed to have been issued by Porsche's West Coast distributor. It detailed three impressive wins by George Follmer at Road Atlanta, Mid-Ohio, and Road America. Because the poster was not widely distributed, it is relatively rare today.

THE PHOTOGRAPHS used on Porsche posters became almost exclusively four-color starting in 1974. That year, Martini was Porsche's racing sponsor and partner, and they took responsibility for a series of six posters that commemorated the major European championships and Le Mans, all of those won by Martini-Porsche cars. One favorite is the poster that featured a 2.1-liter "baby" Turbo Carrera RSR, the direct progenitor of the fire-breathing 934s and 935s.

THIS VICTORY POSTER for the 1989 24 Hours of Daytona is one much sought after. The Busby-Miller team had two colorful cars entered. Derek Bell, the late Bob Wollek, and young John Andretti drove this car, number 67. John's uncle and cousin, Mario and Michael Andretti, were in the number 68 car. The reflective numerals and decals create a memorable image against the nightscape.

IF THE CAN-AM 917 ERA WAS POPULAR with Porsche racing fans, then the 956–962 era was very popular. There are many, many victory posters from these years, 1982 to 1991, but perhaps the one that epitomized this era was this "Porsche 962: 0 to 50 [victories] in 4.6 years" poster issued in 1990. It is readily available, not expensive, and tells a story. It also benchmarked the end of Porsche's surprising string of racing dominations. With the financial disciplines required of a small public company, and with a lot of Porsche family mouths to feed, the factory did not fund a racing campaign in the dozen-plus years after the 962 faded away.

WHILE THE RACING POSTERS were sent to dealers for showroom display as well as for sale or gifting to customers, there were other posters clearly intended for showroom use. They featured advertising copy and demonstrated marketing features. Porsche issued one of the earlier suites of showroom posters over the months between August 1961 and April 1962. At 33 inches by 46.5 inches, they are the largest size that Porsche ever used, and they are very colorful.

These posters put 356s in several sporting and lifestyle contexts. The posters featured golf ("the sport for men with personality"), skiing ("the perfect sporting partner"), hunting ("for carefree country life"), and horseback riding ("a real pleasure in sports car driving")—a notable non se-quitur. The factory also issued a postcard set that used these images.

PORSCHE of America produced one of the most intriguing posters in 1964. Collectors believe that PoA originally planned a suite of four posters, featuring 356s in scenes depicting the four seasons, but only the winter scene was ever printed. It is a stylish poster, with attractive artwork. It is quite rare and desirable today.

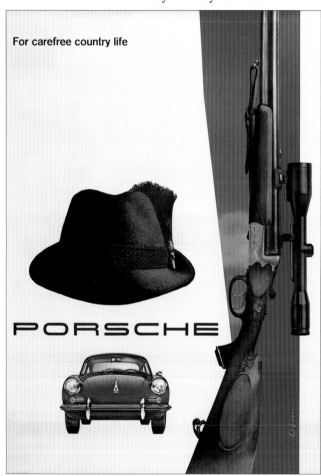

For carefree country life

PORSCHE

PORSCHE

(RIGHT) **PORSCHE STEPPED UP** the pace of issuing showroom posters with the arrival of the 911 series. In the mid-1960s the factory issued several "introductory" posters for the 911. This one featured several views of the 911 with the legend "A new coupe for the man who has 'arrived,' " plus fulsome technical specifications.

(LEFT) **THIS 1967 POSTER** was a lovely example that sold the dual uses of the relatively new Porsche 911. It was a large poster (30 inches by 40 inches), and—like most showroom posters—it was in "landscape" format versus the vertical format typically used for racing posters.

THIS POSTER IS ALSO FROM 1967 and is noteworthy for its brilliant colors that will dominate a wall when framed and displayed. It featured the new soft-window Targa.

THE 1973 CARRERA RS was an epochal model for Porsche-philes. The literature and memorabilia associated with the car are all very collectible, but this poster is perhaps the most scarce and desirable, despite its lack of color. It exists in at least two forms: this plain one, and a second one overprinted with performance specifications (in German only).

THIS SHOWROOM POSTER was published by Porsche Cars North America in 1991. It featured the Turbo and used a tag line that became a classic: "There are leaders and there are followers. Life is really quite simple, isn't it?"

EVEN COLLECTORS who do not highly value showroom posters often want this red Turbo example. The "flying Turbo" poster was actually mailed out as a consumer promotion by Porsche Cars North America with the recipient's name printed in the license plate area. Evidently many collectors either did not receive or did not save this poster because literature and poster dealers are frequently asked for it.

There are leaders and there are followers.
Life is really quite simple, isn't it?

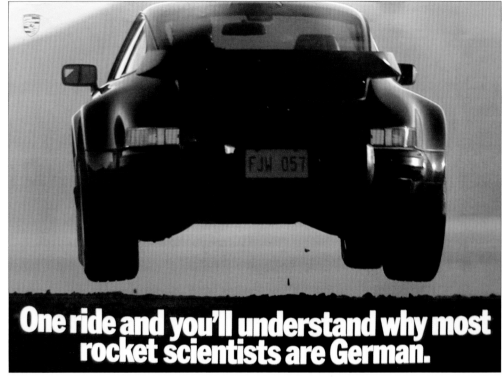

One ride and you'll understand why most rocket scientists are German.

STARTING IN THE EARLIEST DAYS, many Porsche owners kept the sales literature they picked up when they bought a new car. Other Porsche fans regularly visited dealerships and picked up promotional brochures to feed their interest in the marque. A few dedicated aficionados attentively sought all known sales literature for their collections. That all changed in 1978 when Susann Miller and Dick Merritt put together a sourcebook: *Porsche: Brochures and Sales Literature, 1948–1965*. This book (silver cover), published by John Barnes, then of Scarsdale, New York, illustrated fifty-seven different pieces from the 356 era. Ms. Miller subsequently obtained the copyright and published a revised hardback edition (white cover) in 1985 that added twenty-

eight more sale brochures. Now known as "Merritt-Miller," or simply "M & M," these editions illustrated the breadth of the available 356 pieces. The book spurred collecting Porsche sales literature to become a big hobby. Of course, 911, 914, 928, and 924/944 owners and enthusiasts went their own ways, and fortunately the factory and the aftermarket were happy to help.

THE VERY FIRST PORSCHE SALES brochure was issued in 1949 to promote the VW-based, aluminum-bodied prototypes that the war-exiled Porsche firm built in Gmünd, Austria. Printed in Vienna by H. Kapri & Company, the piece featured interpretative artwork of a coupe and cabriolet, although only the Beutler Brothers Karosserie in Thun, Switzerland, ever built a convertible on a Gmünd chassis. When the factory returned to Stuttgart to start series production in 1950, this piece was reissued with changed specifications, moving from an aluminum body, mechanical brakes, and an engine of 1,131 cubic centimeters to a steel body, hydraulic brakes, and 1,098 cubic centimeters.

LATER, IN 1950 OR EARLY 1951, the third factory sales brochure was issued. This piece is Porsche's first full-color sales brochure. Called "1900–1945," it draws attention to the automotive design heritage of Ferdinand Porsche, Sr., by illustrating on its cover his historic designs for the Lohner-Porsche chaise, Austro-Daimler Prince Henry, Mercedes-Benz SSK, the Auto Union land speed record racer, and the Volkswagen. The copy inside goes even further by detailing the parallels between these great cars and the new car bearing the professor's surname.

IN LATE 1951, Erich Strenger painted his first sales folder. It featured handsome painterly artwork of a bent-window coupe. This brochure was evidently printed in huge quantities because later, when the 1500 Super engine was introduced, the factory adroitly glued a new engine specs panel on the back cover and continued to use this brochure through 1952.

THE STANDARD PIECE for 1953 and for 1954, with a cover color change from green to blue, was a large foldout that had a marvelous inside spread. This spread was reformatted and used for the 1954 introductory brochure for the Speedster. Measuring a fulsome 17 inches by 18 inches, the spread had a new element: profiles of four men who were key to the design of the 356: In addition to Ferry and his father, chief engineer Karl Rabe and body designer Erwin Komenda were featured. This piece also increased the range of historic designs used versus the earlier "1900–1945" piece to include the NSU prototype (predecessor to the VW), the Cisitalia Grand Prix racer, and an additional Auto Union, a Grand Prix race car.

IN 1954, Porsche also issued a dealer showroom book designed for potential retail customers to look through. This wonderful and most rare collectible is hand-assembled with photographs that are glued on sheets and inserted into plastic page holders. Both the new Spyder and the new Speedster are featured, complete with specifications and photographs. Also included are exterior paint, seat material, and rug material samples for the colors in which the Speedster was introduced: red, white, and blue. Updated or new showroom books were issued for each new model through the 356 era. In between issues, Porsche produced new specification sheets and fresh photographs so that dealers could update their books. As a result, it is rare to find absolutely identical 356 and 356A showroom books.

IN 1955 four separate A4-sized (8.25 inches by 11.625 inches) single sheets were used to promote the four models: coupe, cabriolet, Speedster, and Type 550 Spyder. These sheets used both new and older photographs, some retouched. Collectors especially prize the Speedster and Spyder sheets. The Spyder sheet featured one of the prototype, flat-front, factory team cars at the August 1954 running of the 1000km of Nürburgring.

SOME OF THE RAREST Porsche literature pieces are the single sheets and folders issued to help sell and explain factory-available accessories. The 1950s pieces for Blaupunkt radios, sunroofs, and luggage racks are very rare and expensive, but not especially attractive or interesting. The attractive 1956 piece on accessory luggage, however, is readily available and covers one of the most sought-after period accessories. It was one of the first sales pieces printed with trilingual text—German, English, and French—in order to use the same printing broadly.

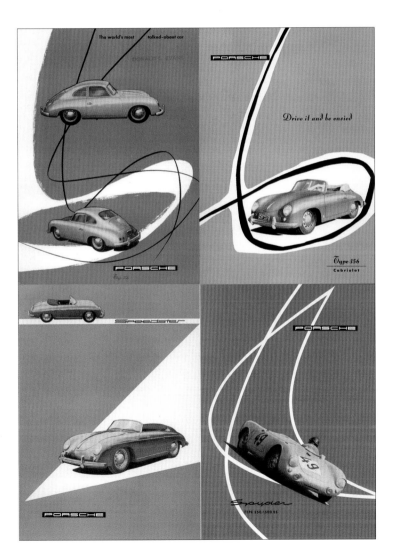

275

ONE OF THE MOST BEAUTIFUL and desirable sales brochures ever produced by the factory was the 1957 Carrera piece featuring a very painterly and interpretative cover by Erich Strenger. The piece was printed in at least German, English, and French. Today four-cam, 356, and general automobile literature collectors all want this attractive piece. The inside spread talked about both the Carrera GT (125 horsepower SAE) and the Carrera Deluxe (115 SAE horsepower), and the back cover was devoted to specifications. The cover explained that the name for the Carrera model was taken from the Mexican road race where Porsche achieved those mid-1950s competition successes.

THERE WERE NOT A LOT of Karosserie-built Porsche specials, certainly not when compared to many famous French, English, or Italian marques. One coach builder did have an early tie to Porsche—the Thun, Switzerland–based Beutler brothers. In the late 1940s, Beutler bought six of the Gmünd chassis and built the first Porsche cabriolets on them. Later, from 1956 through 1959, Beutler used both Volkswagen and Porsche pans with Porsche running gear to make extended-pan, four-passenger, aluminum-bodied coupes and one 1959 cabriolet. In 1960, Beutler built a series of cars that looked much more Porsche-like than their earlier specials. These earlier Beutler-Porsches had been sold off typed sheets and loose photographs put together in "sales kits" and mailed to individual inquiries, but for the 1960 model, Beutler issued this four-page sales brochure.

STARTING VERY EARLY in the firm's existence, Porsche had standard, lower-cost sales sheets and brochures for broad-scale dealer handout, and more elaborate and more expensive "deluxe" sales brochures for "serious" customers. The deluxe brochures were larger, had more pages, had more four-color printing, and sometimes had special die cuts or glued-in enclosures. The 1962 deluxe brochure had a die-cut window in its cover through which showed a 356 coupe on the road in front of a black Volkswagen coupe, although it was late in the day for Porsche to acknowledge the VW heritage of their expensive sports car. Was Porsche still grateful for the financial support that Volkswagen extended when they started paying royalties on the Beetle in the early 1950s?

PORSCHE DID NOT ISSUE SALES brochures for all of its race cars. After the mid-1950s pieces on the 550 Spyder, the factory did not issue individual ones for later Spyders. For the 1964 introduction of the 904, however, Porsche printed a four-page brochure, although only in the German language. Issued in three editions of small quantities, this brochure is relatively available but still quite desirable. In 1969, Porsche issued another plain black-and-white race car sales brochure for the prototype run of twenty-five short-tail 917 coupes. It was never widely distributed because Porsche moved on to different 917 configurations almost immediately.

(BELOW) THE 356C/SC was the most common of the bathtubs, coming at the end of the run of the model. With so many of the model extant, its sales literature is very popular—and readily available. For the 356C, Porsche of America issued its own sales literature in addition to importing and distributing the pieces developed by the factory. One of the popular Porsche Club of America pieces is this twelve-page brochure with a glossy white card stock cover, a readily available brochure. Most often it had a die-cut window looking through to the rear end of a New Jersey–registered 356C. Although this brochure was printed in Germany, many other Porsche Club of America–developed pieces were printed in the United States. They tended to be simple black-and-white creations.

(RIGHT) ANOTHER very collectible piece for the 1973 Carrera RS is the only sales brochure issued for the car. It is an interesting piece, with a unique cover that showed many very small photos of an RS on a test road course, perhaps the Weissach test track. Throughout the brochure, prototype RS models are displayed with side decals that were abandoned before the production car was finalized. As a result, the factory included a black-and-white sheet that explained the new side decals. Another very desirable RS piece is the small blue owner's manual supplement that detailed the changes in the RS versus stock 911s (not shown).

THE 1971–77 DELUXE SALES BROCHURES for the 911 were handsome pieces of impressive size, almost 10 inches by 14 inches. These pieces were expensive to produce and had glued bindings, heavy coated stock, and lacquered covers, and were typically sixteen glossy pages. The first editions featured close-ups of rear-engine lid grilles; the later ones focused on front fenders. These brochures usually included separate four- or six-page folders of technical data that were inserted inside the back cover.

IN 1994 THE FACTORY BEGAN TO USE small-format books, in both hardcover and soft, as deluxe sales brochures. These pieces are very popular with owners of the models covered and have a budding following among literature collectors as well. They had high production values and are certainly durable. The 1994 and 1995 editions had stylized covers, especially the colorful Speedster piece.

PORSCHE FACTORY PRESS KITS go back to at least the early 1950s. The earliest widely distributed ones typically used heavy vellum folders with gold-embossed *Porsche* in logo script on the cover. Inside were technical descriptions, road test reprints (*Sonderdrucks* in German), photographs, and, in later years, marketing or sales write-ups as well.

This press book was put together in 1955 to introduce the prototypes of the Type 597 Jadgwagen, or "Hunter," as the factory later dubbed it in English. Mimeographed sheets in German, French, and English provide the technical description in front of photographs glued onto heavy vellum pages to illustrate the vehicle.

THIS FACTORY 1963 PRESS KIT was for the Frankfurt Auto Show. It featured the new 901 (later the 911) and the 356C model with disc brakes. It included the first 901 sales brochure, press releases on the 901 and 356C disc brakes in both English and German, and five photographs.

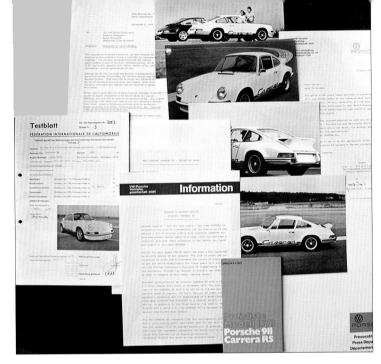

THE INTRODUCTORY PRESS KIT for the 1973 Carrera RS had a cover letter signed by Huschke von Hanstein on VW/Porsche letterhead that reflected the merged distribution agreement. Included were one page of copy, a technical specs sheet, three photos of a prototype RS, and one belatedly added RSR photo.

FULL-LINE PRESS KITS became an annual issue in the late 1970s. This 1999 kit was a prime example. It had an embossed, printed, heavy vellum cover; six double-image sheets of photos; "Selection"—the catalog of lifestyle accessories; four multipage press releases: "Design Evolution: Four Generations of the 911" (two pages), "A Porsche Chronology" (eleven pages), "The 1999 Porsche 911 Carrera" (twenty pages), "The 1999 Porsche Boxster" (twelve pages); and single sheets on prices, features and options, and technical specifications for both the Carrera and the Boxster. The printed sheets alone were about half an inch of material.

Today, Porsche press kits sent to the automotive and print media contain, in addition to color transparencies, a CD-ROM with high-resolution digital images. It may not have the glamour or the feel of a beautifully printed page, but don't be surprised if one day you hear collectors discussing trades: "I'll give you a 2025 model year CD-ROM for you original 2002 disk."
And it will probably still be for a 911 model.

INDEX

A

Abarth, Carlo, 54
ABC *Wide World of Sports*, 164
Ahrens, Kurt, 98
Aichele, Tobias, 171
airbags, 197
Alan Johnson Racing, 173
Alfa Romeo, 77, 78, 130
Allard, 83
Allison, Bobby, 164
all-wheel drive, 52, 136, 180,
    186, 189
    192, 194, 197, 198,
    203–219, 255
Alpine Rally, 236
American Le Mans series, 236
amphibious vehicles, 37, 41, 204
Anciens Etablissement d'Ieteren
    Frères S.A.,122
Andretti, John, 267
Andretti, Mario, 267
Andretti, Michael, 267
Auburn, 77
Audi, 24, 26, 205
audio system, 197, 198
Austro-Daimler, 4–11, 13, 23,
    58, 203, 234, 258, 273
Austro-Daimler 28/36PS sports
    touring car, 7–8,
    10–11
Auto, Motor und Sport, 104, 106,
    130
Auto Age magazine, 87
Auto Union, 24, 26–28, 30, 32,
    42, 54, 55, 93, 234, 235, 258,
    273, 274
Auto Velo, 48
Autocar, 147
automatic brake differential
    (ABD) system, 186, 194–195,
    197, 198, 201

Autosport, 93
Avus Ring, 131

B

Baracca, Paolina, 95
Barbour, Dick, 229
Barnes, John, 272
Becker six-speaker AM/FM
    cassette audio system, 197,
    198
Begue, Rene Le, 78
Behra, Jean, 82, 261
Belgian Speed Trial, 17, 234
Bell, Derek, 237, 252, 267
Bentley, 77
Bentley, John, 83, 87
Benz, Karl, 3
Benz & Cie., 9, 13
Berlin Motor Show, 28
Berlin-Rome race, 34, 36, 43, 47,
    49
Bertone, Nuccio, 149
Beutler Brothers Karosserie,
    272, 276
Blank, Bernhard, 62, 63, 72
Blaupunkt radio, 275
BMW, 48, 78, 125, 127
BOAC, 241
Bosch, 103, 105, 153, 160, 170,
    196
Bott, Helmuth, 154, 205, 207
Boxster. *See* Porsche Boxster
Brands Hatch, 243
Brauchitsch, Manfred von, 14,
    234
Braun, Lawrence, 131
Brendel, Heinz, 97
Büchi, Alfred, 167
Buehrig, Gordon Miller, 143
Buenos Aires 1000km, 238
Buzzetta, Joe, 248, 263

C

Cadillac, Eldorado, 99, 145
Camel GTP/GX
    Championship (IMSA), 236,
    252
Can-Am racing program, 151,
    158, 160, 167, 221, 245, 248,
    261, 265–266
Canepa, Bruce, 162–163, 166
Car and Driver, 139,
    147, 150, 151,
    223–224, 231
Caracciola, Rudolf, 10, 12, 13,
    14, 17, 234
Carrozzeria Ghia, 221–222
Cars Are My Life
    (Ferry Porsche), 4
Castrol, 260
catalog, first, 73
Chinetti, Luigi, Sr., 78
Chiron, Louis, 54
Christophorus, 131, 203, 259
Chrysler, 41, 222
Circuit de La Sarthe, 79, 93, 140,
    252, 255
    See also Le Mans 24 Hours
Circuit de Mugello, 252
Circuit of Savio, 95
Cisitalia, 52, 54, 55–56, 204, 274
Claes, Jon, 259
Consorzio Industriale Sportivo
    Italia,54–55
Cord, 77
Cunningham, Briggs Swift, 78,
    83, 87, 236, 258
Czech Grand Prix, 28, 234

D

Daimler, Gottlieb, 5, 6
Daimler, Paul, 3, 5–6, 8, 11, 13,
    20, 24

Daimler Phoenix, 6
Daimler-Benz AG, 13–14, 17, 20
Daimler-Motoren Gesellschaft,
    4–6, 9, 10, 11, 13, 17, 75
Datsun 240Z, 231
Daytona 6 Hours, 245
Daytona 24 Hours, 162, 183,
    233, 236, 242, 243, 248, 267
De Tomaso, 157
Dean, James, 100
Delahaye, 77
Dijon, 163, 248, 252
DKW, 24
Donohue, Mark, 164, 167, 170,
    237, 245, 247
Dr. Ing. h.c. F. Porsche. *See*
    Porsche (company)
Drauz, 116, 122
Dreyfus, Rene, 78
Dubonnet, André, 142
Duesenberg, 77
Dunlop, 159, 260
Dusio, Piero, 54–56

E

Edmonton, 245
Einspritzer fuel-injected four-
    cylinder engine
    (Volkswagen), 223
Elcosine, 17
electric motorcars, 3, 5, 6, 203
Elford, Vic, 151, 154, 237, 244,
    248, 263, 264
emblem design, 93–95
emissions standards, 145, 173,
    223, 231
Erich Heuer Body Factory, 76,
    87, 90
European GT Trophy, 245
European Hillclimb
    Championship, 263

Exner, Virgil, 222

F

F. Hetterich, 71
Farina, Battista "Pinin," 55–56,
    63
*Fascination of the Compressor,
    The*, 14
Fédération Internationale de
    l'Automobile (F.I.A.),
    101, 160, 163, 166, 171, 172,
    227, 243, 245, 248
Ferrari, 139, 150, 157, 218, 223
Ferrari, Enzo, 78, 94–95, 158,
    221, 241
Fiat, 54–56
    500, 158
    2300 S, 130
    Dino, 21, 223
Fichtel & Sachs, 150
Fittipaldi, Emerson, 164
Fitzpatrick, John, 163, 166, 173,
    248
Follmer, George, 164, 173, 245,
    266
Ford, Henry, 32, 33, 93
Ford Model A, 93
Ford Model T, 32
Ford Motors, 41, 100, 109, 126,
    157
Formula One racing, 192
four-wheel drive. *See* all-wheel
    drive
Foyt, A. J., 164
Frankenberg, Richard von, 98,
    99, 109, 130, 258
Frankfurt Auto Show, 62, 101,
    118, 126, 130, 134, 137, 280
Franzen, Torre, 42, 48
French Comit, International de
    Promotion et de

Prestige, 146
Frère, Paul, 98, 109, 161
Frick, Dennis, 31, 125
Fröhlich, Karl, 23
front-wheel-drive technology, 3,
    5, 6
Fuhrmann, Ernst, 91, 98, 158,
    248

G

Gallieni, Joseph-Simon, 8
Garretson, Bob, 229
Garretson, Fred, 229, 230–231
Gelo (Georg Loos Racing), 163,
    248
General Motors, 23, 41, 126, 205,
    208
Geneva Automobile Show, 73,
    130, 149
Geneva Rally, 241
German Auto Union, 24, 26, 27,
    28, 30, 32, 33, 42, 54, 55, 93,
    234, 235, 258, 273, 274
German Automobile
    Manufacturers Association
    (Reichsverband der
    Automobilindustrie, RDA),
    28–30
German Classic Cars (New
    Cumberland, PA), 125
German Labor Front, 30, 33, 34
German Motor Show, 37
German NSU motorcycle
    factory, commission from, 24
German Sports-Racing
    Championship, 98
Gestapo, 51–53
Giacosa, Dante, 54
Ginther, Richie, 83
Gläser, 76, 79, 87, 90
Glöckler, Helm, 97–98

Glöckler, Walter, 97–98, 99
Goertz, Albrecht, 125
Granturismo Berlinettas, 56
Granturismo movement, 56
Gregg, Peter, 161, 162, 172–173, 228, 233, 237, 245, 248
Guderian, Heinz, 39
Gugelot Design GmbH, 222–223, 226
Gulf Oil Company, 243
Gurney, Dan, 237

H

Hall, Jim, 151
Hanstein, Huschke von, 82, 98, 99, 146, 237, 261, 281
Hart, E. W., 3, 5
Haywood, Hurley, 161, 162, 170, 173, 228, 233, 237, 245, 248
Healey, 83
Herkomer Trials, 7–8
Herrmann, Hans, 98, 109, 237, 248, 260
Hezemans, Toine, 163, 248
Hibbard & Darrin, 18–19
Hild, Wilhelm, 98
Hill, Phil, 237
Hitler, Adolf, 17, 25–26, 28, 30, 32, 33, 34, 35, 36–37, 39, 42, 77
Hockenheim, 241
Hoffman, Maximilian, 76–79, 80, 83, 86, 87, 93–95, 99,106, 109–110, 116, 123, 125, 164
Hoffman & Huppert, 77
Hoffman Motor Car Company, 77–78, 83
Holbert, Al, 173, 237, 252
homologation, 158, 160, 203, 241
Horch, 24
Hotchkiss, 77
Hruska, Rudolf, 54, 56
Hulme, Denis, 164
Huslein, Otto, 57

I

Ickx, Jacky, 205, 207, 237, 248, 251, 252, 255

d-Ieteren, 122
Imola, 163
IMSA (International Motor Sports Association), 227–228, 252, 261
    Camel GTP/GX Championship, 236, 252
    Drivers Championship, 186
    GT Series, 228
    Manufacturers Championship 186
Indianapolis 500, 252
internal combustion engine, 3–5, 203
International Race of Champions/IROC, 163, 164, 167, 168
Interserie Championship, 245
Irwin, James B., 4, 5

J

Jaguar, 77, 83, 87, 139, 150
Jantke, Mannfred, 251
Jensen-Healey, 231
Johncock, Gordon, 164
Jolson, Al, 20–21

K

Kaes, Ghislaine, 16, 41
Kaes, Herbert, 50, 51
Kales, Josef, 23
Karl Baur, 157
Karmann, 224, 230
    Ghia (VW), 122, 136, 221–222
Karosserie C. H. Weidenhausen, 97
Karosserie Drauz, 116, 122
Karosserie Gläser. *See* Gläser
Karosserie Reutter. *See* Reutter
Karosserie Wendler, 98
Karosserie Wilhelm Karmann GmbH. *See* Karmann
Kathrein, Hermann, 97
Kelly, Prescott, 257
Kimes, Beverly Rae, 8
Klett, Arnulf, 75
Koch, Gerhard, 245

Kolowrat, Alexander Graf, 234
Komenda, Erwin Franz
    arrest of, 49
    in brochure, 274
    design of Porsche Model 32, 24
    Porsche 356, 47, 56, 58, 63, 66, 69, 75–76, 81, 105, 146
    and Porsche 901/911, 123, 125–126, 207
    Porsche emblem design, 95
    Spyder 550, 98, 106
    Volkswagen design and, 30, 31, 34, 36, 37–38
Kommandeurwagen, 204
Korean War, 95
Kremer Brothers, 173
Kühnle, Kopp & Kausch (KKK) turbocharger, 170, 172
Kunz, Heinrich, 62
Kussmaul, Roland, 207

L

Laguna Seca, 245, 265
Lamborghini Diablo VT, 218
Lamis, Colonel, 51
Lancia, 77
Lapine, Tony, 205, 207, 208, 210
Le Mans 24 Hours, 79, 93, 98, 109, 140, 163, 166, 172, 212, 228, 233, 235–239, 241, 243–244, 247–249, 251, 252, 255, 258–260, 266
LeComte, Henri, 50–51
Leffingwell, Randy, 205, 207
Leiningen, Prince of, 28, 234
Lightweight-Stable-Agile (LSA) multi-link, subframemounted rear suspension system, 195
Loewy, Raymond, 125
Lohner motorworks (Vienna), 3–5
Lohner-Porsche electric car, 3–4, 5, 6, 234, 258, 273
Lohner-Wagen, 3
Lovely, Pete, 108
Ludvigsen, Karl, 99, 171, 172, 243, 245

Ludwig, Klaus, 172–173
Luftfahrzeug-Motorenbau GmbH, 7
Luftwaffe, 48
Lunar Rover (moon car), 4, 5

M

Maiffre, Major, 51
Mairesse, Willy, 245
Marathon de la Route, 151
Marshall, George C., 72
Marshall Plan, 72
Martini, 172, 266
Maserati, 78, 139
Masetti, Giulio, 10
Mass, Jochen, 248, 251, 252
Maybach, Karl, 7
Maybach, Wilhelm, 3, 5, 6–7
Maybach Motorenbau Gesellschaft, 7
McAfee, Jack, 83, 108
McCluskey, Roger, 164
McQueen, Steve, 183
Mechanix Illustrated, 104, 106
Meluzio, Don, 131
Mercedes-Benz
    450SLC, 230
    engine first positioned in front, 3
    Hitler and, 26
    Mercedes-Benz Model K, 12, 20
    Mercedes-Benz Model S, 12, 13, 20–21
    Mercedes-Benz Model SS, 14–15, 17, 234
    Mercedes-Benz Model SSK, 14, 17, 234, 258, 273
    Mercedes-Benz Model SSKL, 17, 258
    Mercedes-Benz Type 170H, 30
    Porsche's impact on, 93
    post-World War II, 48
    sunroof and, 142
    U.S. distributors, 78
    during World War II, 42
Merritt, Dick, 272

Merz, Otto, 10, 14, 234
Metge, Ren,, 207, 255
Mezger, Hans, 130
MG, 83
Mickle, Josef, 23
Mid-Ohio, 245, 266
Miles, Ken, 238
military vehicles, 37–41, 48, 203–205
Mille Miglia, 60, 99, 162
Miller, Susann, 272
Mitter, Gerhard, 263
Momberger, August, 28, 234
Monte Carlo Rally, 154, 243, 251, 265
Monza, 11, 236, 241, 243
moon car (Lunar Rover), 4, 5
Morgenthau, Henry, Jr., 50
Morgenthau Plan, 50
Moss, Stirling, 237, 238
Motor Trend, 227–228
Mouche, Edmond, 79, 93, 258
Müller, Herbert, 245
Müller, Petermax, 99, 248
Mussolini, Benito, 34

N

National Sporting Authority (ONS), 34
Neerpasch, Jochen, 151, 248
Neubauer, Alfred, 7, 10–11, 13, 23, 234
Neumann, John von, 83, 100, 149
Neumann, Josie von, 83
New York International Auto Show, 189
Newman, Paul, 229
Nibel, Hans, 17
Nordhoff, Heinz, 221–222
Norisring, 248
Nürburgring, 158, 163, 234, 241
Nürburgring 1000km, 100, 243, 244, 275
Nürburgring Eifel Races, 98
Nürburgring Grand Prix, 12, 13, 17, 26, 27, 28, 234
Nürburgring Marathon de la

Route, 151
Nuvolari, Tazio, 54
Nye, Doug, 237

O

OBD II (onboard diagnostics, second generation), 192
Ongias, Danny, 173
Opel GT, 222
Orsini, Hans, 62
Osterreichissche rally, 241
Osterreichring, 241, 243

P

Packard, 41
Palm Beach Shores, 236, 258
Paris Auto Salon, 8, 98, 99, 137, 167, 179
Paris Motor Show, 76, 78, 160
Paris-Dakar Rallye, 203, 205, 207, 255
Paul, Marcel, 50–53
Paul Ricard Circuit (France), 164
Pearson, David, 164
Penske, Roger, 137, 164
Petty, Richard, 164
Peugeot, 51–53, 137
Pharaohs Rallye in Egypt, 205, 207
Piëch, Anton, 16, 24, 25, 37, 50, 51, 52–53, 54, 78, 110, 204
Piëch, Ferdinand, 62, 127, 130, 146, 151, 155, 205, 238, 247–248
Piëch family, exclusion of, 146, 154–155, 205, 247
Polak, Vasek, 140
Pon, Ben, 244
Pontiac, 77
Porsche (company)
    establishment of, 17, 23–24, 95, 110
    motto of, 126
Porsche, Aloisia, 6, 83
Porsche, Anna, 25
Porsche, Ferdinand Alexander "Butzi," III, 62, 80, 81,123,

125–126, 128, 129, 134, 136, 137, 142, 144, 157, 181, 207, 222, 233

Porsche, Ferdinand Anton Ernst, II, "Ferry"
  on Berlin-Rome, 36
  Carreras and, 118, 128
  Cisitalia grand prix car and, 204
  death of, 49, 155
  Dusio and, 54, 55–56
  emblem and, 93–95
  on end of war, 8–9
  exclusion of family and, 146, 154–155, 205
  on father, 11, 23, 29
  as father's assistant, 24
  as head of Porsche KG, 75–79
  Hitler and, 33, 35, 37, 39
  Hoffman and, 106
  imprisonment of, 50, 51, 52–53
  on Lohner-Porsche electric car, 4
  as manager of Stuttgart-Zuffenhausen design office, 37
  photographs of, 7, 9, 16, 22, 25, 58, 59, 62, 80–83, 94, 98, 99, 137, 138, 146, 186–187, 200, 227, 236
  Porsche 356 and, 56, 58, 63, 66, 73, 86, 91, 93, 95, 100–101, 236
  and Porsche 901/911, 123, 125–126, 127, 130, 139, 142
  and Porsche 914, 221
  as race-car driver, 28
  racing and, 235, 237, 245, 247
  on Speedster, 116
  on success, 72
  in United States, 32
  Volkswagen and, 34, 39
  World War II and, 41, 42, 48–49

Porsche, Ferdinand, Sr.
  at Austro-Daimler, 4–11
  birth, 3
  citizenship of, 8–9
  company reorganization and, 76
  at Daimler-Benz AG, 13–17, 30, 234
  at Daimler-Motoren Gesellschaft, 11
  death of, 91, 93
  design heritage of, 273
  establishes Porsche GmbH, 17, 23–24
  as father, 9
  honors for, 8
  imprisonment of, 49–54
  at Lohner motorworks (Vienna), 3–4
  murder accusation against, 49
  origins of all-wheel drive, 203
  photograph of, 16, 25, 61, 62
  racing success and, 258
  as Reich auto designer, 37, 39
  at Steyr, 17
  in United States, 32
  Volkswagen development and, 17, 28–39
  Weber and, 58
Porsche, Gerd, 80
Porsche, Peter, 80, 146
Porsche, Wolfgang, 80, 110
Porsche 356, 29, 56, 57, 69–71, 73, 126, 136, 137, 142, 204, 236, 237, 260, 263, 268, 272, 274,276
  356-1 Gmünd roadster, 56, 58, 61, 64, 65–66, 75–76, 93
  356-2, 47–48, 58–59, 60, 61, 63
  356A, 79, 89, 101–104, 105, 110, 112, 146
  356A Carrera, 105, 110, 118, 162, 183
  356A Convertible D, 116–117, 122
  356A Speedster, 122
  356B, 116, 122, 123
  356B Carrera GTL, 239
  356C, 119–122, 123, 134, 140, 151, 278, 280
  1600 GS, 113
  1600S Speedster, 110–111, 118, 122

2000 GS, 123
America roadster, 83–87, 97, 106
Carrera 2, 123, 128, 130
Carrera 4, 131
Carrera 356 Speedster, 83, 86, 103, 106, 109–110, 112, 113–115, 116, 122, 176–178, 226
Carrera 1600GS, 122–123
Carrera Deluxe, 118, 122
Carrera Grand Sport, 106
Carrera Grand Sport models, 123
Carrera GT, 118, 122, 241
Hoffman as U.S. dealer, 77–79
Porsche 901/911 as replacement for, 123, 125–126
Pre-A Series, 79, 89, 92–93, 103, 104, 105, 106, 112
T-2 series, 118
Volkswagen components, 56, 78, 91, 221
Porsche 901/911, 124–127
  See also Porsche 911
Porsche 904, 130, 137, 222, 241, 262
  Carrera 904 GTS, 140, 142, 233, 238, 240–241, 242
Porsche 906, 142, 238, 241, 244, 245
Porsche 907, 242–243, 247–248
Porsche 908, 158, 242–243, 248, 264
Porsche 910, 241–242, 263
Porsche 911, 119, 137, 139–154, 158–160, 176–201
  901 prototype and test models, 124–126
  911 SC RS, 255
  911E, 143, 151, 153–154, 224
  911L, 141, 150, 151
  911R, 151, 157, 158, 159, 163, 248
  911S, 140, 141, 145–147, 150–151, 153–154, 157–158, 160, 170, 224, 227, 229, 241, 245, 247, 249

911SC Weissach, 177, 178
911T, 150, 151, 153, 154, 224, 226, 227, 228, 229, 230, 243
C4 Lightweight, 251
Carrera 2, 183, 186, 190, 191
Carrera 4, 180–181, 189, 192, 194–196, 208, 210–216, 218–219
Carrera 4S, 189, 197–198
Carrera RS. See Porsche Carrera RS
Carrera RS Club Sport, 183, 185
Carrera S, 196
Carrera Speedster, 179–180, 183, 190, 191
Carrera Turbo, 166–167
GT1, 233, 255
GT2, 183
as replacement for Porsche 356, 123, 125–126, 136
Targa, 144–146, 186, 197, 200
test car 13 327, 127, 129–131, 134, 136
Porsche 912, 137, 140, 145, 150, 151, 154, 175–176
Porsche 914, 175, 221–231, 233, 265, 272
Porsche 917
  Porsche 917/10, 160, 233, 245
  Porsche 917/30, 245
  Porsche 917K, 243
Porsche 924, 272
Porsche 928, 186, 195, 272
  928 GTS, 230
  928 S, 230
  928 S4, 230
Porsche 930, 167–168, 170–171, 173, 180, 190
Porsche 934, 171–172, 186, 229, 233, 266
Porsche 935, 171–173, 186, 229, 233, 249, 251, 252, 254–255, 266
Porsche 936, 171, 233, 248, 251, 252
Porsche 944, 272
Porsche 953, 207, 255

Porsche 956, 205, 233, 249, 252, 267
Porsche 959, 180, 186, 203, 205–215, 218, 251, 255
Porsche 961, 212, 251
Porsche 962, 233, 252–253, 255, 267
Porsche 964, 179, 180–181, 218
Porsche 993, 181, 186–187, 195, 216, 218
Porsche 996, 186
Porsche AG, reorganization as, 154–155
Porsche Boxster, 58, 180, 192, 281
Porsche: Brochures and Sales Literature, 1948- 1965 (Miller and Merritt), 272
Porsche Carrera RS, 157–167, 172, 179, 183, 186, 190, 248, 249, 252, 278, 281
Porsche Carrera RSR, 161–164, 167, 248, 266
Porsche Cars North America, 271
Porsche Club of America, 185, 227, 257, 278
Porsche Competition Department, 163–164, 166
Porsche Design, 155
Porsche: Excellence Was Expected (Ludvigsen), 172, 243
Porsche family, exclusion of, 146, 154–155, 205, 247
Porsche Jagdwagen, 280
Porsche KG, reorganization as, 33, 75, 76
Porsche Konstruktionen GesmbH, 54
Porsche Model 32, 24
Porsche of America Corporation, 123, 278
Porsche Panorama, 131, 257
Porsche RS 60, 100
Porsche Spyder
  550, 58, 97–100, 106, 108–110,

154, 162, 221, 237–238, 259–260, 261, 263, 274, 275 718
RSK, 100, 221, 238, 241, 242
Porsche Type 64 60K 10 sports racing car, 34, 36–38, 43–47, 48, 56
Porsche-Diesel-Motorenbau GmbH, 95
Porsche-Piëch, Louise, 7, 9, 16, 53–54, 62, 83, 146, 154, 155
Posey, Sam, 241
Prince Henry Time Trials, 7–8
Prinzing, Albert, 75, 76

R
Rabe, Karl, 23, 29, 42, 48, 49, 53, 56, 58, 61, 66, 80, 81, 146, 203–204, 274
Rahal, Bobby, 229
Ramelow, Herman, 97, 99
Recaro GmbH Company, 126
Redman, Brian, 229, 237, 243, 264
Reeves, G. C., 42, 48
Renault, 53
Rennsport (sports racing), 150
Resnick, Paul, 131
Reutter, 34, 35, 36, 42, 75–76, 78, 79, 90, 95, 110, 122, 123, 126, 128, 142
Revson, Peter, 163, 164
Riverside, 163, 245, 265
Road & Track, 122, 147, 150, 172, 227, 228
Road America, 245, 266
Road Atlanta, 245, 266
Rodriguez, Pedro, 243
Rolls-Royce, 8, 41, 77
Roosevelt, Franklin D., 50
Roosevelt Raceway, Vanderbilt Cup Race, 27
Roots, Francis, 13

Roots, Philander, 13
Roots supercharger, 13
Roots-type supercharger, 17
Rosemeyer, Bernd, 27, 32
Rosenberger, Adolf, 13, 14, 23, 24, 25–26, 110, 234
rotary engine, 8

S

Sailer, Max, 13
Saoutchik, Jacques, 142
Sascha, 10–11, 13, 28, 234
Sauerwein, Rudolf, 93
Savonuzzi, Giovanni, 54
Schlesser, Joe, 248
Schloss Kransberg, 50
Schoch, Ernst, 62
Schröder, Gerhard, 175
Schuppan, Vern, 252
Schurti, Manfred, 251
Schweden, Bertil von, 236
Scott, David R., 4, 5
Sebring 12 Hours, 183, 233, 236, 242, 262
Seiffert, Reinhard, 130, 203
Senegal Grand Prix, 260
Siffert, Jo, 243, 248, 264
Skoda, 23
Solitude Rally, 241
Sommer, Raymond, 54
Soviet Union, 24
Spa-Francorchamps, 236
Special Works Department, 180
Speer, Albert, 50
Sportomatic transmission, 143, 150–151
Sports Car Club of America (SCCA), 87, 140, 173, 185, 227, 231, 24
Sports Car Graphic, 151
Spyder. *See* Porsche Spyder
Star and the Laurel, The (Kimes), 8
Stasse, Paul, 259
steam-powered cars, 3, 203
Steyr, 17, 23, 25
Stommelen, Rolf, 229, 248, 251

Strenger, Erich, 258–259, 260, 261, 262, 273, 276
Stuck, Hans, 14, 26, 27, 28, 234
Swedish Rally, 236, 243
Swiss Grand Prix, 28, 234
Swiss Hill Climb, 261

T

Talbot, 77
Talladega, 247
tanks, 8, 37, 39, 48
Targa Florio, 10–11, 12, 13, 143, 234, 236, 238, 242, 243, 245, 248, 261, 264
Targa Version II, 146
Taruffi, Piero, 54
Tasco, 143
Teitgen, Pierre-Henri, 51, 53
Telefunken radio, 79, 91
30 Jahre commemorative series, 181
Tiptronic automatic transmission, 180, 192, 196, 197, 201
Titus, Jerry, 140
Toivonen, Pauli, 154
Tomala, Hans, 127, 146
Tour de France, 236
tractors, 40, 55, 62, 95
Travemünde Rally, 236
Trevoux, Major, 51
Tripps, Wolfgang von, 261, 263
trucks, 5, 39, 203
Tulip Rally, 241
12 Hours of Sebring. *See* Sebring 12 Hour
24 Hours of Daytona. *See* Daytona 24 Hours
24 Hours of Le Mans. *See* Le Mans 24 Hours
Type D46 Monopostos, 54, 55

U

Unser, Bobby, 163, 164

V

van Lennep, Gijs, 162, 244, 248
Vanderbilt Cup Race, 27, 32

Varioram, 189, 191
Vatter, Joe, 146
Vauxhall, 77
Veuillet, Auguste, 79, 93, 258
Villa d'Este Concourse d'Elegance, 55
Vingt-Quatre Heures du Mans. *See* Le Mans 24 Hours
Volkswagen
 Beetle, 66, 93
 components and, 56, 73, 78, 91, 136–137
 as dealers for Porsche 356, 76
 development and, 28–39
 development of, 16
 and France, 51–53
 Karmann Ghia, 122, 136, 221–222
 KdF-Wagen, 35, 39
 Kommandeurwagen, 204
 Kübelwagen (bucket car), 37, 39, 40
 Model 32 and, 24
 origins of, 17
 People's Car, 28–30, 33, 91
 Porsche + Audi Division dealerships, 223
 and Porsche 914, 221–223
 Porsche 914 and, 221
 prototypes and test cars, 29–33, 35, 42
 Sascha as forerunner of, 28
 Schwimmwagen (amphibious version), 37, 41
 Type 60, 31, 36
 Type 114, 34, 36
 VW-Porsche Type 64 60K 10 sports racing car, 34, 36–38, 43, 47, 49, 56, 235
Volvo, 77
von Delius, Ernst, 27
Von Senger, Rupert, 63
von Veyder-Malberg, Hans, 25

W

Walters, Phil, 83
Wanderer, 24

Watkins Glen, 78, 79, 241, 243
Webasto, 142
Weber, Friedrich, 58, 66, 72
Weidenhausen, 97
Weissach, 157, 158, 170, 171, 177, 203, 205, 248, 251, 255, 278
Wendler, 98
Werner, Christian, 10, 12, 14, 234
"whale tail," 168, 170, 211
Whittington brothers, 172
Wieselmann, Uli, 104, 106
Willrett, Elmar, 171
Wollek, Bob, 267
World Championship for Production Sports Cars, 251
World Championship for Race Cars, 251
World Championship of International Endurance Racing, 236
World Championship of Makes (WCM), 171, 172, 243, 249, 251, 252
World GT Trophy, 243
World Rally Championship, 243
World War I, 8, 9, 11, 24–25
World War II, 36–37, 39–41, 42, 47–48, 203–205
Wütherich, Rolf, 100
Wyer, John, 243

X

Xenia Coup,, 142

Z

Zagato, 239
Zandvoort, 241, 244
Zeltweg, 243
Zeppelin, Graf Ferdinand von, 6–7

ABOUT THE AUTHOR

Award-winning author, photographer, and historian DENNIS ADLER is recognized as one of the leading automotive photojournalists in the world. His work has appeared in publications ranging from *Motor Trend*, *Road & Track*, *Automobile*, and *AutoWeek* to *Forbes*, the *Los Angeles Times*, *European Car*, the *Robb Report*, and *Automobile Quarterly*. Adler is editor in chief of *Car Collector* magazine and senior contributing editor to *The Star*, the official publication of the Mercedes-Benz Club of America. A leading authority on the marque, he has written more than one hundred articles on Mercedes-Benz models and three books on the history of the company. Adler's previous books include *Mercedes-Benz Silver Star Century*, *Porsche: The Classic Era* and *The Art of the Sports Car: The Greatest Designs of the 20th Century*. *Porsche: The Classic Era* is Adler's twentieth book.